SOVIET REGIONAL ELITE MOBILITY AFTER KHRUSHCHEV

Soviet Regional Elite Mobility after Khrushchev

WILLIAM A. CLARK

PRAEGER

New York
Westport, Connecticut
London

Library of Congress Cataloging-in-Publication Data

Clark, William A., 1958–
    Soviet regional elite mobility after Khrushchev/
William A. Clark.
        p. cm.
    Bibliography: p.
    Includes index.
    ISBN 0-275-93124-2 (alk. paper)
    1. Elite (Social sciences)—Soviet Union. 2. Social mobility—
Soviet Union. 3. Soviet Union—Politics and
government—1953–1982. 4. Soviet Union—Politics and
government—1982– I. Title.
HN530.Z9E425 1989
305.5'2'0947—dc19   88-36973

Library of Congress Catalog Card Number: 88-36973
ISBN: 0-275-93124-2

First published in 1989

Praeger Publishers, One Madison Avenue, New York, NY 10010
A division of Greenwood Press, Inc.

Printed in the United States of America

The paper used in this book complies with the
Permanent Paper Standard issued by the National
Information Standards Organization (Z39.48-1984).

10 9 8 7 6 5 4 3 2 1

For Jayna Elizabeth Ihrig

CONTENTS

TABLES

PREFACE

At the end of a long project it seems appropriate that acknowledging those who were instrumental in its completion should come first. Numerous professional debts are owed to several colleagues who read and commented on various draft chapters of the manuscript. Gerasimos Augustinos, John D. Basil, Donna Bahry, Erik P. Hoffmann, and Henry Morton each provided insights in specific areas that significantly improved the quality of the work. Special thanks go to Gordon B. Smith, James A. Kuhlman, Mark E. Tompkins, and William A. Welsh for willingly giving their time and energy in helping me work through a labyrinth of conceptual and methodological issues. Any weaknesses that remain in the manuscript are certainly more a reflection of my own inability to heed their advice than a commentary on the wisdom of their counsel.

Charles W. Kegley, Jr., of the James F. Byrnes International Center, and William Mishler, of the Department of Government and International Studies, both at the University of South Carolina, provided the financial support that allowed the project to proceed apace. Also, Mary Joyce Burns contributed significantly to the preparation of the final version of the manuscript. I thank them for showing continuous faith in the project.

I would also like to take this opportunity to thank my editors at Praeger, Dan Eades and Omar Dahbour, for their role in bringing this book to print.

Finally, I thank my wife, Jayna Ihrig, for putting up with me and my work schedule during this project. She was deserving of more attention than she received, and was subjected to far too many of my diatribes about esoteric quantitative techniques, troublesome computer programs, and the like. I dedicate the book to her.

SOVIET REGIONAL ELITE MOBILITY AFTER KHRUSHCHEV

INTRODUCTION: THE CONCEPT OF POLITICAL ELITE MOBILITY IN THE SOVIET SYSTEM

THE SETTING

The study of political elite mobility in various societies has a long, distinguished pedigree. From the time of Aristotle's Lyceum and the categorization of governments, through the analyses of the classic "elitists" Pareto and Mosca, to the present studies of social and elite mobility, scholars interested in social dynamics have focused their attention on the recruitment, circulation, and replenishment of political elites. These classic approaches to the study of society have had as an implicit, if not explicit, assumption that the very crux of civil society is largely defined by these processes.

The distinctions that scholars draw between "traditional," "developed," "industrial," "feudal," "democratic," "authoritarian," "open," and "closed" societies revolve around differences in the opportunity structures for political mobility in those societies. That is, the distinctions that are drawn in how differing social systems recruit, circulate, and replenish political elites enable them to differentiate types of political systems. An "open" society differs from a "closed" society in that the elite strata of the former is marked by a demonstrably higher degree of permeability than the latter. Conversely, closed societies are "closed" in the sense that membership in the system's political and social elite is blocked off to the vast majority of the population. The recruitment, circulation, and long-term maintenance of the elite take place almost entirely within a small, homogeneous, and temporally stable social group.

Studies of political elite mobility, then, necessarily reveal the broader issues of the larger social system under consideration. The present examination into Soviet political mobility trends, therefore, should not be a sterile exercise. The particular findings about the Soviet regional (obkom) political elite are not merely the gristle of an esoteric group of scholars;

instead, they seek to contribute to an understanding of the larger issue: the dynamics of Soviet politics.

WHAT IS "POLITICAL MOBILITY"?

This study focuses on political mobility narrowly defined in terms of the movement from one position in the sociopolitical administrative structure to another. It is only peripherally concerned with the much more inclusive concept of "social mobility" as construed by sociologists. The latter concept considers generational movement along indices of social class, socioeconomic status, educational levels, and the like. Soviet sociologist N. A. Aitov (1986: 254) defines social mobility as "the transition of individuals from one social group to another or from one stratum within a social group to another. It connotes a change in the individual's social affiliation." The concept of "political mobility" does share the focus on movement through a hierarchy. However, the hierarchy of importance in this study is not that of class or status, per se. Rather, we are interested in the movement of individuals, and groups of individuals, through a specific hierarchy of political posts.

Certainly, the movement of individuals through this political hierarchy might carry with it changes in class, and/or socioeconomic status, yet these variables are not the primary focus of this examination. Instead, this study centers on changes in political power, defining the political hierarchy, and assessing the political implications of different mobility patterns. The movement of Soviet political elites from one part of the socioadministrative structure to another connotes a change in the individual's political status, defined in terms of political power. These changes over time reveal much about the dynamics of the political system itself.

Almost by definition, the level of social mobility is usually quite high during periods of rapid change, and this general tendency is often reflected in the nature of political elite composition. As a result, political mobility trends are a good barometer of more aggregate-level societal changes. For example, Stalin's assault on Soviet society during the 1930s was mirrored in his devastating purge of virtually all public organs. In January 1934, the 17th Party Congress convened with 1,966 delegates. The so-called Congress of Victors, and the Central Committee it nominally elected, however, fared quite poorly in the resultant period of cleansing. Over the next five years leading up to the outbreak of World War II, 1,108 of the 1,966 delegates (56 percent) and 98 of the 139 members of the Central Committee (70 percent) had been shot (Conquest 1968: 36; 38). Robert Conquest reports that between 1934 and 1940, nineteen members (or ex-members) at the highest echelons of the Politburo were killed by Stalin (1968: 83n). This period of self-destruction certainly resulted in great mobility for many lower apparatchiki (party functionaries). Indeed, those members of the post-Stalin Soviet leadership that lasted into the late 1970s were precisely those members of the party apparatus who rose quickly to the top as a consequence of Stalin's purges.

Even as the Soviet system has moderated its political infighting, leadership changes at the very top have rapidly increased the opportunities for political advancement and decline. As newly emergent general secretaries attempt to consolidate power and build authority, the upward movement of cadres, or key personnel, in support of the leader's agenda becomes prominent. In a word, periods of social and political change—from the most revolutionary to the most moderate—affect the opportunity structure for elites to move from position to position. Given this trend, the study of political elite mobility in the Soviet Union provides a keen indicator of change of a more systemic nature.

Elite turnover not only provides an indication of a leader's progress in building his personal authority, but it also sheds light on the likelihood of policy changes as well. One may assume that building personal authority is not, even in the Soviet Union, an end in itself. A leader's attempts to consolidate power usually have direct policy implications. Gorbachev's rather ambitious policy agenda cannot be realized if he is unable to secure his own personal role in the leadership of the system. That is, a leader's ability to consolidate his power through a rigorous personnel replenishment is a necessary prerequisite to the adoption of his policy preferences. As a result, therefore, the study of Soviet cadres policy also allows the observer to evaluate the likelihood of any significant policy shifts that would come with a leader's regime consolidation.

Finally, the analysis of cadres policy per se highlights key aspects of any political system. Being sensitive to the nature of the governmental elite— how that elite changes over time, the types of skills, training, and experiences prevalent among the elite, and how these characteristics vary from time to time—provides students of any political system with crucial insights into that system.

In assessing the value of any analysis of Soviet political elite mobility, it is perhaps wise to trust the words of the most skillful political infighter in Soviet history. In May 1935, just five months after the assassination of Sergei Kirov precipitated the massive series of purges in the Soviet Union, Iosef Stalin revealed the rationale for the great cleansing: "Cadres decide everything." While, to be sure, the political use of cadres policy in the Soviet Union has become less deadly over the intervening decades, it still plays a significant role in the operation of the Soviet political system. As such, it requires our serious attention.

1

OBKOM FIRST SECRETARIES, POLITICAL MOBILITY, AND *SEILSCHAFTEN*

INTRODUCTION

Since the death of long-time Communist Party (C.P.S.U.) General Secretary Leonid Brezhnev on 10 November 1982, a new phase in Soviet cadres policy has been strikingly evident. Following almost two decades of the ultra-conservative Brezhnev policy of "Faith in Cadres," characterized by the extremely slow rate of turnover among political elites at all levels of the Soviet system, the post-Brezhnev cadres policy has been marked by a level of activity not seen since the time of Nikita Khrushchev.

Yurii Andropov, between November 1982 and February 1984, and Mikhail Gorbachev, since the death of Konstantin Chernenko in March 1985, both pursued a cadres policy aimed at the replacement of personnel in both the party and state hierarchies. Nowhere is this elite turnover more evident than among the regional (oblast) party elite. More than eight out of every ten regional party committee (obkom) first secretaries have been replaced since 1983. On average, a different regional party first secretary has been replaced every two or three weeks since November 1982. Certainly, the policy of "Faith in Cadres" was put to rest with Brezhnev.

This change in the Soviet cadres policy with respect to the regional party elite necessitates a reevaluation of the seemingly dormant western scholarship dealing with oblast-level political elite mobility. The importance of these regional party officials to the smooth operation of the Soviet system has long been acknowledged. Through the study of this new cadre of regional party first secretaries, then, much can be learned about the political orientations of the emerging Gorbachev era of Soviet politics.

THE OBKOM FIRST SECRETARY

A significant body of literature examining the various functions, roles, background characteristics, and career patterns of the Soviet regional (oblast) elite has been developing for over a quarter of a century. The early pioneering works of Merle Fainsod (1958), John Armstrong (1959), Jerry Hough (1961), and Grey Hodnett (1965), each focusing their attention on oblast-level elites and politics, coincided not surprisingly with the early stages of what Thomas Kuhn called a "paradigmatic shift" in sovietology. While what sovietologists "shifted" *to* in terms of a new paradigm for the study of Soviet politics may still be open to debate, it seems clear that the early research of the Soviet regional elite was a significant part of a more general reevaluation (and at least partial rejection) of the totalitarian model. The assumptions, which not only governed the concept of totalitarianism but also guided the so-called "normal" science of sovietology since its inception, were seen as increasingly invalid in the late 1950s and early 1960s and, from a research perspective, unproductive. In this reappraisal, researchers, inter alia, shifted from a strict national (all-union) level-of-analysis perspective, and found "politics" in the Soviet Union existed below the All-Union Central Committee.

Spurred by the initial works of Fainsod, Armstrong, Hough, and Hodnett, an increasing number of researchers throughout the 1960s and early 1970s focused their efforts on regional political elites and cumulatively shed new light on Soviet politics at this level. Scholars investigated above all the most significant political post at the regional level, the oblast party committee (obkom) first secretary. For a number of reasons, this position within the Communist party hierarchy (as well as the individuals filling these slots) seemed the natural point of departure for all investigations into Soviet politics at the regional level. Nothing discovered since these early studies seriously challenges this assumption.

First, at the oblast level these men (there has never been a woman obkom first secretary) are the most ubiquitous and powerful actors in Soviet politics. This fact is reflected in the labels attached to them by sovietologists: "bosses of the apparatus" (Armstrong, 1959: 45), "prefects" (Hough, 1969), "fast trackers" (Blackwell and Hulbary, 1973: 735), "regional satrap[s]" (Rigby, 1980: 57), "the influentials" (Stewart, 1968: 194), and so on. Indeed, Iosef Stalin himself referred to these regional party secretaries as the "generals" of the Communist party (Avtorkhanov, 1966: 153). Sufficient biographical data on the individuals filling the position of obkom first secretary are available to enable the researcher to examine their educational background, vocational training, career history, job tenure, and political mobility. The oblast level is the lowest administrative level within the Soviet system where these data are available in sufficient number for such general statements. This research has produced a relatively clear picture of the functions of the first secretary post as well as of the individuals who have held this position within the party hierarchy.

While the obkom first secretary has traditionally occupied the dominant political position at the regional level in the Soviet Union, his policy prerogatives, even at that level, are significantly constrained. His discretionary power is checked by the "dual authority" invested in the oblast representatives of the state and police bureaucracies, with whom he must interact on a wide array of issues (Moses, 1974: 126). Moreover, in the non-Russian areas of the Soviet Union, there is weighty evidence that the increased authority of the obkom second secretary (Miller, 1977) constrains his power. Finally, the prerogatives of the regional secretary vis-à-vis local party and government officials are often constricted by the dictates of city managers and officials (Lewis and Sternheimer, 1979). Even at the oblast level, then, the first secretary does not enjoy total autonomy.

Armstrong (1959: 45), anticipating the "prefect" concept later employed by Hough (1961, 1969), refers to the obkom first secretary as a "line official." This terminology highlights the hierarchical command structure of the C.P.S.U. and serves well to point out the additional constraints placed on the regional "boss" by the party's tenet of democratic centralism. Party Rule 19 dictates that (a) party bodies must report periodically to superior bodies, and (b) the decisions of higher party bodies are obligatory for lower ones. These "firm Leninist principles" are, of course, vertically delimiting forces on the discretion of the obkom first secretary. Despite these vertical and horizontal constraints, however, the post of regional first secretary possesses a significant power base. The power and discretion inherent in the post are functions of the position's key role in the implementation of national party dictates as well as the specific demographic, economic, and political characteristics indigenous to the respective oblast.

The regional first secretary has tended over the years to be what Robert Blackwell (1972b: 133) has called a "generalist" in training and orientation. Qua generalist, the obkom first secretary is expected to ensure the integration and coordination necessary for the effective political, economic, and social functioning of his oblast (Hough, 1969: 124). Rigby (1980: 63) summarizes the responsibilities and power of the obkom first secretary as follows: "It is at his desk that the 'buck' still stops, especially, as before, in economic matters but also if the problem is one of education, housing, personnel, security, or anything else." As the regional prefect, the first secretary is held responsible for the overall state of affairs in his oblast.

While other secretaries of the typical oblast committee may possess and utilize a more specialized technical training (agronomy for the secre-

tary in charge of agriculture, or ferrous metallurgy for the industrial secretary, for example), the first secretary, usually highly educated, tends not
to utilize a technical orientation toward his work duties (Hough, 1969:
46). Although Philip Stewart's research (1968: 168) lends further support
to this position, there is some evidence (Moses, 1974: 18) that over time
this situation may be changing, with technical expertise becoming increasingly valued in a first secretary.

Specifically, the responsibilities of the first secretary include the general oversight of the obkom bureau, its secretariat, and the party apparatus of the region. Each oblast party committee is governed by a party
bureau (usually consisting of nine to eleven members) and a Secretariat.
While the memberships of these two bodies overlap significantly, the
party secretariat at the oblast level is clearly the structure with more
power and responsibility. Reviewing the captured Smolensk party ar-
chive, Fainsod (1958: 67) concluded that "one searches in vain for any aspect of oblast activity which does not find its reflection and point of
control in one or another division of the secretariat."

Each of the 129 obkoms[1] in the USSR has, at any one time, five party
secretaries, each (with the exception of the first secretary) with a particular functional specialization. In addition to the first secretary, who over-
sees the whole array of activities of the oblast, the four other obkom
secretaries oversee (1) cadres, or leading personnel, (2) agriculture, (3) industry, and (4) ideology, respectively. The obkom first secretary, though,
is clearly primus inter pares among the regional party and state leadership. As Hough (1969: 104) asserts, "it is he [the obkom first secretary]
rather than the committee who is the real prefect."

The first secretary alone can represent the oblast committee to its superior organs, and does so with some frequency as he attempts to adjust the
directives of the republic and all-union Central Committees to suit the
specific conditions indigenous to his oblast (Avtorkhanov, 1966: 162). In
addition, while having no formally defined authority over most economic enterprises, the first secretary is held responsible for the success of
plan implementation in his region (Hough, 1969).

Wary of charges by industrial managers of undue interference into the
prerogatives of state officials *(podmena),* the first secretary is sometimes
left with only crude tools of economic oversight. Nominally, his role is "to
aid, to stimulate, to observe, and to check," economic activity, both industrial and agricultural (Armstrong, 1959: 60). However, inasmuch as
politics and economics are part of the same Soviet wholecloth, party
"oversight" frequently becomes party "management." In sum, the obkom
first secretary plays a crucial role in the operation of the Soviet political
system and possesses significant (given the generally centralized nature
of power in the USSR) power and discretion within his region. These
facts account for the central leadership's long-standing fear of the oblasts

being turned into the personal "fiefdoms" of the incumbent first secretaries. The revelations that emerge from the periodic trials of corrupt obkom "satraps" attest both to the power inherent in these posts as well as to the center's commitment to maintain close scrutiny over its cadre of regional bosses.

Second, while the regional party first secretaryships are, in many ways, middle-level positions within the party hierarchy, they have traditionally been a stepping stone to republic-level and all-union-level leadership slots. Indeed, this post can be viewed as the most crucial position for promotion to the "center" (Rigby, 1978a: 1). Consistently, well over half of the obkom first secretaries have been either voting or candidate members of the All-Union C.P.S.U. Central Committee (Frank, 1971: 189). The 27th Party Congress of 1986 elected approximately 70 percent of these regional first secretaries into the party's Central Committee (Tatu, 1986: 3). Across time, moreover, both the number and the percentage of Politburo members who served as obkom first secretaries has tended to increase. For the 1951 Politburo, for example, this figure was 55 percent; in 1971, 87 percent of the Politburo members had some tenure as an obkom first secretary (Stewart and Town, 1974: 7).

Today, even in the aftermath of the rigorous post-Brezhnev cadre policy, these figures, although reduced, remain significant. Fifty percent (six of twelve) of voting Politburo members in 1987 were at one time regional "bosses," and 45 percent (five of eleven) of the Central Committee secretaries were first secretaries of an oblast-level party committee immediately prior to being promoted into leadership positions at either the republic or all-union level.[2] In addition, except for the fifteen-month Andropov interregnum, every Communist Party general secretary of any significant tenure since the death of Stalin in 1953 held this obkom post.

Finally, evidence has suggested for many years that the post of obkom first secretary is a "make or break" assignment for rising party functionaries. Armstrong (1959: 52–54) argues that a "trial period" or "period of probation" of approximately three years exists for newly appointed regional first secretaries before a decision regarding promotion to a higher administrative level is considered. In this manner, approximately 50 percent of the aspiring party apparatchiki are weeded out from those who will experience upward political mobility from the post of obkom first secretary. In sum, this post offers its incumbents great opportunities for upward, lateral, or downward political mobility. Of course, how and on what criteria these decisions are made from above constitute crucial questions for political scientists, sociologists, and other scholars of the Soviet system.

POLITICAL MOBILITY AND SOVIET *SEILSCHAFTEN*

Political mobility is one of the most studied topics in social science. Sociologists, historians, economists, and others have led the way for political scientists interested in studying the distribution of power in societies. Many key figures in the social sciences have generally investigated the question of political mobility. The study of trends in elite/political mobility allowed Marx, Weber, Pareto, Michel, and Mosca, to cite just a few, to make significant contributions to the analysis of various societies.

Beginning with Aristotle, most taxonomists of political systems have based their analyses, in one way or another, on differences in political mobility. Indeed, the distinction between "open" and "closed" systems is, in large part, based on the extant opportunities for political mobility. A long-time student of Soviet politics, Alfred G. Meyer (1969: 191) argues that a crucial feature distinguishing "democratic" from "bureaucratic" systems is "the egalitarian ethos which expresses itself foremost in the virtually universal opportunities for upward political mobility" in democratic or open societies. In sum, the specific mix of mobility opportunities operating in any given social setting greatly determines the distribution of power within that setting. Those racial, ethnic, religious, and geographic groups that rise to positions of power in any given society reflect the structural biases which inhere in that society. For this reason, the study of political mobility has been a traditional focus for researchers in the social sciences.

Following Stewart (1972: 1273), this study conceives of "mobility" as movement (upward, downward, or lateral) within the Soviet political hierarchy. As such, it must be distinguished from the concept of "political recruitment." This latter phenomenon involves the process of initial selection ("recruitment" or "co-optation") into the party apparatus. Thus conceived, "recruitment" is primarily a unidirectional concept concerned with admission into the hierarchy, whereas "mobility" is multidirectional in nature. This key distinction allows for a more thorough investigation of trends in the movement of political personnel within the Soviet system.

Orthodox explanations of Soviet regional elite mobility (and Soviet elite mobility generally) have been primarily based on the analysis of idiosyncratic variables. The literature of this specific subfield of sovietology has been dominated by idiographic accounts of political mobility predicated on the explanatory value of personalistic forces. Whether the analysis is labeled "patronage," "patron–client," "patron–protege," "regional cohort analysis," or "clientelism," the core tenets of this school of thought are perhaps best represented by the concept of *seilschaften*. As Jozsa (1983: 139) describes it: "In mountaineering jargon the term *seilschaften* stands for a 'roped-party' of climbers whose mutual aid, protection and support enable them to scale heights that would be beyond their individual powers." This metaphor aptly describes the conventional wisdom on political elite mobility at the regional level in the USSR. The patronage-based account, more specifically, entails the following:

A patron–client relationship is a vertical dyadic alliance, i.e., an alliance between two persons of unequal status, power or resources each of whom finds it useful to have as an ally someone superior or inferior to himself . . . Patron–client relationships . . . (1) involve the direct personal attachment of two individuals to each other . . . (2) exist for the purpose of exchanging favors and providing mutual assurances of aid . . . (3) are easy to create, but . . . (4) have some distinctive features which set them off from alliances between persons of equal socioeconomic status (Lande, 1977: xxi).

The upward, lateral, or downward political mobility associated with obkom first secretaries has been viewed, then, as largely the result of political maneuvering at a higher level of the political hierarchy. The careers of subnational political elites throughout the Soviet system are seemingly tied to the successes and/or failures of their ultimate benevolent patron. For example, the upward political mobility currently enjoyed by Vsevolod S. Murakhovskii (chairman of the USSR State Agroindustrial Committee, and a first deputy chairman of the USSR Council of Ministers) is presumably to be explained by reference to his long-standing relationship with Mikhail Gorbachev. Murakhovskii was Gorbachev's subordinate during the latter's tenure as first secretary of the Stavropol regional party organization; when Gorbachev was elevated to the All-Union Secretariat in 1978 (by *his* patrons, Yurii Andropov and Mikhail Suslov), Murakhovskii succeeded Gorbachev as party first secretary in the Stavropol region. As Gorbachev rose through the system, his protégé rose with him. However, in important respects, dyadic relationships such as this are reciprocal in nature. Gorbachev's relative power vis-à-vis his rivals, for example, is buttressed by just this ability to place allies (protégés) in various key posts throughout the Soviet party and state hierarchies.

Grey Hodnett (1975: 11) goes a long way in delineating the essence of the *seilschaft* dynamic as it exists in Soviet politics. The patron–client relationship is extant and operating when both the patron and the client are simultaneously engaged in "(a) promotion of one's interest as a continuing member of the leadership; (b) promotion of one's factional interests; (c) promotion of functional sympathies; (d) promotion of interests associated with one's general policy sympathies; (e) promotion of sectoral ('party,' 'governmental,' etc.), organizational (departmental, ministerial, etc.), or geographic (province, region, republic) interests; (f) promotion of interests associated with one's past career experiences; [and] (g) promotion of interests arising from one's membership in various age, social background, ethnic, and educational categories." As this suggests, the Soviet system offers numerous sources and diverse opportunities for the creation of patron–protégé relationships.

Given these assumptions, explanations of regional political elite mobility require the identification of the various *seilschaft* cohorts that exist within the Soviet system. That is, if political mobility below the republic level is to be seen as part of a complex "string" of *seilschaft* movements, then it becomes necessary for analysts interested in the explanation and prediction of these movements to identify the members of the different "chains" of patrons and protégés that combine to produce political elite mobility in the Soviet Union. To this end, scholars have noted two necessary (but not sufficient) conditions that must exist in order to establish such a relationship between members of the *seilschaft:* (1) The individuals must have been in geographic proximity for a given time period; and (2) there must be a positive correlation of the promotions and advancements of both patrons and protégés (that is, that as patron P rises through the hierarchy, his protégés p^1, p^2, p^3, . . . , also rise with him, though they are at various levels and may rise at different rates) (Willerton, 1979: 164). Several key studies have done just this.

Joel Moses (1976) analyzed the career-paths of twenty-four officials associated with the Dnepropetrovsk region of the Ukrainian SSR. These individuals represented the *seilschaft* headed by then-General Secretary Leonid Brezhnev, who served as that obkom's first secretary between 1947 and 1950. Moses found that the Dnepropetrovsk regional political cohorts advanced more rapidly than did even the upwardly mobile "climbers" of other regional party and state apparatuses. Not surprisingly, he also found the political mobilities associated with the rival Ukrainian Kharkov apparatus (headed by Brezhnev's politburo rival Nikolai Podgorny) to be negatively correlated with those of the Brezhnev-led Dnepropetrovsk group. Moses's claim was simple: "The opportunities for political advancement among Dnepropetrovsk officials had significantly improved since a native and former regional committee [obkom] first secretary, L. I. Brezhnev, had assumed leadership of the Communist Party in October, 1964 . . . " (p. 7).

While Moses focused his attention on a single patron–client chain, the so-called "Dnepropetrovsk Gang," John P. Willerton (1979), utilizing the same key assumptions of the *seilschaft* school, sought to identify the memberships of several patronage networks. He examined Soviet "clientelism" by treating the eighteen full members of the 1966–1976 Politburo as patrons and all full and candidate members of the All-Union Central Committee (n = 470) as potential clients. Willerton identified 154 Central Committee members (33 percent of the total) as clients of Politburo patrons. The number of clients per patron ranged from twenty-six (Brezhnev) to two (Kulakov and Gromyko), with an average 8.6 clients for each Politburo patron (pp. 166–167). Based on his analysis, Willerton concluded that in relation to clients, patrons are (1) "senior" in decision-making power and influence, (2) "senior" in terms of tenure in the All-Union Central Committee, (3) nearly always older and more experienced, and (4) tend to be similar to their clients in terms of functional career specialization (pp. 166–170). Having established a relationship based on similar bureaucratic interests and/or regional loyalties, patron–client relationships tend to be characterized by these dyadic traits.

Writing more recently, Gyula Jozsa (1983) has sought to identify *seilschaften* within the contemporary Soviet leadership cadre. Jozsa explicitly articulates the research disposition of scholars of the patron–client school of Soviet political elite mobility. "It is our concern," he writes, "to demonstrate that the analysis of *seilschaften* must begin with the open cataloguing and identification of the persons involved" (p. 149). Twenty-one patrons (determined a priori by their posts as either full or candidate Politburo members or secretaries of the 1981 Central Committee) were linked with 106 clients, an average of just over 5 clients per patron. The number of clients per patron found by Jozsa ranged from twenty-nine for Brezhnev to one each for Gorbachev and Dolgikh. Supporting the work of Moses (1976), nine of the evident Brezhnev protégés are associated with the Dnepropetrovsk oblast of the Ukrainian SSR (p. 154). Jozsa's caveat to the reader further elaborates on the *seilschaft* theme: "Every patron has been or is simultaneously a client and any client has been, is, or can become a patron. These fluid, dynamic and often dual roles demand that the political and social context as well as the time factor be taken into consideration" when seeking to untangle the complex of *seilschaft* "ropes" that determine political elite mobility in the Soviet Union.

Having identified through painstaking labors the memberships of the respective Soviet *seilschaften,* scholars relying on this mode of inquiry for the explanation and prediction of political elite mobility are compelled to make a series of implicit (and often explicit) causal statements about the specific instances of upward, lateral, or downward mobility:

John A. Armstrong: "In a sense the Soviet system is a vast collection of personal followings, in which the success of middle-level officials *depends on* the patronage of dominant leaders" (1959: 146; emphasis added).

Frederick C. Barghoorn: " . . . most of the present leaders owe their positions largely to Khrushchev . . . " (1970: 76).

Carl A. Linden: "Most Soviet leaders . . . have gathered personal follow-ings around themselves during their rise by rewarding the faithful and punishing the disloyal" (1966: 13).

Jerry F. Hough: "In the course of each man's [Stalin's and Khrushchev's] rise to power, he removed many old members from the [Central] Com-mittee and expanded its size *in order to* swamp the survivors by his own supporters" (1980: 63; emphasis added).

Thomas H. Rigby: "In establishing his power, Khrushchev had made great use of the Party Secretariat to appoint his supporters to key posi-tions; Brezhnev and his colleagues understood this well, since *this is how* most of them had themselves gotten into the top leadership, as proteges of Khrushchev" (1978b: 47; emphasis added).

Harold R. Swearer: "A striking number of high officials, promoted after 1954 . . . had worked in the Ukraine when Khrushchev had been Party boss there. Some of the more important of these men . . . include: A. I. Kirichenko, L. R. Korniets, R. A. Rudenko, A. I. Kirilenko, V. P. Mzhavanadze, V. V. Matskevich, V. E. Semichastny, L. I. Brezhnev, and I. A. Serov. Several men who served under Khrushchev when he was Party First Secretary of Moscow Oblast also rose to prominence at the same time" (1964: 18).

Myron Rush: "After 1960, Podgorny, Polyansky, Voronov, Kirilenko, and Kosygin were added to the Praesidium. All but Kosygin were in rela-tively minor posts when Khrushchev became dictator in 1957, and there is no evidence that any of these five promotions originated other-wise than with him" (1965: 99).

Joel C. Moses: "In attempting to use his native region of Dnepropetrovsk as a private patronage reserve, Brezhnev would be pursuing the most logical strategy to assure political support for *his* policy initiatives in the bureaucracies responsible for their implementation and to counter the influence of other central leadership figures, who might otherwise attempt to undermine his authority by transferring their own loyal sub-ordinates to the same positions" (1976: 72; emphasis added).

Robert E. Blackwell and William E. Hulbary: "When Khrushchev was re-moved, a sharp drop occurred in the impact of Ukrainian affiliation on mobility . . . Khrushchev's strong ties to this apparatus may have been sufficient to hinder the advancement of those with similar ties at the obkom level" (1973: 741).

Zbigniew K. Brzezinski and Samuel P. Huntington: "[In order] to get off to a fast start in the Soviet Union, *it is necessary* to attract the attention of some upper-level political leader and become his protégé . . . Apart from the old Bolsheviks (who were leaders before they were bureau-crats) every major political leader in the Soviet Union has risen to power under the aegis of a patron and as a member of a clique" (1964: 147).

These ten quotations from prominent contributors to the elite literature are representative of the class of explanations produced by the *seilschaft* approach to the study of Soviet political elite mobility. The statements reflect the idiosyncratic, personalistic, and ideographic mode of explanation that tends to inhere in the patron–client assumptions. Each "explanation" highlights the arbitrariness of the cadre selection process as it exists and operates in the Soviet Union. Combined, they defend a view of the Soviet system as one resembling a political "free-for-all," or a Hobbesian "state of nature" wherein trends in political elite mobility reflect not the dynamics of rational-technical criteria of tenure and advancement, but instrumental, power-building, and arbitrary criteria based on political expediency.

Certainly the more sophisticated accounts of elite mobility of this type (and the above cited scholars certainly *are* equally sophisticated proponents) are careful to integrate into the analysis discussions of public policy and related issues. However, it is clear from even a casual review of the literature that any ties to rational-technical standards of elite mobility are deemed to be of only secondary or tertiary explanatory value. Rather, Soviet apparatchiki experience upward, lateral, or downward political mobility *because of* their membership in a political *seilschaft* that is, in toto, experiencing upward, lateral, or downward mobility based on the fates of those power patrons at the head of the "roped-party of climbers." Low-level client "climbers" may fall from the *seilschaft* for any number of idiosyncratic reasons without affecting mobility chances of the remainder of the cohort, but almost all *upward* political mobility (and a great portion of downward political mobility) have been explained through the *seilschaft* metaphor.

SOVIET POLITICAL ELITE MOBILITY AS A RATIONAL-TECHNICAL PROCESS

Movements of elites, it is implied by the *seilschaft* approach, reflect the outcomes of "power games" played at a higher level of politics. Harold Swearer's account of the Shepilov–Khrushchev relationship clearly imputes an arbitrary, instrumental, and game-like quality to high-level political mobility in the Soviet Union; any connection to "legitimate" rational criteria, such as a concern for public policy issues, job performance, relative differences in worldviews, or even personality clashes, are omitted:

An important aspect of the factional struggle among the leaders is the maneuvering of the contestants to have their supporters placed in key positions and either to woo over the supporters of their opponents or to replace them ... More than once after 1953, important secondary figures apparently switched sides to seek personal advantage. For example, D. T. Shepilov, whose elevation into the Party's inner circles appeared to be closely tied to Khrushchev's patronage, threw his lot with the opposition to Khrushchev in June 1957. It is noteworthy that Khrushchev subsequently characterized him as a "double-dealer." The Shepilov affair further serves to point up the fact that even those close to the power struggle cannot always accurately predict the winner (1964: 17).

This description of the *seilschaft* approach to political elite mobility in the USSR, based on idiosyncratic, personalistic, even Hobbesian assumptions, is *not* meant primarily to be critical of this literature. In many ways, especially during the early years of the Soviet system, these traits *did* indeed dominate the operation of Soviet cadres "policy." The criteria for political fortune or misfortune *were* (and no doubt to some degree still are) non-rational, arbitrary, personalistic, and Hobbesian. Careers were made and unmade by the whim and fancy of such individuals as Stalin, Beria, Malenkov, Khrushchev, Suslov, Brezhnev, Andropov, and Gorbachev (to name only the most obvious). The Soviet Union during the 1930s did resemble a Hobbesian state of nature. The *seilschaft*-based explanations of Soviet elite mobility are not invalid, as far as they go. Patron–client chains exist and affect the career chances of many individuals in party, state, and "public" institutions. These chains of "roped" climbers can and should be identified and analyzed.

Yet, scholars studying Soviet-style systems cannot rely solely on this type of explanation for the generation of a complete understanding of the forces at work in the area of elite mobility. Patronage-based explanations are significantly limited in substantive areas of increasing interest to sovietologists. First, the further one is removed from the machinations of the Thursday afternoon Politburo meetings, the less appropriate these idiosyncratic and personalistic explanations appear. As one descends the levels-of-analysis "ladder" from the All-Union Politburo to the over 425,000 primary party organizations operating at the local enterprise level, the need for more rational-technical explanations of elite political mobility becomes increasingly apparent.

Patronage-based explanations cannot account for much of the political mobility experienced by those individuals below the level of the All-Union Central Committee. Indeed, Willerton (1979), explicitly examining "clientelism in the Soviet Union," could link only one-third of the Central Committee members to a "patron." One is left to wonder how the remaining 316 members of this very powerful party organ ever attained such extraordinary upward political mobility. Jozsa (1983) could identify only 106 protégés in the combined memberships of the Politburo and the

Secretariat. These accounts are not invalid; they are merely limited to a certain class or level of analysis.

Second, even if one is to accept as significant the *seilschaft* links that are identified by Moses, Jozsa, and Willerton, these data do little to unearth the forces operative over the long term which have allowed these special 154 (Willerton) or 106 (Jozsa) or 24 (Moses) apparatchiki to get into a position where they are more or less likely to be either "coopted" or "recruited" by the 18 (Willerton) or 21 (Jozsa) or 1 (Moses) "patrons" that have been identified. To the degree that the investigations of these patron–client relationships are significant (and it is believed that they are), they are so only for the light they cast on the motivations and activities of the "power elite" of the Soviet Union. As Bohdan Harasymiw (1983: 141) admits, *seilschaft* analyses are "concentrated [only] on the 'tip of the iceberg.'"

Third, if the Kuhnian concept of the "paradigmatic shift" is at all a valid description of what went on in the discipline during the first two decades after the death of Stalin, and if this shift in the activities and assumptions of sovietologists is at all reflective of changes that have actually been developing in the Soviet system, then the explanatory value of the *seilschaft*-based depiction of political elite mobility is declining over time. Put succinctly, to the degree that sovietologists have correctly abandoned the totalitarian assumptions of an outdated paradigm, the idiosyncratic and personalistic elements of patron–client explanations are becoming increasingly anachronistic and invalid for a larger percentage of the *nomenklatura,* those key positions throughout the Soviet system controlled by the CPSU. If the Soviet Union is becoming increasingly rational-technical in *its* criteria for judging cadres, then it is incumbent upon sovietologists wishing to explain and predict an increasing portion of elite political mobility in the USSR to alter the assumptions that govern their *own* research efforts.

As Bohdan Harasymiw (1984a: 17) explains, "The process of [elite] recruitment must, in any society, be conceived of as consisting of several component determinants: individual, social, and structural." Using *seilschaften* as an explanation of elite mobility is to focus overwhelmingly on the individualistic determinants of patronage, sponsorships, connections, and friendships. Patronage-based studies of political mobility look at individuals and how their activities create and perpetuate "friends, followers, and factions" (Schmidt et al., 1977). The present study focuses on the social and structural forces affecting elite mobility in the USSR; as such, it is more a complement to than a rival of the large body of literature on the individualistic sources of Soviet elite mobility. If patronage-based explanations focus on the "tip of the iceberg," then the rational-technical orientation adopted here as a point of departure for the study of regional elite mobility seeks to describe the massive structure that lies below the surface and supports the structure's "tip." Scholars of Soviet elite mobility cannot assume that the dynamics that govern mobility at the Politburo/Secretariat level are necessarily identical (or even similar) to those which effect mobility at lower levels.

According to Philip D. Stewart et al. (1972: 1270), this alternative orientation toward political elite mobility involves at least two key propositions: "(1) As economic growth of the industrial sector advances, there arises a need for technical expertise in management to ensure efficiency and progress; and (2) in a state where economic development is a major goal of the political regime, political leaders will tend to be selected for their technical, administrative, and 'bargaining' skills."

Rather than focusing on Kremlinological maneuvering and patron–client *seilschaften,* the rational-technical view of regional elite mobility places much store in Khrushchev's dictum: "Friendship is friendship, but business is business" (Hough, 1969: 277). Friends, followers, and factions are important variables in many individual cases, but the development of an industrialized state and the national political commitment to promote rapid industrial and technical growth both exert significant structural pressure toward creating within the political system a rational-technical set of criteria for governing elite mobility throughout the party, state, and public apparatuses. To the degree that *seilschaft*-based explanations are valid, they are so only within a rational-technical environment that determines the opportunity structures for these personalistic forces.

A complex interplay of rational-technical and personalistic forces operates at all levels of the Soviet system, as well as in other systems. Explanations of political elite mobility couched almost solely in terms of personalistic forces (to the relative neglect of rational-technical factors) are not overly consistent with the view of the USSR as a highly-bureaucratized political and economic system that annually produces the world's second ranking economic output. Patron–client relationships exist, if you will, only by being superimposed upon a rational-technical system that over the long run colors that climate of expectations and affects the "career chances" of elites.

Jerry F. Hough (1969) has provided a comprehensive set of case histories describing the rational-technical model of Soviet elite mobility. Focusing on the obkom first secretary's role in industrial decision making, Hough examines the significant impact that rational-technical criteria (such as the oblast's economic performance) have on the career mobility of the regional "prefect." Hough views the development of the Soviet system as moving away from non-rational, non-technical, and idiosyncratic characteristics and toward a modern system based on a rational-technical foundation.

The model of rational-technical society suggests that there are rational-technical solutions to most of society's problems and that these solutions are fairly apparent to the man with the proper specialized preparation .... From a thirty- to forty-year perspective, perhaps the most basic development in the Soviet administrative system has been the increased specialization in administrative and Party structure and personnel (Hough, 1969: 306; 274).

Hough's research clearly calls for the development and testing of other analytic approaches to the study of Soviet regional elite mobility. These rival explanations must be based on rational-technical/structural forces if they hope to explain the key processes of elite mobility in an increasingly modern, industrial, and technocratic Soviet Union.

Stewart et al. (1972), following the lead established by Hough, provide a "partial test" of these two models of elite mobility. Two of the major conclusions of their quantitative analysis are: (1) " ... while patronage is relevant to succession struggles, its significance is probably overestimated"; and (2) "within the Russian republic [the focus of the study], as the level of economic development increases, the patronage model tends to explain less and the performance model tends to account for more of the variance in mobility" (p. 1284). Yet, despite the promise of these studies, research into the rational-technical determinants of elite mobility has not been pursued.

William A. Welsh (1973: 3), after surveying the extant literature on the subject, discerned three major trends within the area of Soviet elite mobility: (1) an increase in the use of "rational-technical" criteria in the recruitment of elites, (2) a decline in the importance of ideological considerations in decision making, and (3) the emergence of a new kind of elite, a "managerial class." His analysis showed a decline in the importance and explanatory value of patronage as a force in political elite recruitment as the Soviet system moved toward the creation of a ruling "technocracy." The conflict evident in the preceding discussion of the *seilschaft*-based school of political mobility is made clear in Welsh's treatment. It is contradictory to assert, as many have done, the rise of the bureaucratic state in the USSR, yet maintain a view of political cadres policy based on the "anything goes" assumptions of the patronage model of elite mobility. Few scholars of the patron–client school directly address this inconsistency.

Despite these early efforts advocating the adoption of the rational-technical approach to Soviet elite mobility, very few significant works have appeared since the mid-1970s that seek to explicate the non-idiosyncratic factors at work in this area. This trend away from the study of elite mobility generally and away from research on regional elite mobility more narrowly can be explained in the main by the extremely conservative cadres policy adopted by Brezhnev. His "trust-in-cadres" policy slowed elite turnover almost to a standstill:

Notwithstanding a party rule that still mandates a steady level of turnover within the elite, this objective has not been attained, nor for that matter has it even been aggressively pursued ... The turnover rate for obkom first secretaries has also been much lower under Brezhnev, roughly half what it was under Khrushchev ... While the degree of decline in obkom leadership turnover varies by region, each republic shows a lower rate in the post-Khrushchev period (Blackwell, 1979: 31; 34).

Scholars interested in elite mobility soon became interested in the ramifications of elite *non*-mobility in the Soviet Union. They abandoned the search for the structural determinants of mobility, and focused instead on the dysfunctional effects of elite ossification and generational conflict (for example, Hough, 1980; Bialer, 1980).

CONCLUSION

The personnel policy of "trust in cadres" died with Brezhnev. Except for the short interlude of Konstantin Chernenko, regional elite mobility and elite mobility generally have been steady and significant. Whereas the 1965–1978 period witnessed on average only thirteen removals of obkom first secretaries per year (Blackwell, 1979: 34), the post-Brezhnev period has been marked by a rigorous pattern of regional elite mobility. During Andropov's rule between November 1982 and February 1984, thirty-two obkom first secretaries were replaced; since Gorbachev's rise to the post of general secretary in March 1985, an average of almost three regional party bosses per month have been moved. These two figures parallel the twenty-seven per year average of the Khrushchev years. Indeed, in the first four years following the death of Brezhnev, 101 of the 129 regional first secretaries (78 percent) were moved out of the obkom tier.

If the cadres flux usually associated with Khrushchev warranted the greatly increased attention of scholars interested in elite mobility, then certainly it is time to reopen the investigation that virtually ended over a decade ago. This present study attempts to contribute to the search for non-idiosyncratic, rational-technical variables affecting regional elite mobility in the Soviet Union in the post-Khrushchev period. It seeks through both quantitative and qualitative analysis to (1) construct a political mobility hierarchy of the 129 oblast party committees of the USSR; (2) identify "correlates" of political mobility from a statistical analysis of oblast-level economic, demographic, political, and sociocultural data; (3) ascertain and measure differences in political mobility associated with obkom first secretaries of differing functional career specializations; and

(4) chronicle and analyze the changes in the regional elite that have taken place under Andropov, Chernenko, and Gorbachev.

The research orientation embraced herein is one that views the generation and testing of structural, rational-technical hypotheses of Soviet elite mobility and politics as preferable, both philosophically and intellectually, to those based on totalitarian, Kremlinological, and/or idiosyncratic variables. It is hoped that studying Soviet elite mobility in a way similar to studying elite mobility in any other advanced industrial state will yield positive results in both the generation of new knowledge and the further philosophical reorientation of Western scholars of Soviet elite politics.

NOTES

1. For the purposes of this study, the *oblast* (region) and the somewhat larger in size *krai* (province), both directly below the union republic level, are considered "regional" units and are, as such, treated as identical. The oblast is the highest purely administrative unit of the USSR. Above this level, the territorial divisions [autonomous republics (ASSRs) and union republics] of the Soviet Union are based on nationality. As of the end of 1986 there were 123 oblasti and 6 krai in the USSR. The oblast unit does not, however, exist in all union republics; only eight of the fifteen contain oblasti. The specific distribution of oblasti is as follows:

Russian Republic (RSFSR)	49 oblasti + 6 krai
Ukrainian SSR	25 oblasti
Kazakh SSR	19 oblasti
Uzbek SSR	12 oblasti
Belorussian SSR	6 oblasti
Turkmen SSR	5 oblasti
Kirgiz SSR	4 oblasti
Tadzhik SSR	3 oblasti
	123 oblasti + 6 krai

Unless reference is specifically to a krai or kraikom, the term "obkom" will be used throughout to denote both obkoms and kraikoms.

2. Parenthetically, as T. H. Rigby (1978a: 2) demonstrates, the political importance of regional posts is not a strictly Soviet invention. In Tsarist times, both the post of *voevody* and *gubernator* constituted "a common stepping stone to high office in St. Petersburg."

REFERENCES

Armstrong, John A. *The Soviet Bureaucratic Elite: A Case Study of the Ukrainian Apparatus.* New York: Praeger, 1959.

Avtorkhanov, Abdurakhman. *The Communist Party Apparatus.* Chicago: Henry Regnery, 1966.

Barghoorn, Frederick C. "Trends in Top Political Leadership in the USSR," in R. Barry Farrell, ed. *Political Leadership in Eastern Europe and the Soviet Union.* Chicago: Aldine, 1970.

Bialer, Seweryn. *Stalin's Successors: Leadership, Stability, and Change in the Soviet Union.* Cambridge: Cambridge University Press, 1980.

Blackwell, Robert E., Jr. "Career Development in the Soviet Obkom Elite: A Conservative Trend," *Soviet Studies* 24 (July 1972a): 26–39.

_____ . "Elite Recruitment and Functional Change: An Analysis of the Soviet Obkom Elite 1950–1968," *Journal of Politics* 34 (1972b): 124–152.

_____ . "Cadres Policy in the Brezhnev Era," *Problems of Communism* (March–April 1979): 29–42.

Blackwell, Robert E., Jr., and William E. Hulbary. "Political Mobility Among Soviet Obkom Elites: The Effects of Regime, Social Backgrounds, and Career Development," *American Journal of Political Science* 17, no. 4 (1973): 721–743.

Brzezinski, Zbigniew K. and Samuel P. Huntington. *Political Power: USA/USSR.* New York: Viking Press, 1964.

Fainsod, Merle. *Smolensk under Soviet Rule.* New York: Random House, 1958.

Frank, Peter. "The CPSU Obkom First Secretary: A Profile," *British Journal of Political Science* 1, no. 2 (1971): 173–190.

Harasymiw, Bohdan. "Some Theoretical Considerations on Advancement within the Political Elite in Soviet-Type Systems," in T. H. Rigby and Bohdan Harasymiw, eds. *Leadership Selection and Patron-Client Relations in the USSR and Yugoslavia.* London: George Allen & Unwin, 1983.

_____ . *Political Elite Recruitment in the Soviet Union.* New York: St. Martin's Press, 1984.

Hodnett, Grey. "The Obkom First Secretaries," *Slavic Review* 24 (December 1965): 636–652.

_____ . "Succession Contingencies in the Soviet Union," *Problems of Communism* 24, no. 2 (March–April 1975): 1–21.

Hough, Jerry F. "The Role of the Local Party Organs in Soviet Industrial Decision Making." Ph.D. dissertation, Harvard University, 1961.

_____ . *The Soviet Prefects: The Local Party Organs in Industrial Decision-Making.* Cambridge, Mass.: Harvard University Press, 1969.

_____ . *Soviet Leadership in Transition.* Washington, D.C.: Brookings Institution, 1980.

Jozsa, Gyula. "Political 'Seilschaften' in the USSR" in T.H. Rigby and Bohdan Harasymiw, eds. *Leadership Selection and Patron–Client Relations in the USSR and Yugoslavia.* London: George Allen & Unwin, 1983.

Lande, Carl H. "The Dyadic Basis of Clientelism," in Steffen W. Schmidt et al., eds. *Friends, Followers, and Factions.* Berkeley: University of California Press, 1977.

Lewis, Carol and Stephen Sternheimer. *Soviet Urban Management.* New York: Praeger Publishers, 1979.

Linden, Carl A. *Khrushchev and the Soviet Leadership: 1957–1964.* Baltimore: Johns Hopkins University Press, 1966.

Meyer, Alfred G. "The Comparative Study of Communist Political Systems," in Frederic J. Fleron, Jr., ed. *Communist Studies and the Social Sciences.* Chicago: Rand McNally, 1969.

Miller, John H. "Cadres Policy in Nationality Areas: Recruitment of CPSU First and Second Secretaries in Non-Russian Republics of the USSR," *Soviet Studies* 29, no. 1 (January 1977): 3–36.

Moses, Joel C. *Regional Party Leadership and Decision Making in the USSR.* New York: Praeger, 1974.

————. "Regional Cohorts and Political Mobility in the USSR: The Case of Dnepropetrovsk," *Soviet Union* 8, part 1 (1976): 63–89.

Rigby, T. H. "The Soviet Regional Leadership: The Brezhnev Generation," *Slavic Review* 37, no. 1 (March 1978a): 1–24.

————. "Personal and Collective Leadership: Brezhnev and Beyond," in Dmitri K. Simes et al. *Soviet Succession: Leadership in Transition.* Beverly Hills, Cal.: Sage Publications, 1978b.

————. "How the Obkom Secretary was Tempered," *Problems of Communism* (March–April 1980): 57–63.

Rush, Myron. *Political Succession in the USSR.* Boston: Little, Brown & Co., 1965.

Schmidt, Steffen, et al., eds. *Friends, Followers, and Factions: Reader in Political Clientelism.* Berkeley: University of California Press, 1977.

Stewart, Philip D. *Political Power in the Soviet Union: A Study of Decision-Making in Stalingrad.* New York: Bobbs-Merrill, 1968.

Stewart, Philip D., et al. "Political Mobility and the Soviet Political Process: A Partial Test of Two Models," *American Political Science Review* 66 (1972): 1269–1290.

Stewart, Philip D., and Kenneth Town. "The Career-Attitude Linkage among Soviet Regional Elites: An Exploration of its Nature and Magnitude." Paper delivered at the 1974 annual meeting of the American Political Science Association Chicago, Ill.: August 29–September 2, 1974.

Swearer, Howard R. *The Politics of Succession in the USSR.* Boston: Little, Brown & Co., 1964.

Tatu, Michel. "The Central Committee Elected at the Twenty-Seventh Party Congress: Halfway Towards Rejuvenation," *Radio Liberty Research* RL 106/86 (March 10, 1986): 1–3.

Welsh, William A. "Introduction," in Carl Beck et al., eds. *Comparative Communist Political Leadership.* New York: David McKay Co., Inc., 1973.

Willerton, John P. "Clientelism in the Soviet Union: An Initial Examination," *Studies in Comparative Communism* 12, nos. 2–3 (1979): 159–183.

2

TOWARD THE CONSTRUCTION OF A POLITICAL MOBILITY RANKING OF OBLAST COMMUNIST PARTY COMMITTEES

INTRODUCTION

Scholars interested in explicating trends in Soviet political elite mobility are immediately confronted with a methodological problem generic to all mobility studies. In order to assess "upward," "downward," or even "lateral" mobility within any field, one must, by definition, have clearly established criteria against which to judge these movements. That is, the scholar must be able to operationalize the concepts of "upward," "downward," and "lateral" if the statements articulated are to have any validity. The movement from post A to post B can be considered a promotion only if (a) these respective positions have a priori been placed within a comprehensive positional hierarchy or ranking, and (b) post B is superior to post A on this hierarchy.

It is easy to state, and defend successfully, the proposition that post B is superior to post A if B represents the general secretary of the C.P.S.U. Central Committee and A represents the first secretary of the Stavropol kraikom. Even an intuitive understanding of an imaginary and ill-defined hierarchy of posts within the Soviet Union would allow the observer to make such a statement. To say that Mikhail Gorbachev has experienced upward political mobility from post A to post B does not require the rigor of a clearly articulated and comprehensive hierarchy of posts within the Soviet sociopolitical structure. However, when analyzing political mobility trends of a larger number of cases at lower political-administrative levels, using largely undefined, intuitive hierarchies of the Soviet political-administrative structure will not yield a measurable degree of exactness.

This chapter seeks to construct a hierarchical ranking of oblast Communist party committees (obkomy) based on the political mobility opportunities associated with them. More precisely, based upon the career mobility of each unit's first secretaries, quantitative political mobility scores are generated for each obkom. Inherent in the construction of such a ranking, however, is the necessary juxtaposition of actual individuals' career moves and a comprehensive, detailed hierarchy of positions comprising the Soviet sociopolitical structure. That is, any attempt to construct a political mobility ranking of obkomy based upon individuals' career paths is predicated on the validity of a positional hierarchy of posts against which these career moves are judged. It is this positional hierarchy that operationalizes the concepts of "upward," "downward," "lateral," "promotion," "demotion," and so on.

Therefore, the nature of this hierarchy of posts is crucial to the larger project; it represents the methodological problem referred to in the opening lines of this chapter. Unfortunately, little consensus exists among scholars on the best procedure to build an appropriate positional hierarchy against which to judge these career moves. Indeed, much of the research that has attempted to measure elite mobility in the Soviet Union speaks just as much to the methodological dictates of hierarchy-building as to the substantive nature of mobility patterns among elites in the USSR. This present effort is, to be sure, but a variation on that theme.

"THE HUNTING OF THE HIERARCHY": HIERARCHY-BUILDING AS A VOCATION

Several important attempts have been made to rank the regional party apparatuses, the key units in the political-administrative structure, according to their importance within the broader Soviet political system. Of course, different scholars have meant different things when discussing "importance." Chauncy Harris (1970), an economic geographer, constructed what he called a "central-place hierarchy" of regions in the Soviet Union based on economic and demographic variables. He classified Soviet oblasti in three main categories: (1) centers of major economic regions, (2) centers of industrial-management regions (the now-defunct sovnarkhozy), and (3) component oblasti. Explicating a decidedly structural argument, Harris hypothesized that:

the centers of these 3 levels of regions form an approach to a hierarchy of economic-administrative central places of decreasing rank and successively small tributary areas, and that these centers are "nested" so that centers of a higher order have within their tributary areas several centers of the next lower, and so on. Each high order center serves also the functions of lower-order centers but for much smaller areas (1970: 158).

Harris's schema made little mention of the Communist party and the more explicitly political aspects or implications of the variations among oblasti. However, his work provided the foundation for other scholars interested in these aspects of regional differences in the Soviet Union.

Peter Frank (1974) constructed a "classified ranking" of regional party committees utilizing a combination of Harris's administrative position approach and a decidedly more politicized version of "importance." Investigating the career patterns of obkom first secretaries, Frank (1971) discovered a problem that merited separate consideration. Although no differentiation among the regional party committees could be discerned on the surface, Frank quickly found that:

Some units seemed in practice to be more important than others. In other words, although the CPSU *Statutes* do not discriminate between one obkom and another, it seemed to us that to be the first secretary of obkom A was often more prestigious and more "important" than to be first secretary of obkom Z. Certain party obkoms . . . seemed to supply a disproportionately large number of promotees into the all-Union central party apparatus, while others . . . appeared to offer their first secretary only relatively poor prospects of further upward career mobility (1974: 217).

Frank argued further that "the Central Committee Secretariat does not place its cadres randomly, . . . it does have some kind of classification, or ranking, of party units, and . . . it does have certain specific criteria for assessing the importance or standing of obkoms" (1974: 217–18). Seeking to determine the basis for this "importance," Frank looked at such unit variables as area, population, and population density. None of these variables proved to be wholly satisfactory.

Frank's criterion of "importance" settled on the unit's representation in the C.P.S.U. Central Committee. While not defending their importance in any logical sense, the level of Central Committee representation of these regional party units certainly, in Frank's view, reflected their importance. Distinguishing obkomy based on the unit's first secretary's Central Committee status would go a long way toward the construction of a classified ranking of these regional units. While the percentage of "represented" oblasti has grown to a present level of approximately seven out of ten, a longitudinal analysis of the respective units' Central Committee status can reveal significant differentiation among these units.

Frank's analysis produced a ranking of the R.S.F.S.R. regional party units into seven hierarchical groups:

GROUP I: Leningrad, Moscow, Gorkii, Voronezh, Kuibyshev, Rostov, Sverdlovsk, Novosibirsk, Irkutsk, Khabarovsk

GROUP II: Tula, Saratov, Volgograd, Cheliabinsk, Perm, Kemerovo, Krasnoiarsk, Primore (Maritime)

GROUP III: Riazan, Kalinin, Briansk, Orel, Belgorod, Kursk, Tatar ASSR, Bashkir ASSR, Ulianovsk, Krasnodar, Stavropol, Dagestan ASSR, Orenburg, Omsk, Altai Krai

GROUP IV: Arkhangelsk, Murmansk, Ivanovo, Magadan

GROUP V: Pskov, Novgorod, Vologda, Karelia ASSR, Kostroma, Yaroslavl, Vladimir, Kaluga, Kirov, Mari ASSR, Chuvash ASSR, Mordovian ASSR, Lipetsk, Penza, Astrakhan, Kalmik ASSR, Kabardino-Balkar ASSR, Severo-Osetiia ASSR, Tiumen, Kurgan, Udmurt ASSR, Tomsk, Buriat ASSR, Chita, Tuva ASSR, Amur, Sakhalin, Yakut ASSR

GROUP VI: Komi ASSR

GROUP VII: Smolensk, Tambov, Checheno-Ingush ASSR, Kamchatka

Thus, the seventy R.S.F.S.R. units analyzed by Frank congealed into these seven ranked groupings of "importance." Frank was quick to assert the tentative nature of his findings, however, admitting that several possible objections to his particular hierarchy could be raised. Although the research showed great promise, Frank's work at this point represented what he called a "report of the progress made so far" in discriminating among these regional units; its aim was to serve as a "prophylactic aid" to others working in this substantive area (1974: 217).

The most thoroughgoing, and disheartening, critique of Frank's efforts (and of those basing their similar analyses on Central Committee status) has been provided by Mary McAuley (1974). Skeptical of basing any obkom-differentiating scheme on its status in the C.P.S.U. Central Committee, McAuley offers an alternative to Frank's assumptions about the significance of these variables.

The more we searched for something that might serve as the criterion of "importance," the clearer it became that depending upon the sense in which "importance" was being used the hierarchy would differ and that there was no satisfactory way of defining "importance" so as to produce something we could call *the* hierarchy.... When the leaders are concerned with party membership they may rank the oblasts in one way; when agriculture comes up as a pressing problem, the hierarchy would be different ..." (1974: 476).

On this point, McAuley is forced to conclude that, "even if it *were* clear what it means to talk of the leadership's 'assessment of the importance of different posts,' we would not accept that the CC status would, in all cases, correspond to the relative importance of that post" (1974: 479).

However, after a quantitative analysis of the relationship between the major indices cited by Frank (population, party membership, and economic performance) and the Central Committee status of these units,

McAuley conceded some theoretical ground to his key assumption. Although McAuley recognized other factors are clearly at work in the allocation of Central Committee representation to obkomy (especially in the withholding and changing of representation status), she found that "the Secretariat does operate within a *general* framework of awarding the majority of the prestige M [full central Committee membership] places to those with the best indices: the big leaders" (1974: 498). Yet this admission does not compel McAuley to retreat totally from her criticism:

It would be misleading to propose that a hierarchy based on CC status provided a reliable ranking of obkom posts in terms of the "responsibility" of the posts (and hence the incumbents' views on what counts as promotion) or in terms of the amount of attention paid by the leadership to what goes on in the oblast and the views of its first secretary (1974: 499).

Within the much broader general hierarchy of posts that comprise the overall Soviet political structure, then, the exact ranking of this subgrouping of regional party committees remains problematical.

Stewart et al. (1972), in their important analysis of two models of Soviet political mobility, utilize a comprehensive positional hierarchy that is adopted, in part, herein. Within this hierarchy, Stewart and his colleagues make no attempt to differentiate along any continuum the various oblast party committees (1972: 1287). The coding scheme adopted by the researchers in their mobility study assigns to *all* oblasti the identical numerical score. In this way, Stewart's team avoids the tough issues confronted by Frank and McAuley.

While Frank and McAuley could agree on the general proposition that Central Committee status is, to some degree, correlated with obkom "importance" (however defined), the Stewart index scores Leningrad and Moscow oblasti equally with Sakhalin and Kamchatka. The adoption of this position, however, while avoiding the methodological maelstrom faced by McAuley and Frank, skirts a crucial consideration. Stewart's coding scheme would generate identical numerical scores for each of the following hypothetical career moves: (1) the first secretary of the Belgorod city party committee (gorkom) becomes first secretary of the Leningrad obkom; and (2) the first secretary of the Belgorod gorkom becomes first secretary of the Magadan obkom. Such an equation of these mobility dyads seems, prima facie, indefensible. Neither Frank nor McAuley, it is argued, would agree with Stewart's coding results in this case. Indeed, McAuley views Stewart's assignment of equal standing to all obkomy as a weakness in his analysis (1974: 475n).

The debates among these scholars seem to revolve around the fundamental assumptions, or first steps, of the construction of positional heirarchies. Indeed, they reveal the significant methodological problems confronting all efforts to measure systematically political elite mobility trends in the Soviet system. To overcome these barriers in practice, of course, requires the resolution of a vast array of separate and thorny methodological issues.

These weaknesses notwithstanding, however, Stewart's approach has much merit. His hierarchy of posts comprises a wide array of posts and positions throughout the entire Soviet political/administrative structure, not just at the oblast-level. Second, his scheme is parsimonious (without being overly simplistic) with respect to the coding of actual career moves. As shall become clear below, the modifications of Stewart's hierarchy adopted for this study address its major structural shortcomings.

The most obvious weakness of Stewart's scheme is the structural rigidity that renders it unable to differentiate among base positions falling within the same coding category. The examples of Moscow-Sakhalin and Leningrad-Kamchatka cited above are instances of this overly rigid coding scheme. In this regard, it is argued, Frank's fundamental assumption cannot be resisted. "It seems commonsensical," he writes, "that if a structural tier contained about 150 units then some would have a greater intrinsic importance than others" (1974: 217). McAuley's criticisms do not deal with this aspect of Frank's work. Rather, she is concerned with Frank's criterion of "intrinsic importance." McAuley herself concurs with Frank on the general issue of obkom differentiation:

If one is looking at personnel movements with the aim of explaining promotions and demotions, it does seem commonsense to differentiate between the obkomy, or rather to suggest that the secretariat and the obkom secretaries themselves think of them as "different" units (1974: 475).

In creating a comprehensive hierarchy of Soviet political-administrative posts, one cannot equate key structural subunits like obkomy without threatening the validity and utility of the hierarchy. No matter how problematic, some method of distinguishing between the Leningrads and Moscows, on the one hand, and the Sakhalins and Kamchatkas, on the other, must be devised. McAuley's skepticism not withstanding, the most parsimonious indicator of these distinctions remains the unit's representative status in the C.P.S.U. Central Committee. This argument can, of course, be expanded to apply to *all* the coding categories of the hierarchy of posts.

McAuley's skepticism does, however, raise a critical point. Not only would the Soviet leadership's assessment of "importance" vary with respect to issue area, but Western scholars engaged in constructing a valid hierarchy of positions within the Soviet political-administrative system would no doubt argue among themselves over the exact placement on this hierarchy of many of its constituent posts. Western analysts with exper-

tise in Soviet local politics, for example, might argue that the first secre-
ittee (gorkom) was placed too low on the
the scholar specializing in Politburo-level
:ademician with a research interest in the
ight advise the elevation on the hierarchy
terial posts. Other specialists in the field
; to the original. In a word, disagreements
itive hierarchies as the number of scholars
)e proferred as "valid."
the validity of her criticisms (she is essen-
dard of exactness she expects. Recalling a
. . there was no satisfactory way of defining
ə something we could call *the* hierarchy"
nal). Attempts to produce a hierarchy of
t is intrinsically correct at all times, for all
irs, are futile. Indeed, this was never, nor
ɔal. Rather, Frank produced a hierarchy of
:ceptable and defensible criteria.
g has long been used by scholars in soviet-
istribution of political power (Tatu, 1986;
)onaldson, 1972). Full membership in that
in accurate measure of discretionary power

for the incumbent, but such membership is reflective of a general privileged status for the post itself. Indeed, research has shown that, in essence, Central Committee status is a reflection less of the *individual* characteristics of the post incumbent than of the status of the post itself. That is, certain levels of Central Committee representation go with certain *posts,* no matter who occupies them. McAuley herself argues this very point. In her view, it is the *withdrawing* or *lack* of representation on the C.P.S.U. Central Committee that is important in this regard. At worst, she believes that certain aspects of oblast Central Committee membership can be utilized to indicate the importance of the respective oblasti. For these reasons, Central Committee status is herein considered an appropriate variable to be used in the differentiation of Soviet regional party committees.

As the above treatment reflects, considerable work in what McAuley calls "hunting the hierarchy" has been undertaken. The lack of agreement among those working in this substantive area, however, points to the fact that much more work has yet to be done. Serious doubt remains as to whether it is possible to create and utilize for further research a hierarchy of posts of the Soviet administrative structure that can be considered immune from all serious threats to valid inference. When evaluating a positional coding scheme, different scholars will discover different strengths and different weaknesses. In a word, the positional hierarchy that would be deemed satisfactory by all interested scholars is yet to be constructed. Anyone interested in engaging in research in this substantive area is forced to employ a hierarchy that avoids as many of the most serious threats to validity as possible. Avoiding all threats, given the subject matter at hand, is impossible.

This methodological fact, however, does not at the outset doom any and all efforts to analyze systematically Soviet elite mobility patterns. The problems of method, formidable as they may be, do not render the subject matter any less important or worthy of investigation. The methodological positions that support these research efforts reflect hundreds of micro-choices that are unavoidable. It is far more the nature of the choices themselves, rather than the researchers' actual resolution of them, that makes systematic inquiry into Soviet political elite mobility so problematic.

RESEARCH DESIGN AND DATA

The present study, then, utilizes Stewart's positional hierarchy as a point of departure.[1] This hierarchical arrangement of key political-administrative posts has, however, been altered substantially and, in its present form, embraces the methodological position articulated by Frank. That is, Stewart's equation of all regional party units has been rejected through the employment of a variation of Frank's regional differentiating scheme. It is believed that the resultant positional hierarchy and mobility coding index better reflect the disparities of power and prestige that inhere in the various party, state, and "public" institutions of the Soviet system.

The original positional hierarchy utilized by Stewart is a ten-part index of positions in the Communist party of the Soviet Union, the executive apparatus of the Soviet government, and the more ceremonial parliamentary organs of the Soviet state (see Appendix I). The posts represented range from "student" to "first secretary" of the C.P.S.U. Central Committee, and are simply coded from 0 to 9 in ascending hierarchical order. The lowest category is reserved for individuals who have left posts due to retirement, illness, or death. Each of the remaining nine levels is divided into various party and government categories. Stewart sought to provide a "partial test" of the rational-technical and patronage models of Soviet elite mobility by using this positional hierarchy to code the career moves of regional party committee first secretaries. Interested in movement out of the obkom tier, he examined the mobility of 224 persons who had left the position of first secretary in 58 oblasti of the R.S.F.S.R. between 1955 and 1967. In its skeleton form, Stewart's hierarchy is adopted, but significant alterations in the coding schemes seemed advisable.

The positional hierarchy employed for this study is structurally similar to Stewart's, but, due to several important changes, functions differently (see Appendix II). Like Stewart's, the present mobility index includes a ten-part hierarchy of the party, executive, and parliamentary posts of the Soviet political-administrative structure. In essence, the posts of each respective level of the hierarchy remain consistent with Stewart's. However, other scoring mechanisms are included that further sensitize the coding scheme.

Unlike Stewart, who coded all obkom first secretaries equally as a 5 in his 0 to 9 hierarchy, the revised hierarchy seeks, after Frank, to differentiate obkomy through attention to their respective representative status in the C.P.S.U. Central Committee. To this end, a "supplementary scores" mechanism has been included that enhances the standard score assigned to the post of obkom first secretary. That is, through the scoring of additional "points" based on Central Committee status, the present hierarchy distinguishes among obkomy that carry various levels of Central Committee membership.

While Stewart's scheme is indiscriminate in scoring the post, the revised hierarchy will score differently the obkom first secretary with full Central Committee membership, with candidate membership, and with no representative status at all. Moreover, the largely ignored parliamentary posts (for example, member of the Presidium of the USSR Supreme Soviet, member of the Presidium of the Ukrainian SSR Supreme Soviet, and so on) are included in this supplementary scores mechanism to enhance the coded scores of individuals who have been awarded (simultaneous with a more substantive post) membership in these bodies. This added criterion allows further distinctions to be drawn between post incumbents.

Of course, in embracing Frank's predisposition to weigh Central Committee status in scoring career mobility, we apply these supplemental scores not solely during the tenure as obkom first secretary, but throughout the individual's career. Thus, a deputy USSR minister with full status in the C.P.S.U. Central Committee would be scored differently from another deputy minister with lesser standing. If the Central Committee standing can distinguish obkom first secretaries, logically it can be used to differentiate an array of posts throughout the hierarchy.[2]

To accommodate for the addition of these supplemental scores, it was necessary to alter Stewart's original coding scores in order to retain the proper scaling of the hierarchy. The revised index, then, while still a ten-part scale, ranges from 0 to 18, ascending in units of two. Very simply, Stewart's mobility index scores were doubled to accommodate the use of the supplemental scores mechanism. Because these index coding scores are arbitrary numerical values in the first place, no injury is done to the scale by doubling them for present purposes. In the mobility hierarchy employed here, then, the basic score assigned to the post of obkom first secretary is 10. Like the model hierarchy, this sole post occupies the middle stratum in the mobility scale.

Unlike Stewart's scheme, where its isolated rank of 5 made the obkom post totally unique (no other post could receive a score of 5), in the present hierarchy, through the use of its supplemental scores mechanism, no such presumption of uniqueness exists. That is, whereas Stewart's coding scale assumes that no other position (or combination of positions held simultaneously) in the Soviet political-administrative structure falls into the same category of "importance" as the obkom first secretary, the revised coding scheme does not. For example, using Stewart, an obkom first secretary with no status in the Central Committee would receive a score of 5, while a candidate member of the Politburo of the Ukrainian Communist party with full C.P.S.U. Central Committee membership would receive a score of 4 (see Appendix I). In the present scheme, the scores generated would be 10 (10 + 0) for the regional secretary and 10 (8 + 2) for the Ukrainian party official (see Appendix II). The latter scheme, it is believed, is more accurate and flexible than Stewart's.

As amended, then, the coding sensitivity of the adopted scheme is over twice as high with respect to post differentials than Stewart's original. His coding scores ranged from 0 to 9. The reconstructed hierarchy utilized herein can distinguish among base posts from 0 to 18. When the supplemental scores mechanism is included, this range increases from 0 to over 25. These scores are added to enable the researcher to distinguish among individuals whose "base" positions fall within the same coding category. That is, individuals occupying the identical base post (for example, obkom first secretary) do not necessarily receive the identical coded score. Thus, the revised coding scheme seeks to avoid artificially equating certain posts within the Soviet administrative hierarchy.[3] While this range of variance is, to be sure, a simplification of Soviet reality, it is nonetheless an improvement on the parent Stewart scheme.

This chapter analyzes the mobility of 281 officials who have left the post of obkom first secretary in the post-Khruschev period. Unlike Stewart et al. (1972), Blackwell and Hulbary (1973), and most other mobility studies of this type that examined only R.S.F.S.R. oblasti, here the first secretaries of the 129 oblasti of the 8 union republics with such units are studied. This focus more than doubles the sample of a study focusing solely on the R.S.F.S.R. Such a broad examination allows for much more comparative analysis and sheds light on a wider array of national political phenomena in the Soviet Union.

A lengthy directory of the career paths of individuals who have held the post of obkom first secretary since the reunification of the regional party apparatuses in 1965 has been compiled from a variety of sources.[4] These data were coded according to the above described positional hierarchy and coding scheme. The career posts held by these elites since serving as regional first secretary were assigned the appropriate mobility scores. Combining each individual's career position scores produced a "raw score" of mobility. This raw score was then divided by the number of posts held to produce that individual's "mobility score." Dividing by the number of positions held eliminates the tendency of the raw score to be weighted in favor of those individuals who simply held many different posts. The division produces, in essence, the mean score for all positions held since (and including) that of obkom first secretary. As such, it does not favor those obkom first secretaries who, subsequent to that post, experienced frequent transfers from job to job.

Finally, because the unit of analysis of this study is not the individual per se but the unit itself, the mobility scores of the individuals for each unit are aggregated to produce a *unit* mobility score. That is, the mobility scores of the various regional units are derived from the aggregation of their individual party first secretaries' personal mobility scores. Theoretically, of course, the careers of other representative individuals connected to the oblast (for example, chairmen of the oblispolkom, obkom second secretaries, capital city gorkom first secretaries) could be similarly analyzed to produce more comprehensive mobility scores. Practically, however, the paucity of biographical data on these less notable regional officials precludes any such study on that scale. For the reasons elaborated in Chapter 1, as well as the inherent data collection problems, focusing on obkom first secretaries seems both methodologically valid and practical.

FINDINGS: THE POLITICAL MOBILITY RANKING

Based on consistent themes in the general literature on the distribution of political power in the Soviet Union, certain expectations about the results of this mobility study present themselves. First, scholars interested in the issue of nationalities and the politics of ethnicity in the USSR would hypothesize that the mobility scores associated with the oblasti within the Slavic republics (the Russian Soviet Federated Socialist Republic, the Ukrainian Soviet Socialist Republic, and the Belorussian Soviet Socialist Republic) would be greater than those associated with the oblasti of the five non-Slavic republics (Lapidus, 1984; Miller, 1977). This expectation is supported by the results of the mobility study (see Table 2.1). The scores of the Russian, Ukrainian, and Belorussian republics are each higher than any of those of the other non-Slavic republics. Combined, the Slavic republics score 12.35 on the mobility index, compared to an aggregate 10.86 for the five non-Slavic republics.

Table 2.1
Political Mobility Scores by Republic

SSR OBLASTI	# POSTS	RAW SCORE	MOBILITY SCORE
R.S.F.S.R.	204	2655	13.01
BELORUSSIAN	31	357	11.52
UKRAINIAN	105	1190	11.33
KIRGIZ	24	270	11.25
KAZAKH	79	879	11.13
TURKMEN	12	130	10.83
UZBEK	56	585	10.45
TADZHIK	8	80	10.00
All Oblasti	519	6146	11.84
Slavic Oblasti	340	4202	12.35
Non-Slavic Oblasti	179	1944	10.86

Second, within the Slavic bloc of republics, also reflecting themes in the literature on the Communist party and the Soviet system in general (Hill and Frank, 1983; Schapiro, 1971), the mobility score of the aggregated Russian republic oblasti is significantly greater than those of even the Ukrainian SSR and the Belorussian SSR. In fact, the high mobility associated with the 55 R.S.F.S.R. oblasti raises the mean all-oblasti mobility score above even the aggregated scores of these other two Slavic republics' oblasti. The results indicate that the mobility scores of the Russian oblasti are by far the most impressive. Indeed, the gap between the R.S.F.S.R. score and the next highest score (Belorussian SSR) is essentially equal (1.49) to the gap between that of the Belorussian republic and that of the least upwardly mobile (Tadzhik) republic (1.52). These data support the notion that upward career mobility within the Soviet public hierarchy is dominated by those individuals whose careers are associated with party posts in the Russian republic apparatus (see Table 2.2).

At the aggregate, union-republic level, then, the results of this mobility study generally confirm the expectations culled from the literature. One surprise, however, can be found in the overall variance in terms of mobility of the Ukrainian and Belorussian oblasti. Contrary to a significant body of literature that would predict a higher relative score for the Ukrainian oblasti (Moses, 1974, 1976), the combined Belorussian oblasti generate a higher mobility score (11.52) than the Ukrainian oblasti (11.33). However, although the career of every post-Khruschev obkom first secretary of the Belorussian SSR was analyzed, the number of cases is small. The Belorussian republic contains within it only six oblasti, compared with twenty-five in the Ukrainian SSR. These six oblasti combined generated only sixteen coded regional first secretaries and only

Table 2.2
Republic Mobility Scores

| SSR OBLASTI | RSFSR SCORE | As a Percentage of: | | NON- |
		SLAVIC OBLASTI SCORE	ALL OBLASTI SCORE	SLAVIC OBLASTI SCORE
R.S.F.S.R.	100	105	110	120
BELORUSSIAN	89	93	97	106
UKRAINIAN	87	92	96	104
KIRGIZ	86	91	95	104
KAZAKH	86	90	94	102
TURKMEN	83	88	91	100
UZBEK	80	85	88	96
TADZHIK	77	81	84	92

fifteen coded positions beyond that post. For the Ukrainian republic, the numbers are much larger (fifty-six first secretaries and forty-nine additional coded posts) and the results for this republic seem more reliable, given the larger number of coded cases. Only the additional personnel changes within the Belorussian public apparatus that come with time can provide a test of the validity of the mobility scores generated using this relatively small number of cases. In fact, this same caveat must be raised for at least three other republics (Kirgiz SSR, Turkmen SSR, and Tadzhik SSR) that contain neither the necessary number of oblasti nor the sufficient number of coded personnel moves to guarantee the long-term validity of the mobility scores generated.

Third, as Table 2.2 discloses, the mobility scores at the union republic level reveal three distinct aggregate-level mobility groups. The first group is comprised of the oblasti of the R.S.F.S.R. These regional units' scores combine to produce a republic score significantly higher than the others and merit a separate class. The score of 13.01 for the R.S.F.S.R. oblasti is 10 percent above the all-oblasti mean and a full 20 percent above the aggregate score of the non-Slavic oblasti. The second group of oblasti represent a middle stratum in terms of political mobility. The oblasti of the Belorussian, Ukrainian, Kirgiz, and Kazakh republics generate aggregate scores that fall within 89 percent to 86 percent of those of the R.S.F.S.R. oblasti and 97 percent to 94 percent of the all-oblasti score. Finally, the third group identified at the union republic level is comprised of oblasti of the Turkmen, Uzbek and Tadzhik republics. The aggregate scores of these units are much lower than those of the second tier of oblasti, each scoring below even the mean associated with the non-Slavic oblasti. However, an ecological fallacy must be avoided when observing these republic-level data. The individual scores of the component oblasti within these eight republics cannot accurately be predicted using aggregate-level mobility scores. A closer look at the data at the oblast level-of-analysis is necessary to uncover more accurate political mobility trends.

At the oblast level, the primary level of analysis of this project, a wide disparity exists in the associated mobility scores. The scores generated for individual oblasti range from a 15.62 for Stavropol kraikom (R.S.F.S.R.) to a 9.33 for Sumy (Ukrainian SSR) obkom. Again, the mean mobility score for all 129 oblasti of the Soviet system is 11.84. The Stavropol score, then, is 31.9 percent greater than the national average, while the latter obkom generates a mobility score only 78.8 percent of the all-oblasti mean.

Table 2.3 shows the obkom mobility scores by republic and reveals the rather wide range of mobility scores generated within each republic, including the R.S.F.S.R. In fact, the variance in numerical scores between Stavropol (15.62) and Smolensk (9.50) is the largest gap between a republic's high and low obkom scores. This is to be expected given the relatively high scores generated by many of the Russian republic oblasti. However, Smolensk oblast continues to be anomalous; its mobility score is the sole R.S.F.S.R. score generated by the analysis that falls clearly into the category of negative political mobility. This finding, however surprising, is supported in the previous work of McAuley (1974). She found that Smolensk stood out as "the 'oddest' obkom of the period" (1974: 495). The examined economic characteristics of the oblast did not coincide with its lack of Central Committee status between 1965 and 1971. The present analysis, which shows only 2 of 129 oblasti with a lower mobility score, lends further evidence of the poor position of the Smolensk oblast party organization, especially given its R.S.F.S.R. affiliation.

Table 2.4 represents the all-oblasti political mobility ranking for the eight union-republics within the oblast subdivision. Certain findings immediately present themselves from this ranking. First, the oblast party organizations that produced the two dominant C.P.S.U. general secretaries of the post-Khruschev period (Dnepropetrovsk and Stavropol) generated high political mobility scores. Interestingly, however, the calculation of the Dnepropetrovsk score does not include the career of Leonid Brezhnev, as he was obviously the obkom's first secretary prior to the time frame of this study. Brezhnev's "Dnepropetrovsk gang," though, did experience high (14.25) upward mobility (Moses, 1976). Three of the four Dnepropetrovsk first secretaries analyzed here (V. V. Shcherbitskii, A. F. Vatchenko, Ye. V. Kachalovskii, and V. G. Boiko) each experienced significant upward mobility from this obkom post.

The Stavropol mobility score (15.62) includes not only Gorbachev's obviously high score (17.33), but also the strong mobility scores generated by the analyses of the career paths of his predecessor, L. N. Yefremov (14.50), and his successor, V. S. Murakhovskii (14.67). For both of these highly upwardly mobile units, though, it is far from clear that political

Table 2.3
Oblast Political Mobility Scores
(by Union Republic)

UZBEK SSR

1.	Andizhan	11.30
2.	Tashkent	11.00
3.	Namangan	10.60
4.	Samarkand	10.50
5.	Syr-Daria	10.44
6.	Bukhara	10.20
7.	Ferghana	10.00
	Dzhizak	10.00
	Kashka-Daria	10.00
	Navoi	10.00
	Surkhan-Daria	10.00
12.	Khorezm	9.80

KAZAKH SSR

1.	Alma Ata	13.60
2.	Uralsk	13.00
3.	Kustanai	12.00
	North Kazakhstan	12.00
5.	Karaganda	11.80
6.	Turgai	11.50
7.	Kzyl-Orda	11.20
8.	Dzhambul	11.17
9.	Tselinograd	11.00
10.	Taldy-Kurgan	10.71
11.	Mangyshlak	10.67
	Pavlodar	10.67
13.	Kokchetav	10.57
14.	Aktyubinsk	10.50
	East Kazakhstan	10.50
	Semipalatinsk	10.50
17.	Chimkent	10.40
18.	Dzhezkazgan	10.00
19.	Gurev	9.80

TADZHIK SSR

1.	Kuliab	10.67
2.	Kurgan-Tuibe	10.00
3.	Leninabad	9.50

TURKMEN SSR

1.	Ashkhabad	11.17
2.	Mary	11.00
3.	Chardzhou	10.00
	Krasnovodsk	10.00
	Tashauz	10.00

BELORUSSIAN SSR

1.	Minsk	14.67
2.	Brest	13.25
3.	Vitebsk	12.00
4.	Gomel	10.67
5.	Mogilev	10.50
6.	Grodno	10.00

KIRGHIZ SSR

1.	Issyk-Kul	11.67
2.	Osh	11.55
3.	Talass	10.00
4.	Naryn	9.50

UKRAINIAN SSR

1.	Dnepropetrovsk	14.25	14.	Rovno	10.83
2.	Lvov	13.33	15.	Kirovograd	10.75
3.	Kharkov	12.75	16.	Khmelnitskii	10.50
4.	Kiev	12.50	17.	Ivano-Frankovsk	10.27
	Donetsk	12.50	18.	Nikolaev	10.17
	Zaporozhe	12.50	19.	Transcarpathia	10.00
7.	Vinnitsa	12.25		Cherkassy	10.00
8.	Crimea	12.17		Zhitmoir	10.00
9.	Chernigov	12.00		Chernovtsy	10.00
	Voroshilovgrad	12.00	23.	Ternopol	9.67
11.	Kherson	11.75	24.	Volyn	9.60
12.	Odessa	11.00	25.	Sumy	9.33
	Poltava	11.00			

Table 2.3 (continued)

R.S.F.S.R.

1.	Stavropol	15.62		29.	Saratov	12.40
2.	Leningrad	15.25		30.	Ivanovo	12.33
3.	Krasnoiarsk	15.00		31.	Tambov	12.17
	Omsk	15.00		32.	Arkhangelsk	12.00
5.	Rostov	14.37			Vologda	12.00
6.	Moscow	14.00			Briansk	12.00
	Orenburg	14.00			Kalinin	12.00
	Sverdlovsk	14.00			Kaluga	12.00
	Vladimir	14.00			Kirov	12.00
10.	Tomsk	13.75			Lipetsk	12.00
11.	Krasnodar	13.62			Novosibirsk	12.00
12.	Kuibyshev	13.50			Sakhalin	12.00
	Primore	13.50			Yaroslavl	12.00
	Pskov	13.50			Tula	12.00
	Volgograd	13.50			Amur	12.00
16.	Cheliabinsk	13.43		44.	Chita	11.67
17.	Perm	13.33			Kostroma	11.67
	Riazan	13.33			Murmansk	11.67
19.	Gorkii	13.25		47.	Kamchatka	11.33
20.	Altai	13.00			Kurgan	11.33
	Belgorod	13.00		49.	Novgorod	11.20
	Penza	13.00		50.	Astrakhan	11.00
	Ulianovsk	13.00			Magadan	11.00
24.	Voronezh	12.80			Khabarovsk	11.00
25.	Irkutsk	12.67		53.	Kaliningrad	10.00
	Kemerovo	12.67			Kursk	10.00
	Orel	12.67		55.	Smolensk	9.50
28.	Tiumen	12.50				

patronage of the respective general secretaries is the sole (or even most significant) force at work.

Both of these units produced significant national political figures prior to the obkom tenure of their future C.P.S.U. general secretaries. For Dnepropetrovsk, Demian Sergeevich Korotchenko, obkom first secretary between 1938–1939 (eight years before Brezhnev), became chairman of the Ukrainian SSR Council of Ministers with no "help" from Brezhnev and later rose to become a candidate member of the C.P.S.U. Central Committee Politburo and was chairman of the Presidium of the Ukrainian Supreme Soviet for fifteen years. While it is true that the careers of Brezhnev's successors Andrei Kirilenko, Vladimir Shcherbitskii, and Aleksei Vatchenko flourished at various times during Brezhnev's tenure as general secretary, it is not clear how their respective careers would have developed in isolation from Brezhnev's.

In the case of Stavropol krai, a long list of national figures predates even the twenty-year focus of this study. Mikhail Suslov (1939–1944),

Table 2.4
Aggregate Political Mobility Scores by Oblast

	OBLAST	SSR	SCORE
1.	Stavropol	RSFSR	15.62
2.	Leningrad	RSFSR	15.25
3.	Krasnoiarsk	RSFSR	15.00
	Omsk	RSFSR	15.00
5.	Minsk	Belorussian	14.67
6.	Rostov	RSFSR	14.37
7.	Dnepropetrovsk	Ukrainian	14.25
8.	Moscow	RSFSR	14.00
	Orenburg	RSFSR	14.00
	Sverdlovsk	RSFSR	14.00
	Vladimir	RSFSR	14.00
12.	Tomsk	RSFSR	13.75
13.	Krasnodar	RSFSR	13.62
14.	Alma Ata	Kazakh	13.60
15.	Kuibyshev	RSFSR	13.50
	Primore	RSFSR	13.50
	Pskov	RSFSR	13.50
	Volgograd	RSFSR	13.50
19.	Cheliabinsk	RSFSR	13.43
20.	Perm	RSFSR	13.33
	Lvov	Ukrainian	13.33
	Riazan	RSFSR	13.33
23.	Brest	Belorussian	13.25
	Gorkii	RSFSR	13.25
25.	Altai	RSFSR	13.00
	Belgorod	RSFSR	13.00
	Penza	RSFSR	13.00
	Ulianovsk	RSFSR	13.00
	Uralsk	RSFSR	13.00
30.	Voronezh	RSFSR	12.80
31.	Kharkov	Ukrainian	12.75
32.	Irkutsk	RSFSR	12.67
	Kemerovo	RSFSR	12.67
	Orel	RSFSR	12.67
35.	Donetsk	Ukrainian	12.50
	Kiev	Ukrainian	12.50
	Tiumen	RSFSR	12.50
	Zaporozhe	Ukrainian	12.50
39.	Saratov	RSFSR	12.40
40.	Ivanovo	RSFSR	12.33
41.	Vinnitsa	Ukrainian	12.25
42.	Crimea	Ukrainian	12.17

Table 2.4 (continued)

	OBLAST	SSR	SCORE
	Tambov	RSFSR	12.17
44.	Amur	RSFSR	12.00
	Arkhangelsk	RSFSR	12.00
	Briansk	RSFSR	12.00
	Chernigov	Ukrainian	12.00
	Kalinin	RSFSR	12.00
	Kaluga	RSFSR	12.00
	Kirov	RSFSR	12.00
	Kustanai	Kazakh	12.00
	Lipetsk	RSFSR	12.00
	North Kazakhstan	Kazakh	12.00
	Novosibirsk	RSFSR	12.00
	Sakhalin	RSFSR	12.00
	Tula	RSFSR	12.00
	Vitebsk	Belorussian	12.00
	Vologda	RSFSR	12.00
	Voroshilovgrad	Ukrainian	12.00
	Yaroslavl	RSFSR	12.00
61.	Issyk-Kul	Kirgiz	11.87
62.	Karaganda	Kazakh	11.80
63.	Kherson	Ukrainian	11.75
64.	Chita	RSFSR	11.67
	Kostroma	RSFSR	11.67
66.	Osh	Kirgiz	11.55
67.	Turgai	Kazakh	11.50
68.	Kamchatka	RSFSR	11.33
	Kurgan	RSFSR	11.33
	Murmansk	RSFSR	11.33
71.	Andizhan	Uzbek	11.30
72.	Novgorod	RSFSR	11.20
	Kzyl-Orda	Kazakh	11.20
74.	Dzhambul	Kazakh	11.17
	Ashkhabad	Turkmen	11.17
76.	Astrakhan	RSFSR	11.00
	Khabarovsk	RSFSR	11.00
	Magadan	RSFSR	11.00
	Mary	Turkmen	11.00
	Odessa	Ukrainian	11.00
	Poltava	Ukrainian	11.00
	Tashkent	Uzbek	11.00
	Tselinograd	Kazakh	11.00
84.	Rovno	Ukrainian	10.83
85.	Kirovograd	Ukrainian	10.75
86.	Taldy-Kurgan	Kazakh	10.71
87.	Gomel	Belorussian	10.67
	Kuliab	Tadzhik	10.67
	Mangyshlak	Kazakh	10.67
	Pavlodar	Kazakh	10.67

Table 2.4 (continued)

	OBLAST	SSR	SCORE
91.	Namangan	Uzbek	10.60
92.	Kokchetav	Kazakh	10.57
93.	Aktyubinsk	Kazakh	10.50
	East Kazakhstan	Kazakh	10.50
	Khmelnitskii	Ukrainian	10.50
	Mogilev	Belorussian	10.50
	Samarkand	Uzbek	10.50
	Semipalatinsk	Kazakh	10.50
99.	Syr-Daria	Uzbek	10.44
100.	Chimkent	Kazakh	10.40
101.	Ivano-Frankovsk	Ukrainian	10.27
102.	Bukhara	Uzbek	10.20
103.	Nikolaev	Ukrainian	10.17
104.	Surkhan-Daria	Uzbek	10.00
	Chardzhou	Turkmen	10.00
	Cherkassy	Ukrainian	10.00
	Chernovtsy	Ukrainian	10.00
	Dzhizak	Uzbek	10.00
	Dzhezkazgan	Kazakh	10.00
	Ferghana	Uzbek	10.00
	Grodno	Belorussian	10.00
	Kaliningrad	RSFSR	10.00
	Kashka-Daria	Uzbek	10.00
	Krasnovodsk	Turkmen	10.00
	Kurgan-Tuibe	Tadzhik	10.00
	Kursk	RSFSR	10.00
	Navoi	Uzbek	10.00
	Talass	Kirgiz	10.00
	Tashauz	Turkmen	10.00
	Transcarpathia	Ukrainian	10.00
	Zhitomir	Ukrainian	10.00
122.	Gurev	Kazakh	9.80
	Khorezm	Uzbek	9.80
124.	Ternopol	Ukrainian	9.67
125.	Volyn	Ukrainian	9.60
126.	Naryn	Kirgiz	9.50
	Smolensk	RSFSR	9.50
	Leninabad	Tadzhik	9.50
129.	Sumy	Ukrainian	9.33

Ivan Boitsov (1945–1956), Nikolai Beliaev (1960), Fedor Kulakov (1960–1964), and Leonid Yefremov (1964–1970) preceded Mikhail Gorbachev as party boss in this R.S.F.S.R. region and later became national figures of significance. In fact, Gorbachev seems to be the beneficiary of the upward mobility associated with the Stavropol kraikom rather than the originator of it. As a result, it is more difficult to argue that the strong mobility score of Gorbachev's successor Vsevolod Murakhovskii (14.67) has been caused by Gorbachev.

Second, as mentioned above, the R.S.F.S.R. oblasti dominate the higher end of the mobility ranking. Twenty of the twenty-five highest mobility scores are generated by Russian republic units. Only one of the fifty-five R.S.F.S.R. oblasti is associated with a downward mobility value and 80 percent of this group received scores of 12.00 or higher. This phenomenon becomes more evident when it is considered that only two Ukrainian oblasti (Dnepropetrovsk and Lvov) and two Belorussian oblasti (Minsk and Brest) are ranked among the twenty-five most upwardly mobile regions, seven of twenty-five Ukrainian oblasti generated a score of 10.00 or below, and only thirty-six percent of Ukrainian regions scored at 12.00 or above. The comparative numbers for the other union-republic oblasti are even less competitive.

Third, two oblasti score unexpectedly high. The Minsk oblast (Belorussian SSR) registers the fifth highest mobility score (14.67) of any region in the USSR, almost 24 percent above the national mean. This unit score is based on the career mobility scores of its two post-Khruschev first secretaries (excluding the present incumbent). Ivan Poliakov (1964–1977) became a full member of the Politburo of the Belorussian Communist Party Central Committee, the chairman of the presidium of the Belorussian Supreme Soviet, a deputy chairman of the presidium of the USSR Supreme Soviet, and scored a 15.00 on the mobility scale. His successor in Minsk, Vladimir Mikulich (1977–1985), generated a score of 14.00 by virtue of his simultaneous standing in the C.P.S.U. Central Committee and Belorussian party's Central Committee Politburo. A review of the pre-Brezhnev period seems to validate this rather unexpectedly high mobility score.

Several Minsk obkom first secretaries, including Vasilii Chernyshev (1948–1950), Kirill Mazurov (1950–1953), Petr Masherov (1955), Fedor Surganov (1955–1956), Vasilii Shauro (1956–1960), and Sergei Pritytskii (1960–1962) later filled key union-republic and all-union party and state posts. Indeed, both Mazurov and Masherov made it to the C.P.S.U. Central Committee Politburo, and Suganov, Shauro, and Pritytskii each became chairman of the presidium of the Belorussian Supreme Soviet. The Minsk score, then, given the long-term trends of the unit's party leaders, seems to be based in a tradition of upward political mobility.

The second seemingly anomalous score is assigned to the Kazakh

SSR's Alma Ata obkom. Alma Ata's score of 13.60 is close to that of the expectedly strong scores of four R.S.F.S.R. oblasti: Moscow, Orenburg, Sverdlovsk, and Vladimir. Yet the high mobility score of Alma Ata, upon closer scrutiny, also seems valid. It is based on the individual scores of first secretaries Sabir Niiazbekov (14.00), Asanbai Askarov (13.00), and Kenes Aukhadiev (14.00), all native Kazakhs. Niiazbekov (1964–1965) later became a full member of the Kazakh Communist party's Central Committee Politburo, chairman of the presidium of the Kazakh SSR Supreme Soviet, a full member of the C.P.S.U. Central Committee, and a deputy chairman of the presidium of the USSR Supreme Soviet. Askarov (1965–1978) coupled his tenure as obkom first secretary with posts on the Politburo of the Kazakh Communist party's Central Committee, and full membership in the C.P.S.U. Central Committee. Finally, First Secretary Aukhadiev (1978–1985) also became a full member of the Kazakh Communist party Central Committee Politburo and a full member in the C.P.S.U. Central Committee. Examining the careers of prior Alma Ata first secretaries reveals a history of upward mobility as well. Masymkhan Beisebaev (1958–1962) later became chairman of the Kazakh SSR Council of Ministers, a full member of the Kazakh party Politburo, and a full member of the C.P.S.U. Central Committee. Petr Kantseliaristov (1963–1964) became chairman of the Kazakh Council of Ministers' People's Control Committee before retiring in 1981. It seems that some grounds exist then, for accepting as valid the two seemingly aberrant scores for Minsk and Alma Ata. Of course, this representation on all-union level bodies may reflect the need felt among the leadership to provide representation for Belorussians (the third largest ethnic group by population in the USSR) and Central Asians. Given the recent rioting in the Kazakh SSR over the promotion of an ethnic Russian to the republic party's top leadership post, the issue of minority representation on major republic and all-union bodies seems no trifling issue.

Fourth, the distribution of obkom mobility scores reveals clustering at both the 12.00 and 10.00 levels (see Table 2.5). Seventeen obkomy registered a mobility score of 12.00, and eighteen regional units generated the score of 10.00. These groupings at the respective scores of 12.00 and 10.00 come as no surprise, given the adopted mobility coding scheme. That is, since an obkom first secretary with no representative status in the C.P.S.U. Central Committee (and receiving no other supplementary points) would be scored at a 10.00 and an obkom party boss who possessed full membership in the Central Committee would be coded as 12.00, the high frequency (n = 35) of obkomy coded as either of these scores seems logical. Moreover, the third highest frequency shown in Table 2.5 is for obkomy receiving the 11.00 mobility score. This finding meshes well with the above explanation. The score of 11.00, which was

Table 2.5
Distribution of Obkom Political Mobility Scores

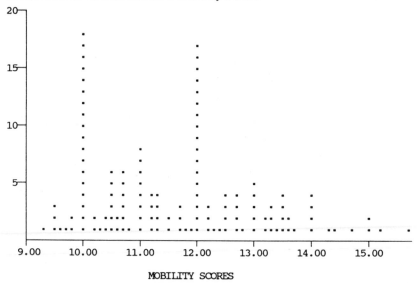

MOBILITY SCORES

generated for eight units, could represent oblasti whose representative party leaders consistently retain candidate membership in the C.P.S.U. Central Committee. While these three high frequency mobility scores do not *necessarily* reflect just that unit's Central Committee status, in many cases they do. Finally, given the codes assigned to posts in the mobility hierarchy (that is, sequenced in units of two), there is some mathematical probability that the scores generated will assume these values, especially when that coding scheme is applied to cases with only a small numbers of coded positions.

Fifth, although in essence measuring different (although related) variables, it is possible to compare Frank's ranking with the mobility ranking constructed in this chapter. This comparison, of course, is limited inasmuch as Frank looked only at Russian republic oblasti and we have excluded the nationality-based autonomous Soviet socialist republics (ASSRs) from this sample. However, it is constructive to compare the results of these two attempts to rank the regional party units of the Soviet Union. There is a rough correspondence of Frank's seven hierarchical groupings of oblasti and the political mobility scores generated herein (see Table 2.6).

When viewed at the oblast level, however, several incongruities emerge between Frank's groupings and the mobility scores generated in this chapter. Stavropol, the highest scoring oblast in the sample, was placed by Frank in Group III. Krasnoiarsk (II), Orenburg (III), Omsk (III),

Table 2.6
Frank's Groupings and Aggregate Mobility Scores

CATEGORY	SCORE
Group I	13.68
Group II	13.41
Group III	13.37
Group IV	11.57
Group V	12.37
Group VI	————
Group VII	11.46

Vladimir (V), Tomsk (V), and Penza (V) are each lower in Frank's rank-ing than they are in this mobility ranking. Conversely, Voronezh, Novosibirsk, Irkutsk, and Khabarovsk certainly do not generate the po-litical mobility scores of any first order oblast; each is higher in Frank's ranking (Group I) than seems to be indicated by their measures of politi-cal mobility. These individual contrasts aside, however, there does seem to be some overlap between Frank's ranking and the present ranking, at least when judged by the broad categories devised by Frank.

CONCLUSION

It is important to reassert the tentative nature of the findings of this chapter. Many of the mobility scores generated for the oblasti are based on the career moves of single individuals. Brezhnev's "trust in cadres" policy created a situation characterized by the very slow turnover among these obkom elites. Since the effort undertaken in this chapter does not, by definition, include the present 129 obkom incumbents (unless they were previously a first secretary of another obkom), mobility scores for several obkomy are based on very small numbers of coded career moves. This problem, of course, cannot be avoided. As will be examined in depth in Chapter 5, the post-Brezhnev period has witnessed the demise of the conservative "trust in cadres" policy; over 80 percent of the regional party bosses have been replaced since November 1982. If the pattern es-tablished over the past four years persists, it will not be long before the in-creased validity that comes with a greater number of examined cases will be achieved.

The results of this exercise have yielded generally predictable findings. The mobility scores of the Russian republic oblasti are consistently higher than those of the other republics, even much higher than those of the Ukrainian SSR and the Belorussian SSR. The scores of the non-Slavic oblasti are relatively weak in comparison. Highly upwardly mobile oblasti (Stavropol, Minsk, Leningrad, Krasnoiarsk, and Omsk) as well as oblasti with relatively poor mobility values (Naryn, Smolensk, Leninabad, and Sumy) have emerged from the application of the adopted methodology. The mobility ranking has revealed some surprisingly strong scores (Minsk, Alma Ata) and several unexpectedly weak mobility scores (Smolensk, Sumy).

Yet, the creation of this ranking in some respects raises an important question. While it goes a long way in measuring the political mobility *associated* with a large number of regional party units, the quantitative political mobility ranking constructed in this chapter in no way establishes either causal or correlational knowledge of the forces at work which *determine* these career mobility chances.

It is still unknown what forces (political, economic, demographic, historical, cultural, and so on) alter the political climate of expectations for individuals associated with these respective regional units. What is it about these individual units that determines their respective political mobility values? Why is it that certain obkomy seem "to supply a disproportionately large number of promotees . . . while others appeared to offer . . . only relatively poor prospects of further upward career mobility?" (Frank, 1974: 217). It is these questions that the following chapter considers.

NOTES

1. For another adaptation of Stewart's original coding hierarchy, see Robert E. Blackwell, Jr., and William E. Hulbary (1973), "Political Mobility among Soviet Obkom Elites: The Effects of Regime, Social Backgrounds, and Career Development," *American Journal of Political Science* 17 (4): 721–743.

2. For a more detailed explanation of how this supplementary scores mechanism is used in practice, see Appendix II.

3. It is necessary to keep in mind the methodological dictates of attempting to arrange a wide array of posts in a manageable coding hierarchy. One alternative to grouping posts into a smaller number of categories would be to construct a hierarchy consisting of *individual* posts from "General Secretary of the C.P.S.U." at the top to "student" (or something else?) at the bottom. Yet, this alternative hierarchy with each post constituting its own category would not be any less prone to criticism than the one employed. We would still be forced to defend the specific arrangement of certain posts, with little consensus among scholars as to the "correct" arrangement. Categorizing the posts, it seems, creates a more manageable and parsimonious methodology that is no more flawed than any alternative scheme.

4. The biographical data of individuals who held the position of obkom first secretary were gathered from an array of English-language sources. They include: Boris Lewytzkyi, ed., *Who's Who in the Soviet Union,* Munich: K. G. Saur, 1984;

Institute for the Study of the USSR (Munich), *Prominent Personalities of the USSR,* New York: Scarecrow Press, Inc., 1968; Institute for the Study of the USSR (Munich), *Biographic Directory of the USSR,* New York: Scarecrow Press, Inc., 1958; various editions of *A Biographic Directory of 100 Leading Soviet Officials,* Munich: Radio Liberty Research, RFE/RL; various editions of *Directory of Soviet Officials,* National Foreign Assessment Center of the Central Intelligence Agency, Washington, DC: U.S. Government Printing Office; Herwig Kraus, *The Composition of Leading Organs of the CPSU (1952–1982),* Munich: Radio Liberty Research, RFE/RL, 1982; various editions of John L. Scherer, ed., *USSR Facts and Figures Annual,* Gulf Breeze, FL: Academic International Press; various editions of United States Information Agency, *Foreign Broadcast Information Service,* Washington, DC: U.S. Government Printing Office; *Current Soviet Leaders,* Oakville, Ontario: Mosaic Press; *Current Digest of the Soviet Press,* Columbus, OH; and *Leaders of the Soviet Republics,* vols. 1 and 2 (vol. 1, 1955–1972 by Grey Hodnett and Val Ogareff; Vol. 2, 1971–1980 by Val Ogareff), Canberra, Australia: Department of Political Science, Research School of Social Sciences, Australian National University, 1973, 1980.

REFERENCES

Blackwell, Robert E., Jr. "Elite Recruitment and Functional Change: An Analysis of the Soviet Obkom Elite, 1950–1968," *Journal of Politics* 34 (1972): 124–152.

———. "The Soviet Political Elite—Alternative Recruitment Policies at the Obkom Level," *Comparative Politics* 6, no. 1 (October 1973): 99–121.

———. "Cadres Policy in the Brezhnev Era," *Problems of Communism* (March–April 1979): 29–42.

Blackwell, Robert E., Jr., and William E. Hulbary. "Political Mobility Among Soviet Obkom Elites: The Effects of Regime, Social Backgrounds, and Career Development," *American Journal of Political Science* 17, no. 4 (1973): 721–743.

Donaldson, Robert H. "The 1971 Central Committee: An Assessment of the New Elite," *World Politics* (April 1972): 382–409.

Frank, Peter. "The CPSU Obkom First Secretary: A Profile," *British Journal of Political Science* 1, no. 2 (1971): 173–190.

———. "Constructing a Classified Ranking of CPSU Provincial Committees," *British Journal of Political Science* 4, no. 3 (1974): 217–230.

Gehlen, Michael P., and Michael McBride. "The Soviet Central Committee: An Elite Analysis," *American Political Science Review* 62 (1968): 1232–1241.

Harris, Chauncy D. 1970. *Cities of the Soviet Union: Studies in their Functions, Size, Density, and Growth,* no. 5 in the monograph series published for the Association of American Geographers. Chicago: Rand McNally, 1970.

Hill, Ronald J., and Peter Frank. *The Soviet Communist Party.* London: George Allen & Unwin, 1983.

Kress, John H. "Representation of Positions on the CPSU Politburo," *Slavic Review* 39, no. 2 (June 1980): 218–238.

Lapidus, Gail Warshofsky. "Ethnonationalism and Political Stability: The Soviet Case," *World Politics* 36, no. 4 (July 1984): 555–580.

McAuley, Mary. "The Hunting of the Hierarchy: RSFSR Obkom First Secretaries and the Central Committee," *Soviet Studies* (October 1974): 473–501.

Miller, John H. "Cadres Policy in Nationality Areas: Recruitment of CPSU First and Second Secretaries in Non-Russian Republics of the USSR," *Soviet Studies* 29, no. 1 (January 1977): 3–36.

Moses, Joel C. *Regional Party Leadership and Policy-Making in the USSR.* New York: Praeger, 1974.

——— . "Regional Cohorts and Political Mobility in the USSR: The Case of Dnepropetrovsk," *Soviet Union* 3, part 1 (1976): 63–89.

Rigby, T. H. "The Soviet Regional Leadership: The Brezhnev Generation," *Slavic Review* 7, no. 1 (March 1978): 1–24.

Schapiro, Leonard. *The Communist Party of the Soviet Union.* New York: Vintage Books, 1971.

Stewart, Philip D., et al. "Political Mobility and the Soviet Political Process: A Partial Test of Two Models," *American Political Science Review* 66 (July 1972): 1269–1290.

Tatu, Michel. "The Central Committee Elected at the Twenty-Seventh Party Congress: Halfway Toward Rejuvenation," *Radio Liberty Research,* RL 106/86 (March 10, 1986): 1–3.

3
SOVIET REGIONAL ELITE MOBILITY: THE SEARCH FOR NON-IDIOSYNCRATIC INDEPENDENT VARIABLES

INTRODUCTION

Writing about political elite mobility in the United States, Joseph Schlesinger attempted to illuminate what he called the "structure of political opportunities" operating within the system (1966: 11–12). Three general propositions articulated by Schlesinger seem equally plausible for the Soviet experience: (1) Opportunities for political mobility are patterned rather than randomly distributed; (2) aspiring political elites must largely accommodate themselves to these established patterns rather than hope to shape them; and (3) these opportunity structures confer differential mobility advantages upon the occupants of certain posts and disadvantages upon others (1966: 194–211).

Having established in the preceding chapter one measure of the "differential mobility advantages" of regional party first secretaries, this chapter seeks to shed some light on the structure of political opportunities extant and operating in the Soviet Union. It is argued that by analyzing the available characteristic data on the regional units of the USSR, the predominant structure of regional elite mobility will be highlighted.

Traditional analyses of political mobility in the Soviet system regard the career moves of individuals in the party and state apparatuses primarily as dependent variables. Specifically, most explanations view the promotion or demotion of middle-level elites as dependent on the dynamic interplay of patronage systems established by both the spatial and temporal overlap of individuals' career paths. Patron–protégé relationships, according to this perspective, develop into self-perpetuating personnel "cohorts" (Moses, 1976) wherein protection and promotion are provided from above as a reward for loyalty and support from below.

John A. Armstrong, in one of the earliest studies of regional political elite mobility in the USSR, best summarizes the philosophical disposition of the patronage school: "In a sense the Soviet system is a vast collection of personal followings, in which the success of middle-level officials *depends on* the patronage of dominant leaders" (1959: 146; emphasis added). Yet, as discussed in Chapter 1, explanations of elite mobility based solely on the patronage phenomenon are incomplete, at best.

The patronage-based analyses of Soviet elite mobility rely fundamentally on idiosyncratic independent variables. That is, the promotion or demotion of individual *apparatchiki* is explained by reference to his personal relationship with another bureaucrat higher up the administrative structure: Ivanov was moved from position A to position B because his patron Smirnov so willed it. Such an explanation of Soviet cadres policy discounts technical criteria for mobility and highlights the arbitrariness of idiosyncratic personalistic factors. While patronage certainly does influence individual career chances in the Soviet Union (as it does in the United States, Great Britain, and every other state in the world), a wide array of less-arbitrary forces are also at work.

This chapter seeks to explicate a number of non-idiosyncratic (non-arbitrary) independent variables that influence the career chances of individual regional elites in the long run in the Soviet Union. While on the one hand these factors may be said to provide the long-term structural environment within which patronage forces (to the degree they are relevant) operate in the USSR, the non-idiosyncratic approach is, on the other hand, potentially injurious to the validity of the patronage-based explanation.

In explaining extended patterns of political elite mobility, this analysis discounts the machinations of clientelism, *seilschaften,* patrons, clients, and so on. Instead, attention is focused on the rational-technical forces structuring mobility opportunities. Since the unit of analysis of this study is the oblast communist party committee (obkom), this chapter looks at the economic, demographic, sociodevelopmental, and political characteristics of these key administrative units in order to explain the variance in political mobility opportunities of these units. It has been established elsewhere (see Chapter 2) that since 1965 significant differences with respect to political mobility chances exist among the regional structures of the Soviet Union. This chapter addresses the nature of these disparities in political mobility opportunities through an analysis of the key structural characteristics of the respective regional units. This approach to the explanation of non-idiosyncratic independent variables better addresses the phenomenon of regional elite mobility in the Soviet Union.

REGIONAL DIFFERENCES AND POLITICAL MOBILITY IN THE USSR

While in some senses the oblasti of the Soviet Union are equivalent administrative units, these regional entities vary significantly in several crucial structural characteristics. For example, the largest Soviet regional unit (Krasnoiarsk krai, R.S.F.S.R.) is over three hundred times as large as the smallest oblast (Andizhan, Uzbek SSR). The most populous region (Moscow oblast) in 1983 had over 14.7 million inhabitants, with 90 percent living in urban areas; the least populated oblast (Naryn, Kirgiz SSR) had less than one-quarter million people, with only 18 percent of the total residing in urban areas. While Moscow lies in the heart of European Russia, fourteen other oblasti lie over 4,000 kilometers from the capital. In a word, the 129 Soviet oblasti, despite some formal administrative equivalence, are quite different in most other respects—size, population, degree of urbanization, ethnicity, language, economic activity, development, and so on (Bandura and Melnyk, 1973: see also Appendix III).

These distinctions among Soviet regions, it can be argued, make some oblasti more important than others politically. That is, some units are more important for the proper functioning of the Soviet system (social, political, economic) than others (Beissinger, 1986: 15). With respect to the question of political mobility, this chapter hypothesizes that the crucial characteristics of the respective Soviet oblasti influence the climate of expectations of individuals associated with these units (Willerton and Reisinger, 1987: 8, 11). Specifically, differences in the structural characteristics of Soviet oblasti, such as demographic trends, economic activity, level of social development, and so on, should be reflected in the long run in the political mobility opportunities of elites tied to these regions (Moses, 1974: 16).

Only a small body of literature directly addresses the issue of the relationship between political elite mobility and the structural characteristics of Soviet subnational political units. Stewart et al. (1972), testing the validity of both the patronage and rational-technical models of political mobility, assert that "the concepts of economic performance and level of economic development constitute the core of the rational-technical model" (1972: 1274). Inasmuch as plan fulfillment data at the oblast level are not available outside the Soviet Union, Stewart utilized the disaggregated *Narodnoe Khoziastvo* data for the R.S.F.S.R. oblasti. Specifically, he constructed a two-part measure for both (a) oblast industrial production, and (b) oblast food and clothing production. From these, his analysis yielded four categories of oblasti: (1) agriculturally/industrially important, (2) industrially important, (3) agriculturally important, and (4) undeveloped (1972: 1288–1289). For our present purposes, Stewart's finding for the R.S.F.S.R. that, "as level of economic development increases, the patronage model tends to explain less and the performance model tends to account for more of the variance in mobility," seems especially important.

Joel C. Moses' research also highlights the impact of structural characteristics on cadres policy and elite mobility in the Soviet Union. He finds

that "regions that have undergone more rapid or fundamental environmental change have higher turnover rates in obkom bureaus and different
kinds of personnel assigned to the bureaus" (1974: 18). According to
Moses, members of the regional leadership cohort will tend to have their
tenures and job placements reflect the degree of modernization of their
host oblast.

Examining the "conditions of opportunity" operating at the union republic level outside the R.S.F.S.R., Grey Hodnett (1978) found some cor-
roborating evidence for the notion that certain elite mobility patterns
should mirror the levels of development/modernization associated with
the unit level-of-analysis. While focusing primarily on the career patterns
of individuals per se (that is, not as indicators of the respective *unit's* mobility opportunities), Hodnett found a correlation between the age of individuals at the time of appointment to jobs in different republics and the
"development" measures of these republics (1978: 391). In addition, his
analysis yielded a "reasonable correlation" between the native occupancy
rates of key positions at the republic level and the "human-resource development" of the native populations (1978: 391). However, Hodnett's
concern with *individuals'* career patterns, background variables, and
transfers limited the adaptability of his findings for present purposes.

A larger literature within the rational-technical school of elite mobility
also sheds light on the relationship between the structural characteristics
of mid-level administrative units and the political mobility opportunities
associated with indigenous elites. The so-called Performance School of
political mobility hypothesizes that a politician's efficiency in advancing
societal goals of economic development is the primary variable explaining his career success.

Barrington Moore (1954) was perhaps the first analyst to state explicitly the characteristics of a rational-technical system in the USSR and its
implications for social and political mobility. Now well over three decades old, Moore's description of this image of the Soviet "future" best addresses the salient features of the emerging system:

First of all, technical and rational criteria would largely replace political ones in
the appraisal of economic activities. . . . There would also be some increase in the
personal security of the officials, inasmuch as conformity with objective rules and
objectively appraised performance would become the chief basis for tenure in office. Social mobility would remain at a high level, as the acquisition of technical
skills provided the major avenue for upward mobility (1954: 224).

In assessing the likelihood of these developments for the Soviet future,
Moore argued that "industrialization exerts very strong pressure toward

creating a society such as this. . . . The criterion of merit is the one that will have to be stressed in the future" (1954: 225, 196).

At the foundation of Moore's conception is the critical role played by the local party organs in the fulfillment of economic production plans. This key role, then, ensures the existence of a considerable degree of meritocracy in promoting/demoting responsible cadres. Indeed, this view provides the logic to the general rational-technical model of Soviet cadres policy. If the obkom first secretary, for example, is to be judged from above according to a rational-technical, or performance, criteria, he will, in selecting cadres for responsible positions in the oblast nomenklatura, then, make his selections based on these standards as well. The performance model articulated has found significant support elsewhere.

David Granick, in an important study of executive organizational affairs in Soviet industry, details the unique relationship that exists between party and state officials. His description highlights the criterion by which party officials are judged:

The build-up of industry is a fundamental ingredient in the program of expanding the strength of the Soviet system and thus of the Soviet Communist Party. The Party committees are there to protect the interest of the "stockholders" [i.e., party members], and they themselves are judged by their success in this regard (1961: 174).

As Granick and other analysts have attested (Schapiro, 1960; Hill and Frank, 1983), the relationship between the party secretary and the plant manager is both one of the most important and one of the most problematic in Soviet administration. That the party's role vis-à-vis the state officials goes beyond "guidance" *(rukovodstvo)* has been well established.

Indeed, consistent with the secretary's role in a rational-technical system is his responsibility over economic affairs within his geographic domain. According to Granick,

When a director follows the instructions of his Party Committee, and his actions later prove to be wrong in the eyes of the government representatives supervising the plant, the director is personally held at fault. He cannot slough off responsibility. At the same time, if things go badly in the plant, the higher Party authorities will hold the Party secretary to account. Thus, willy-nilly, the two must form a team. . . . But if they cannot work together in any fashion, one or both will be removed by higher-ups (1961: 25–26).

Jerry F. Hough's work on the Soviet "prefects" has consistently reinforced the basic tenets of the meritocratic view of elite mobility (1969: 280–285; 1972: 62). Referring to Moore's rational-technical picture as "the most successful model of Soviet society" (1969: 280), Hough argues that "being held responsible for the performance of their area, [the local party officials], like the managers they supervise, have an interest in any action improving performance" (1969: 256). More precisely, Hough asserts that as "the local party organs soon were given responsibility for the economic development program, . . . the performance of the party officials came to be judged primarily by the success or lack of it in this field" (1969: 6). In essence, when weighing the validity of the performance model vis-à-vis that of the patronage model, Hough concludes that "the evidence still strongly suggests that the selection of personnel . . . is basically conducted on the basis of a proverb . . . 'Friendship is friendship, but business is business' " (1969: 277).

The work of Joel C. Moses lends further support to this notion. In estimating the influence on policy of what he calls "environmental factors," he argues that the regional party official shares the responsibility for industrial performance with the local enterprise directors, adding that the "party officials alone are likely to be held accountable for failing to meet [certain] quotas" (1974: 76). Moses, however, does not explicitly address the counterfactual: What benefits, if any, accrue to the regional secretary if quotas are met? That is, is the incentive described by Moses strictly negative, or will a strong economic performance accelerate a climber's career?

More recently, Mark R. Beissinger (1986), without discounting the explanatory value of clientelism, directly addresses the nature of these performance incentives. He argues that "aspiring provincial party officials could be motivated to engage in behavior conducive to economic success in their territory because poor performance inhibited their prospects for promotion" (1986: 18–19). Yet, he finds that during the late Brezhnev period, the validity of the performance model declined as the cadres policy in the USSR became increasingly conservative:

In the 1976 to 1982 period, promotions were distributed regardless of economic performance, while demotions were reserved for officials with poor economic records. In short, the criteria for personnel decision-making increasingly shifted in the late Brezhnev era from reward-centered motivation to punishment-centered motivation, as economic performance throughout the Soviet system declined. . . . In a period of declining economic performance, "trust-in-cadres" was bound to undermine performance incentives, for it led to a declining number of mobility opportunities and perverted the criteria used for personnel selection (1986: 23, 22).

Finally, Willerton and Reisinger (1987) note that in the Soviet Union "system support and programmatic success increasingly require economic productivity. As a result, leadership effectiveness is increasingly determined on the basis of the fulfillment of directives" (1987: 1). While more committed than the other scholars cited above to the patronage-based explanation of Soviet elite mobility, Willerton and Reisinger hypothesize that there is a positive correlation "between a region's good economic and political performance and the promotion of local cadres to top party positions" (1987: 8).

As the brief review of the literature provided above attests, broad agreement exists among scholars on the importance of performance or meritocratic criteria in the evaluation of regional party elites. Even those scholars (for example, Willerton and Reisinger, 1987) who discount to some degree the explanatory value of the rational-technical approach to elite mobility and who remain firmly in the patronage school are nonetheless convinced of the link between performance variables and mobility opportunities.

Recalling Stewart's description of the bases of the rational-technical model, however, a neglected area of research seems evident. He argued that the rational-technical model consists of two "core" concepts: (1) economic performance and (2) level of economic development (1972: 1274). The extant literature in the area of regional elite mobility generally ignores the latter of these two core elements, focusing instead on the links between oblast economic performance (usually measured by the percentage increase in disaggregated economic measures from the prior plan period) and the career paths of individuals associated with the oblast. Few attempts have been made to establish the exact relationship between a unit's *developmental* characteristics and its long-term "structure of political opportunities."

More precisely, additional study is necessary to link analytically the variances among Soviet oblasti with respect to (a) level of economic and social development and (b) political mobility opportunities. The approach adopted in the present study, therefore, includes but goes beyond a strict performance model. A more structural line of investigation is embraced herein and looks more to the developmental and demographic characteristics associated with the units under scrutiny than to a pure economic performance criteria. Such an approach will, it is hoped, help close a gap in the literature on the structural factors of political elite mobility in the Soviet Union.

RESEARCH DESIGN AND DATA

The data utilized in this study were collected from a variety of primary sources. Longitudinal oblast figures for population (urban, rural, and total), area, and administrative substructure were provided by *SSSR administrativno-territorialnoe delenie soiuznikh respublik v 1983 goda.* This source provided three sets of the above data categories (1963, 1976,

1983) and therefore allows for the calculation of various demographic growth rates.

Additional demographic data were contained in *Itogi vsesoiuznoi perepisi naselennia 1970 goda.* This reporting of the 1970 Soviet census data contained oblast-level values for ethnic composition by urban, rural, and total populations. It therefore enables the researcher to identify the respective Russian and non-Russian saturation rates for areas within each USSR oblast. In addition, *Itogi* provides the important workforce data, which break down the Soviet labor force into the three traditional categories: workers, employees,[1] and *kolkhozniki.* Two years of these data (for 1959 and 1970) allow for comparison over time as well. Although the latest Soviet census was taken in 1979, the 1970 census data are the most recent census results available in aggregate form.

The bulk of the economic and social development data were compiled from various republic editions of *Narodnoe khoziastvo.*[2] The most recent available editions of *Narkhoz* for each of the 8 union republics containing oblasti were consulted and produced almost 40 separate socioeconomic variables for each of the 129 Soviet oblasti. Moreover, in most cases, data were collected for these oblast variables for three different years (one year each in the 1960s, 1970s, and 1980s) over the time frame of this study. This allows for the computation of growth rates for various indicators.

Of course, the Soviets have traditionally been rather recalcitrant in publishing any heavy industrial output figures. Only very indirect indicators of heavy industrial activity are available. However, rather comprehensive data are provided for social development estimations. The much utilized figures for doctors per capita, hospital beds per capita, level of retail sales, maternity/child care clinics, student enrollments at various educational levels, and so on are complete in *Narkhoz* and provide a valid indication of social development.

From the large number of variables for which oblast data are available, a much smaller group of variables seems, intuitively, crucial in any determination of oblast levels of socioeconomic development. For each of the 129 oblasti of the Soviet Union, the following variables were included in a statistical analysis aimed at categorizing the regions with respect to development: (1) total population, (2) population growth, 1963–1983, (3) population density, (4) "natives"[3] as a percentage of the total population, (5) "natives" as a percentage of the urban population, (6) degree of urbanization, (7) "workers" as a percentage of the labor force, (8) "collective farmers" as a percentage of the labor force, (9) "employees" as a percentage of the labor force, (10) the value of retail sales, (11) the amount of increase in the living space available to the population, (12) the number of children in day-care facilities, (13) the number of maternity/child-care clinics, (14) the number of doctors per capita, (15) the number of hospital beds per capita, and (16) the number of college students. Combined, these variables provide a sound measure of the level of modernity or development attained in each region of the Soviet Union.

Certain aspects of oblast development are highlighted by these data. The population growth figures allow researchers to ascertain crucial demographic trends in the Soviet Union. The data indicate that certain regions of the USSR are experiencing significant increases in population over time while others are experiencing long-term population losses.

Data on the ethnic composition of oblasti are also important, especially with respect to political mobility. Most research on ethnonationalism in the Soviet Union relies on union republic-level figures that tend to gloss over significant intra-republic variation in ethnic composition. For example, the Ukrainian Republic is approximately 74 percent native Ukrainian, but the oblast-level data reveal that wide variation exists within the Ukrainian SSR. The population of Ternopol oblast, for example, is 96 percent Ukrainian (and 2 percent Russian) while only 27 percent of the Crimean oblast is ethnically Ukrainian (and 67 percent Russian). Indeed, several other Ukrainian oblasti are less than 60 percent "native." This range of variance in these demographic data is even more striking in Kazakhstan. Due to migration patterns, Russians outnumber native Kazakhs in Kazakhstan by approximately 41 percent to 36 percent.

Close examination of the oblast-level data reveals important differences among the nineteen Kazakh oblasti. Kzyl-Orda oblast is over 70 percent native, but eight other Kazakh regions fall below even 30 percent native. These differences, it is argued, are potentially important when discussing political mobility opportunities in a multinational system noted for its traditional political, economic, and military suzerainty by ethnic Russians.

Comparing oblast population density figures with the degree of urbanization sheds light on the distribution of the population throughout the geographic boundaries of the region and allows for a more accurate description of the extant social conditions in a given oblast. For example, the overwhelming bulk (82 percent) of the population of Magadan oblast in the far northeastern part of the R.S.F.S.R. lives in urban settings, yet the region's population is not at all dense (40 persons per square kilometer). These data describe a region that is quite large in size (almost 1.2 million square kilometers) wherein the population is strongly concentrated in only a relatively small number of established urban sites.

The juxtaposition of these data allows the observer to resist the temptation to equate oblasti with similar "urbanness" measures that are, in reality, quite different demographic types of regions. The populations of Kamchatka oblast (82 percent urban) and Dnepropetrovsk oblast (82 percent urban) are, by one measure, equally "urban," yet their population density figures belie this first statistical similarity. The population of

Table 3.1
Developmental Variables of Soviet Regions

VARIABLE	MEAN	STANDARD DEVIATION
Population	1925.55	1710.11
Population Growth	259.15	454.22
Population Density	4.22	4.51
Native Population (%)	35.36	33.16
Urban Native Population (%)	29.45	29.40
Urban Population (%)	63.16	14.34
Workers in the Labor Force (%)	58.51	11.96
Kolkhozniki in the Labor Force (%)	19.81	15.29
Employees in the Labor Force (%)	21.48	51.81
Value of Retail Sales	2033.38	2674.06
Increase in Available Living Space	3197.49	2428.12
Children in Day-Care Centers	108.23	98.73
Maternity/Child-Care Centers	177.34	118.81
Doctors per Capita	361.20	90.53
Hospital Beds per Capita	131.77	10.63
University Students	412.85	796.44

KEY:
- Population: 1983 data (x 1,000)
- Population Growth: 1963 -- 1983 (x 1,000)
- Population Density: 1983 data (x 1,000/sq. km.)
- Native Population: 1970 data [For units inside the RSFSR, "native" connotes all non-Russians; outside the RSFSR, "native" connotes the titular ethnic group of the respective Republic].
- Urban Native Population: 1970 data
- Urban Population: 1983 data
- Labor Force statistics: 1970 data
- Value of Retail Sales: 1980 data (x 1,000,000 rubles)
- Increase in Living Space: 1980 data (x 1,000 sq. meters)
- Children in Day-Care Centers: 1980 data (x 1,000)
- Maternity/Child-Care Centers: 1980 data (#)
- Doctors per Capita: 1980 data (# per 100,000 population)
- Hospital Beds per Capita: 1980 data (# per 10,000 population)
- University Students: 1980 data (x 100)

Kamchatka oblast is distributed throughout the region at a rate of 90 persons per square kilometer while the territory of Dnepropetrovsk region is quite dense, with 11,750 people per square kilometer. The combination of these two oblast indicators allows important distinctions to be drawn among regions of the USSR.

In the absence of published indicators of Soviet economic activity, researchers are forced to rely on more indirect measures. Statistical breakdowns of oblast workforce figures are published and they permit inferences to be made about the mix of economic activities taking place in respective regions of the Soviet Union. Knowing the percentages of blue-collar workers, collective farmers, and white-collar employees that comprise a region's workforce assists in describing the predominant types of economic activity in the oblast.

Several variables indicate the age distribution of the oblast population. The number of children in full-time, day-care facilities, and maternity/child-care clinics are both indicators of the number of young people (both children and young adults) in the population. Moreover, the number of college students statistic bolsters these figures and provides a clue about the development of the higher educational system of the respective oblast.

The final four variables reveal the level of social infrastructural development by focusing on the degree of indigenous activity in internal trade, construction, and health care. Variations in the volume of retail trade and new housing construction can reveal much about the level and pattern of activity within and among Soviet regions. The number of doctors and hospital beds per capita allow inferences to be drawn about the level of development of the health care industry as well as the level of modernity of the oblast itself. These numerous measures, when combined, provide a solid basis for differentiating the Soviet oblasti by level and type of socio-economic development.

These sixteen oblast variables were factor analyzed to produce developmental characteristic measures. That is, developmental patterns in the oblast data were sought in an effort to create categories or types of oblasti. Basically, factor analysis is a means for delineating order and regularity in phenomena. It is a method that highlights the interrelationships among the observed variables in order to discover and delineate distinct patterns of shared variation in the data. By extracting from the data values a number of separate factors, or dimensions, factor analysis untangles the pattern of interrelationship among the variables, sorts the variables into distinct classes, and determines the extent to which each variable is related to these different sources of variation. That is, it establishes the basic dimensions necessary to account for the principal relationships among the variables.

As a statistical tool, factor analysis "assumes that the observed (measured) variables are linear combinations of some underlying source variables (or factors). That is, it assumes the existence of a system of underlying factors and a system of observed variables" (Kim and Mueller, 1978: 8). Specifically, it assumes that the sixteen observed variables listed above for each oblast are representative values of a much smaller quantity of *underlying* factors (or developmental measures that tend to coalesce).

Factor analysis, then, is founded on the premise "that some underlying factors, which are smaller in number than the number of observed variables, are responsible for the covariation among the observed variables" (Kim and Mueller, 1978: 12). Specifically, the observed variance among the values for each of the 16 variables across 129 cases is due to several underlying factors. Factor analysis, then, explicates these underlying factors and describes their respective characteristics.

In addition, the analysis provides a "degree of fit" for each oblast to each of the factors. That is, each oblast may be scored with respect to its position on each respective factor continuum, defined by the characteristics that comprise them. In this way, it is possible to create different developmental categories of oblasti, depending on their respective scores for each of the generated factors.

It is possible, moreover, having generated a series of factor scores for each of the 129 Soviet oblasti, to correlate these scores (in this case, factor scores for level and type of development) and oblast political mobility scores. In this way, the non-idiosyncratic-independent variables that affect regional elite mobility in the Soviet Union can be made explicit.

FINDINGS: OBLAST DEVELOPMENTAL FACTORS AND POLITICAL MOBILITY

The analysis of the selected oblast characteristics produced three underlying factors that account for approximately 80 percent of the variance in the observed values of these oblast traits.[4] The first factor, essentially a measure of modern, yet still rapidly developing oblasti, is characterized by (1) large absolute population, (2) high population density, (3) significant increases in population during the 1963–1983 period, (4) sizable increases in the living space available to the population, (5) a large volume of retail trade, (6) a large number of doctors per capita ratio, (7) a high number of children in day-care facilities, (8) a significant number of maternity/child-care clinics, and (9) a sizable college student population. Oblasti possessing high scores for this first factor, then, are likely to be characterized by relatively younger, larger, and growing populations, living in relatively urban settings with strongly developed social infrastructures. Oblasti fitting this measure can be considered modern units that, despite the significant degree of modernity already attained, are nonetheless experiencing still further rapid development and growth.

The second underlying factor produced by the analysis essentially describes characteristics of a rural, agrarian life. The developmental variables significant for this factor are (1) very low percentages of blue-collar workers in the unit's labor force, (2) correspondingly high numbers of collective farmers engaged in agricultural labor, (3) moderate population density, with a relatively small fraction of the total oblast population residing in urban settings, (4) significant percentages of non-Russians (for R.S.F.S.R. oblasti) or titular ethnic natives (for oblasti outside the R.S.F.S.R.) in the unit total population, with (5) similarly high percentages of these groups in the oblast's urban environs. Those oblasti scoring

Table 3.2
Rotated Factor Scores for
Oblast Developmental Variables

VARIABLE	FACTOR 1	FACTOR 2	FACTOR 3
Population	.98049	-.07147	.05232
Population Growth	.86550	-.02672	.23820
Population Density	.76255	.44416	-.04561
Native Population	-.03847	.92928	-.03461
Urban Native Population	.00998	.94380	-.03246
Urban Population	.38054	-.47159	.58745
Workers in the Labor Force	.01237	-.80564	.38521
Kolkhozniki in Labor Force	-.10760	.75200	-.55270
Employees in the Labor Force	.30417	-.38408	.74863
Value of Retail Sales	.95266	-.05889	.15266
Increase in Living Space	.63078	-.23933	-.10407
Children in Day-Care Centers	.94684	-.17163	.14501
Maternity/Child-Care Centers	.91379	.02875	.03168
Doctors per Capita	.52904	.06924	.67819
Hospital Beds per Capita	-.27426	-.12885	.71134
University Students	.90042	-.00288	.16890

Note: The factor scores are rotated according to a varimax orthogonal rotation technique. According to R. J. Rummel (1970:392), "varimax is now generally accepted as the best analytic orthogonal rotation technique."

high on this factor measure are likely to be agriculturally based, rural units either outside the Russian Republic or the non-European territories of the R.S.F.S.R.

Finally, the third factor highlighted by the analysis is a measure of developed, urban oblasti which are not at this time experiencing significant growth demographically or physically. The characteristics significant for Factor 3 are (1) a low percentage of collective farmers, (2) a high percentage of the population living in urban settings, (3) established health care systems as reflected in a large number of doctors per capita and a large number of hospital beds per capita, and (4) a high percentage of the labor force comprised of white-collar employees. As such, strong oblast scores for Factor 3 would seem to indicate established, yet somewhat stagnant, urban regions with a relatively developed social infrastructure. In addition, despite generating a high factor score for urbanness, this third measure scores rather low for population density. Combined, these characteristics seem to describe relatively large regions whose populations are concentrated in the major urban area(s) of the oblast. This demographic phenomenon would account, then, for the simultaneous high percentage of the populations living in urban environs and low population density scores.

The characteristics described by Factor 1 for measuring the modernity of the respective units intuitively seem to fit the individual oblasti with

Table 3.3
Oblast Developmental Factors

FACTOR 1	FACTOR 2	FACTOR 3
Large Population	Low % Blue Collar	Low % Kolkhozniki
Dense Population	High % Kolkhozniki	High % Urban
Growing Population	Low % Urban	Doctors/Capita
Increase in Living Space	High % Non-Russians	Hospital Beds/
Children in Day Care	High % Natives	Capita
High Retail Sales	High % Urban Natives	High % Employees
Doctors/Capita	Moderate Population	
Maternity Clinics	Density	
College Students		

strong Factor 1 scores (see Appendix IV). The ten highest "degree of fit" scores associated with Factor 1 are Moscow (7.24723), Leningrad (2.30260), Kiev (1.92365), Donetsk (1.88945), Krasnodar krai (1.74343), Rostov (1.27889), Dnepropetrovsk (1.26467), Sverdlovsk (1.10348), Kharkov (0.96481), and Gorkii (0.91251). Each of these oblasti is a well-developed, highly and densely populated, industrial oblast with an advancing social and economic infrastructure.

Factor 2 component characteristics seem to describe rural, agricultural oblasti populated, relative to other oblasti, by significant numbers of non-Russians. The high scores on this measure generated by the respective characteristics of Ternopol (2.36568), Chernigov (2.07915), Vinnitsa (2.03866), Khmelnitskii (1.98201), Volyn (1.97027), Cherkassy (1.92328), Kirovgrad (1.88307), Ivano-Frankovsk (1.73623), Rovno (1.68146), and Chernovtsy (1.58642), all prime agricultural regions of the Ukrainian republic, seem to attest to the validity of the description generated by the factor scores.

The oblast characteristics picked up by Factor 3 combine to depict an urban, developed oblast with an established social infrastructure and a large white-collar workforce. Regions scoring high on this factor measure might well be dominated by the population and activities of the core urban area(s), with the surrounding countryside being sparsely populated. The vital characteristics of Sakhalin (3.15803), Magadan (2.97088), Kamchatka (2.89366), Astrakhan (2.21633), Karaganda (1.93828), Gurev (1.84003), and Khabarovsk krai (1.63545) lend validity to the picture constructed by this factor measure.

Next, these various factor scores were utilized as independent variables in a multiple regression analysis; the respective mobility scores generated in Chapter 2 served as the dependent variables in the analysis. Multiple regression allows for the incorporation of more than one dependent variable into the equation. As a result, it (a) offers a fuller explanation of the dependent variable (since few phenemona are products of a single cause), and (b) clarifies the effect of any single independent variable by removing the distorting influences of the other independent variables (Lewis-Beck, 1980: 47). Inasmuch as the factor analysis described above produced three oblast developmental factors, or variables, multiple regression techniques are called for.

Both Factor 1 and Factor 2 explain statistically significant amounts of the variance in political mobility among the Soviet oblasti (see Table 3.4). Combined, Factors 1 and 2 account for approximately 41 percent of this observed variance. The analysis also showed that the characteristics comprising Factor 1 are positively correlated with oblast political mobility scores, while those comprising Factor 2 are almost equally negatively correlated with these same mobility scores. That is, high oblast scores on the scale defined by Factor 1 characteristics are associated with high political mobility scores, and vice versa. On the other hand, high oblast scores on the Factor 2 scale are associated with low political mobility scores.

Factor 3 by itself explains very little of the observed variance in the political mobility scores generated by the oblasti. It correlates only very weakly ($r = -.02017$) with the calculated mobility scores and thus has no predictive value in this regard. The Factor 3 score generated by each of the oblasti, then, cannot alone serve as an indicator of the political mobility opportunities associated with the respective regions. Table 3.4 shows the relative explanatory power of each of the three factors with respect to regional elite mobility in the Soviet Union.

Mindful of the oblast developmental characteristics that were utilized in the construction of these two factors, certain general statements about their relationship to political mobility opportunities may be proffered. First, oblasti that are modern yet growing rapidly and developing further have been shown to be positively correlated (.465814) with upward political mobility. That is, to the extent that an individual oblast is characterized by a large, dense, and growing population, significantly growing housing construction, high levels of retail trade, an established health care system, and large numbers of both children in day-care facilities and students in colleges, that oblast will tend to have high upward political mobility opportunities associated with it. In a word, modern and rapidly growing regions of the Soviet Union have presented, at least since 1965, the best opportunities for upward political mobility for their respective party leaders.

Second, Soviet oblasti characterized predominantly by rural, agrarian activities tend to be negatively correlated ($-.451391$) with upward political mobility opportunities. More precisely, regions with low percentages of blue-collar workers, high percentages of collective farmers, low urbanness, a high percentage of non-Russians in both rural and urban settings, and only moderate population density tend to present to their party first secretaries only poor prospects for upward political mobility. The

Table 3.4
Relative Weights of Factor Variables
on Political Mobility

VARIABLE	BETA SCORE[*]
1	.46581
2	−.45139
3	−.02017

For Variables 1 and 2: r^2 = .42074
Adjusted r^2 = .40867
F = 34.86382

[*]Significant at 0.05 level

more an individual region approximates the "ideal type" Factor 2 oblast, the more likely it is that its political mobility score will be low, relative to those of other oblasti.

These aggregate findings seem to be supported by examining the individual oblasti themselves. Table 3.5 shows these oblasti that possess the largest numerical gap between their Factor 1 and Factor 2 scores and reveals that those units with high Factor 1–low Factor 2 scores easily outperform on the mobility scale those regions with high Factor 2–low Factor 1 scores. Indeed, for the selected oblasti the former group's mean

Table 3.5
Selected Oblast Factor Scores and Political Mobility

OBLAST	FACTOR 1	FACTOR 2	GAP	MOBILITY SCORE	RANK
Moscow	7.24723	.31595	6.93128	14.00	8
Leningrad	2.30260	−.38589	2.68849	15.25	2
Sverdlovsk	1.10348	−1.37840	2.48188	14.00	8
Rostov	1.27889	−1.05041	2.32930	14.37	6
Gorkii	.91251	−1.08692	1.99943	13.25	23
			MEAN:	14.20	9.4
Ternopol	−.19569	2.36568	2.56137	9.67	122
Chernigov	−.38110	2.07915	2.46025	12.00	44
Kirovgrad	−.45562	1.88307	2.33869	10.75	85
Khmelnitskii	−.10773	1.98201	2.08974	10.50	93
Vinnitsa	−.02415	2.03866	2.06281	12.25	41
			MEAN:	11.12	77.0

ranked position is 9.4 from the top of the scale, while the latter group's mean ranking is far lower, at the 77.0 (of a total of 129) position.

In addition, several advanced regions in the Soviet Union's agricultural breadbasket scored quite well on both Factor 1 and Factor 2 scales. A number of developed and growing regions (strong Factor 1) also supported a significant agricultural economy (strong Factor 2). While when in isolation or combined with a weak Factor 1 score, a high Factor 2 score would tend to produce a relatively low mobility score, those units that score high on both factor scales present solid political mobility opportunities. The economically diverse regions of the Ukrainian SSR are especially noteworthy in this respect. Kiev, with a political mobility score of 12.50, scored high on both measures, as did Dnepropetrovsk (14.25), Kharkov (12.75), Lvov (13.33), and Odessa (11.00). Minsk, of the Belorussian SSR, also scored well on Factor 1 and Factor 2, and generated a strong 14.67 mobility score as well (see Appendix IV).

In terms of explaining the variance among oblast political mobility scores, Factor 3 adds very little to the analysis. Very little statistical correlation $(-.02017)$ exists between the two variables. In essence it seems, at least with respect to the variance in political mobility scores, Factor 3 and its constituent developmental characteristics possess little explanatory value in and of themselves. In all likelihood, whatever Factor 3 is measuring, it is being measured better by Factor 1. That is, concerning the effect on political mobility opportunities, Factor 1 and Factor 3 are essentially measuring the same phenomena. A look at the correlation matrix of Factor 1 and Factor 3 variables confirms this suspicion. Three crucial Factor 3 developmental characteristics exhibit some significant levels of correlation with Factor 1 variables (see Table 3.6).

Conceptually, Factors 1 and 2 are very similar and when viewed as independent variables affecting political mobility, Factor 3 characteristics seem to be captured by the highly compatible nature of Factor 1. By itself, then, Factor 3 explains very little of the variance in political mobility scores not captured by Factors 1 and 2.

The bulk of the explanatory power, such as it is, discerned in this analysis inheres in Factor 1 and Factor 2. These constructs and the oblast characteristics that comprise them speak directly and with significance to the issue of the regional elite mobility patterns that are extant and operating in the Soviet Union.

CONCLUSION

This chapter has sought to explicate non-idiosyncratic independent variables that condition the political elite mobility opportunities of Soviet oblast party officials. It was found, after categorizing the oblasti

Table 3.6
Correlation Matrix of Selected Variables
of Factor 1 and Factor 3

| | Factor 3 Variables: | | |
Factor 1 Variables	PERCENT URBAN	DOCTORS/ CAPITA	PERCENT EMPLOYEES
POPULATION	.42989	.51229	.33355
POPULATION GROWTH	.37995	.61557	.52757
INCREASE IN LIVING SPACE	.49439	.28047	.14359
CHILDREN IN DAY-CARE CENTERS	.52863	.54072	.42544
VOLUME OF RETAIL SALES	.41531	.56408	.41482
MATERNITY/CHILD-CARE CENTERS	.34148	.50160	.26591
UNIVERSITY STUDENTS	.35886	.56807	.41591

according to type and level of socioeconomic development, that modern developing regions marked by (1) large populations, (2) high population density, (3) significant population growth over the past two decades, (4) sizable increases in constructed living space for its inhabitants, (5) a high level of internal retail trade, (6) a large number of doctors per capita, a relatively young population as measured by (7) the number of children in full-time, day-care facilities and (8) the number of maternity/child-care centers, and (9) a sizable number of university students was *positively* correlated (r = .46581) with the quantitative political mobility measures generated in the previous chapter.

It was found, moreover, that oblasti of a second type, one characterized by a rural, agrarian existence with (1) low percentages of blue-collar workers, (2) a correspondingly high percentage of collective farmers, (3) low urbanness, (4) high percentages of non-Russians, even in the urban areas, and (5) only moderate population density, are *negatively* correlated (r = − .45139) with those same political mobility scores.

The analysis indicates that the first type of oblast offers its party incumbents relatively stronger opportunities for upward political mobility while those of the second type offer only relatively weaker opportunities for upward movement in the political-administrative hierarchy. Combined, the characteristics of these two types of oblasti explain approximately 41 percent of the measured variance in the political mobility scores associated with Soviet oblasti.

The factor analysis of the oblast developmental variables also produced a third type of regional unit. Examination of the data indicates that this third oblast type exhibits (1) a high degree of urbanness, (2) a high percentage of white-collar employees in its labor force, (3) negligible agricultural activity as measured by the percentage of collective farmers in the work force, (4) strong doctors per capita and (5) hospital beds per capita ratios. These urban developed, yet perhaps stagnant, regions, it was discovered, are neither significantly positively nor negatively correlated ($r = -.02017$) with the political mobility opportunities of their respective party secretaries. That is, the above Factor 3 characteristics do not explain a significant amount of the variance among the oblast political mobility scores.

As in the previous chapter, this portion of the overall research project must close with a note of caution. Although significant findings have been attained, the tentativeness of their explanatory power must be stressed. If the analysis herein explains 41 percent of the variance in oblast political mobility scores, 59 percent of that variance is left unexplained. Other variables are clearly at work that help condition the structure of political opportunities at the regional level in the Soviet Union. Although this analysis has stressed the structural variations of the oblasti themselves, little attention has been paid to the very individuals experiencing this mobility. While certain kinds of oblasti may be more conducive to an upwardly mobile career path, what individual traits of the secretaries themselves might abet these structural forces? Are certain kinds of individuals, with certain specialized training, or specified career experience, more likely than others to advance in the contemporary Soviet system? These are the questions to which the analysis now turns.

NOTES

1. *Sovkhozniki,* workers on state farms, are considered "employees" in Soviet terminology inasmuch as they receive a fixed salary for their work. *Kolkhozniki,* workers on collective farms, on the contrary, have a fluctuating income that depends on production levels.

2. *Narodnoe Khoziastvo RSFSR v 1984 Godu* (Moskva: Tsentral'noe Statisticheskoe Upravlenie, 1985); *Narodnoe Khoziastvo Ukrainskoe SSR v 1983 Godu* (Kiev: Tekhnika, 1984); *Narodnoe Khoziastvo Uzbekskoe SSR v 1979 Godu* (Tashkent: Izdatelstvo "Uzbekistan," 1980); *Narodnoe Khoziastvo Kirgizskoe SSR v 1981 Godu* (Frunze: Izdatelstvo "Kirgizia," 1982); *Narodnoe Khoziastvo Tadzhikskoe SSR v 1982 Godu* (Dushanbe: Izdatelstvo "Irfon," 1983); *Narodnoe Khoziastvo Turkmenskoe SSR v 1982 Godu* (Ashkhabad: "Turkemnistan," 1983); *Narodnoe Khoziastvo Kazakhstana v 1982 G.* (Alma-Ata: "Kazakhstan," 1983); and *Narodnoe Khoziastvo Beolrusskoe SSR v 1982 g.* (Minsk: "Belarus'," 1983).

3. For the fifty-five R.S.F.S.R. oblasti, "natives" refers to the non-Russian population. For the seventy-four oblasti of the remaining seven republics, "natives" connotes the predominant ethnic national group (for example, Ukrainians in the Ukraine, Kazakhs in Kazakhstan).

4. The three factors combine to confront 80.5 percent of the variance in the data values: Factor 1 = 45.7 percent, Factor 2 = 26.2 percent, and Factor 3 = 8.6 percent.

REFERENCES

Bandera, V. N., and Z. L. Melnyk, eds. *The Soviet Economy in Regional Perspective.* New York: Praeger Publishers, 1973.

Beissinger, Mark R. "Economic Performance and Career Prospects in the CPSU Party Apparatus." Paper presented at the eighteenth annual convention of the American Association for the Advancement of Slavic Studies, New Orleans, LA, November 20–23, 1986.

Cole, J. P., and M. E. Harrison. *Regional Inequality in Service and Purchasing Power 1940–1976.* London: University of London, 1978.

Gleason, Gregory. "Principles of Soviet Federalism and Regional Policy." Paper presented at the eighteenth annual convention of the American Association for the Advancement of Slavic Studies, New Orleans, LA, November 20–23, 1986.

Granick, David. *The Red Executive: A Study of the Organization Man in Russian Industry.* Garden City, N.Y.: Anchor/Doubleday, 1960.

Harris, Chauncy D. "Size Relations, Central Places, and the Administrative Hierarchy," pp. 129–185 in Chauncy D. Harris, *Cities of the Soviet Union: Studies in Their Functions, Size, Density, and Growth.* Chicago: Rand McNally, 1970.

Hill, Ronald J., and Peter Frank. *The Soviet Communist Party.* 2d ed. London: George Allen & Unwin, 1983.

Hodnett, Grey. *Leadership in the Soviet National Republics: A Quantitative Study of Recruitment Policy.* Oakville, Ontario: Mosaic Press, 1978.

Hough, Jerry F. "The Party Apparatchiki," pp. 47–92 in H. Gordon Skilling and Franklyn Griffiths, eds. *Interest Groups in Soviet Politics.* Princeton, NJ: Princeton University Press, 1972.

Hough, Jerry F. *The Soviet Prefects: The Local Party Organs in Industrial Decision-Making.* Cambridge, MA: Harvard University Press, 1969.

Kim, Jae-On, and Charles W. Mueller. *Introduction to Factor Analysis.* Number 13 in the series, *Quantitative Applications in the Social Sciences.* Beverly Hills, CA: Sage Publications, 1978.

Lewis-Beck, Michael S. *Applied Regression: An Introduction.* Number 22 in the series, *Quantitative Applications in the Social Sciences.* Beverly Hills, CA: Sage Publications, 1980.

McAuley, Alastair. *Economic Welfare in the Soviet Union.* Madison, WI: University of Wisconsin Press, 1979.

Moore, Barrington. *Terror and Progress USSR: Some Sources of Change and Stability in the Soviet Dictatorship.* Cambridge, Mass.: Harvard University Press, 1954.

Moses, Joel C. *Regional Party Leadership and Policy-Making in the USSR.* New York: Praeger Publishers, 1974.

Nechimias, Carol. "Regional Differentiation of Living Standards in the RSFSR: The Issue of Inequality," *Soviet Studies* 32 (July 1980).

Rummel, R. J. *Applied Factor Analysis.* Evanston, IL: Northwestern University Press, 1970.

Schapiro, Leonard. *The Communist Party of the Soviet Union.* New York: Random House, 1960.

Schlesinger, Joseph A. *Ambition and Politics: Political Careers in the United States.* Chicago: Rand McNally, 1966.

Schroeder, Gertrude E. "Regional Differences in Incomes and Levels of Living in the USSR," pp. 167–195 in V. N. Bandera and Z. L. Melnyk, eds. *The Soviet Economy in Regional Perspective.* New York: Praeger Publishers, 1973.

Schroeder, Gertrude E., and I. S. Koropeckyi. *The Economics of Soviet Regions.* New York: Praeger Publishers, 1981.

Stewart, Philip D., et al. "Political Mobility and the Soviet Political Process: A Partial Test of Two Models," *American Political Science Review* 66 (July 1972): 1269–1290.

Whitehouse, F. Douglas. "Demographic Aspects of Regional Economic Development in the USSR," pp. 154–166 in V. N. Bandera and Z. L. Melnyk, eds. *The Soviet Economy in Regional Perspective.* New York: Praeger Publishers, 1973.

Willerton, Jr., John P., and William M. Reisinger. "Elite Mobility and Regional Economic Performance in the Soviet Union: Hypotheses and Suggestive Analyses." Paper presented at the eleventh annual meeting of the Mid-Atlantic Slavic Conference, American Association for the Advancement of Slavic Studies, Baruch College, New York, March 7, 1987.

Yanowitch, M., and W. Fisher, eds. *Social Stratification and Mobility in the USSR.* White Plains, N.Y.: International Arts and Sciences Press, 1973.

4

ELITE MOBILITY AT THE OBKOM TIER: THE EFFECTS OF BACKGROUND CHARACTERISTICS AND FUNCTIONAL CAREER TYPES

INTRODUCTION

In Chapter 3, the analysis focused on the "structural" factors of the Soviet regional party units as they impinged on the political mobility opportunities of their respective party elites. Scant attention was paid to the individuals per se as the focus was on the attributes or characteristics of over 125 administrative party units that are in many ways the crucial structures of policy implementation in the Soviet political system. For analytic purposes, the individuals' career opportunities themselves were considered to be determined by the structures over which they exercised power.

Yet a comprehensive account of the forces at work in defining the structure of political opportunities operating in the USSR cannot focus solely on the indigenous characteristics of the oblasti. While certainly the prior analysis *has* shown that these factors do indeed play a significant role in the Soviet opportunity system, it seems ludicrous, prima facie, to believe that the political mobility patterns experienced by individuals are not shaped by their own respective skills, experiences, training, and so forth. That is, it seems commonsensical to assume that the variance of individual political mobility opportunities within a given population of elites can be explained (if only partially) by the variance of backgrounds, skills, and experiences of the individuals that comprise the elite population.

As Grey Hodnett has cogently remarked, "the decision to recruit the occupant of position X to fill position Y is really *only the last in a series* of choices encapsulated, as it were, in the occupancy by this individual of position X" (1978: 225; emphasis added). The analysis of the preceding chapter purposely ignored the important variables that comprise for each individual this "series of choices," and focused instead on the unit's characteristics. In this chapter, then, attention will center on the characteristics of individual oblast party committee first secretaries in the hope of shedding additional light on the nature of regional elite mobility opportunities in the Soviet Union.

While this approach, to be sure, identifies characteristics that cannot help but bear upon the actual performance of the elites in their roles, performance itself is not the focus of the analysis. Nor, for that matter, will explicit attention be paid to the attitudes that supposedly inhere in certain career types, ethnic groups, or in any group of individuals of a given generation (Blackwell, 1973b; Stewart and Town, 1974). The present concern is to establish the type and extent of the relationship between certain "functional" or background characteristics of regional party elites and the political mobility opportunities they experience.

It is assumed at the outset that certain "types" of individuals, who have certain types of education, training, experience, and so on, possess better chances for upward political mobility. It is assumed, moreover, that the analysis will yield generally consistent patterns of opportunity with respect to these individual traits that conform to the rational needs of an evolving complex society. That is, these opportunities within the political system are seen in the main as structured, not primarily as the product of arbitrary personalistic forces. As such, then, this chapter remains faithful to the philosophical orientation of the rational-technical model of Soviet society that has guided this overall project (Moore, 1954: 224; Stewart et al., 1972: 1270; Hough, 1969: 306).

BACKGROUNDS, FUNCTIONAL CAREER TYPES, AND MOBILITY IN THE USSR

The gradual abandonment of the totalitarian model of Soviet politics entailed for scholars a fundamental refocusing of analytic attention away from perceptions of a system-dominated political monolith and toward a view of a subsystem-dominated political dynamic. This philosophical reorientation was manifested in a great increase in research into the nature and diversity of various subgroupings within the Soviet political system.

At the aggregate level, scholars throughout the 1960s and early 1970s engaged in the taxonomical exercise of identifying the key groups that comprise the foundation of political activity in the USSR. Table 4.1 shows which groups were considered by several important scholars to be the key actors in the Soviet political subsystem. However, these efforts at categorizing what Wolgang Leonhard called the "pillars of Soviet society" went beyond mere taxonomy. Underlying this early research into subsystem politics were a number of assumptions about the evolving nature of Soviet political life that continue to guide contemporary scholarly efforts in this area. The underlying philosophical assumptions of the model of

Soviet politics that emerged from these writings are perhaps best articulated by H. Gordon Skilling:

[I]n the . . . years since Stalin's death the Soviet political system has been passing through a period of transition, characterized among other things by the increased activity of political interest groups and the presence of group conflict. Although decision-making in its final stage still remains in the hands of a relatively small group of leaders at the top of the party hierarchy, there has been . . . a broadening of group participation in the crucial preliminary stages of policy deliberation and in the subsequent phase of implementation (Skilling and Griffiths, 1971: 19).

Applying a variant of the Western interest-group approach to the Soviet case, scholars examining aggregate groups have agreed that these groups have tended to be (a) institutionally based, (b) relatively autonomous, (c) only weakly organized as pressure or demand groups per se, and (d) both internally and externally conflictual. The dynamic of group interaction over alternative policy and/or administrative options is, then, the dynamic of the political system. The label applied to this subsystem-dominated political dynamic has varied from "bureaucratic pluralism" (Hammer, 1974: 286) to "institutional pluralism" (Hough, 1969: 27; 1977: 22–24) to "participatory bureaucracy" (Daniels, 1971: 22) to a "pluralism of elites" (Skilling and Griffiths, 1971: 9). However labeled, though, the locus of political activity in the Soviet political system lies within and among groups (Lodge, 1968). The increased interest in aggregate-level groupism in Soviet politics has led to further research into the specific career patterns of various political cadres. Scholarly endeavors into the backgrounds of the Soviet elite, then, further narrow the focus on important institutional or occupational groups.

Frederic Fleron's work in the area of Soviet "career types" has provided a useful point of departure for subsequent scholars working in this substantive area. Fleron draws a careful and important distinction between "recruited" officials and those who are "co-opted" into the political elite. Recruited officials are those individuals who enter the elite at very early stages in their respective careers and thus have "little opportunity to form close ties with a professional-vocational group" (1970: 123). Co-opted cadres, on the other hand, enter the political elite in the middle or later stages of their careers. Given the time of their entry, these co-opted individuals have had sufficient time to establish very close professional ties outside the political elite.

In his initial research, Fleron discovered that the percentage of co-opted officials in the elite was increasing over time. This finding was further defined through additional investigation of career types. Fleron (1973) notes that officials in party staff positions tend to have been recruited, while those in line positions are usually co-opted. Thus, Fleron

Table 4.1
Key Sub-groups in Soviet Politics

Leonhard (1962)	Aspaturian (1964)	Gehlen (1966)
Party Machine Economic Machine State Apparatus Military State Police	Party Apparatus Govt. Bureaucracy Economic Managers Intelligentsia Police Armed Forces	Party Apparatus State Bureaucracy Military Bureaucracy Science Elite Writers Trade Unions Workers Consumers

Dueval (1966)	Fleron (1970)	Skillings & Griffiths (1971)

Central Party Apparatus
Regional Party Apparatus
Central Govt Bureaucracy
Regional Govt Bureaucracy
Armed Forces
Min of Foreign Affairs
KGB, MVD
Supreme Soviet
Trade Unions
Komsomol
Scientists/Academicians
Writers/Artists
Leading Workers/Farmers
	Central Party Apparatus
	Regional Party Apparatus
	Central Govt Apparatus
	Regional Govt Apparatus
	Economic Managers &
	  Planners
	Military
	KGB, MVD
	Komsomol
	Trade Unions & Public
	  Organs
	Scientists/Academicians
	Writers/Artists
	Workers/Farmers
	Foreign Affairs (Govt)
	Industrial Plant Managers
		Party Apparatchiki
		Security Police
		Military
		Industrial Managers
		Economists
		Writers
		Jurists

distinguishes between the party elite of more generalist-oriented staff cadres who were recruited into the party hierarchy and the more specialized line cadres who were co-opted into party work only after establishing strong professional ties outside the party apparatus. Over time the nature of the party elite will change, in Fleron's view, as an increasing percentage of the elite is drawn or co-opted from specialized groups outside the old party cadre.

Michael P. Gehlen has discerned similar patterns among the careers of the party elite. With Michael McBride, he analyzed the backgrounds of the members of the Central Committee elected at the 23d Party Congress of 1966. Such variables as age, sex, education, occupation, career history, place of residence, party status, and foreign travel were studied with a view toward discovering patterns in the careers and backgrounds of these elites. Most important among their findings was the marked increase of technical specialist training among these elite:

The evidence indicates the importance of education to members of the Soviet political elite in terms of influencing how they launched their careers and of influencing their status in the CPSU. Most of this educational preparation was specialized rather than general, with the four largest categories being engineering, agronomy, Party, and military, in that order (Gehlen and McBride, 1968: 1239).

Gehlen then expanded the sample in his analysis to include the career patterns of apparatchiki who attained full membership in the C.P.S.U. Central Committee between 1952 and 1966. Several important trends in the backgrounds of these elites were uncovered. Gehlen's (1970) analysis points to (a) the declining role of the Komsomol (Communist Youth League) experience as a prerequisite for entrance into the party elite (p. 143), (b) the significantly greater role of specialized training vis-à-vis either a general education or Party School preparation for admittance into the party elite (pp. 145, 147–149), (c) the increased co-optation into the higher echelons of the apparat of persons who have functional specializations in the economic sector of Soviet society (p. 147), and (d) the relatively small number of persons recruited into the party apparat from the ranks of the professional governmental bureaucracy (p. 148). For Gehlen, the importance of these trends cannot be underestimated:

Should the trend established in the 1952–1966 period continue . . . it seems likely that there will be a further gradual transformation of the party *apparat* into a coterie of functional elites who maintain close identification with specialist areas of operation. This development would probably even further diminish the distinction of the party from the bureaucracy and make it even more difficult for the Party to justify its dominant role and to maintain its present autonomy (Gehlen, 1970: 156).

Philip Stewart (1968) has focused attention on the background and career characteristics of party elites at the obkom level. While his finding that a pedagogical education "is one of the most direct paths to a career in the Party apparatus" (p. 158) seems to run counter to certain aspects of the above mentioned research, other findings mesh well with those analyses conducted on higher-level elites. On the one hand, he finds an increase in the depth and diversity of the educational backgrounds of obkom first secretaries over time, yet notes that "once these men enter full-time Party work, the patterns of training and testing in Party leadership positions tend to be quite similar" (p. 159).

Second, Stewart's finding that the average age of these obkom first secretaries has been rising over the years supports the notion that turnover in the obkom tier slowed considerably under Brezhnev, thereby causing new cadres to enter the responsible party positions later than under Khrushchev (p. 165). Finally, his analysis also reveals that the less technical the educational background of an obkom secretary, the more likely he is to have a long tenure in that post (p. 168). It is difficult, however, to conclude anything substantive from this finding with regard to the success or failure of these specific party elites' careers. As Stewart remarks, "a short tenure as obkom first secretary may lead equally to either a political future or obscurity" (p. 172).

Jerry F. Hough, in his important study of regional party "prefects," examines the educational backgrounds of these local party secretaries. In his view, two events, the creation of the *sovnarkhozy* (Regional Economic Councils) and the bifurcation of the party apparatus in November 1962, greatly facilitated the influx of more technically trained cadres into responsible party positions:

Although the creation of the sovnarkhozy changed the type of Soviet industrial administrator relatively little [i.e., they were already "technocrats"], it had a much more dramatic impact on the Party officials dealing with industrial questions. In the most industrialized oblasti, the proportion of the obkom first secretaries with technical training increased sharply. . . . The bifurcation of the Party apparatus created conditions in which Khrushchev's policy of increasing the technical qualifications of Party secretaries could be carried through to completion. A year after the reorganization, eighty-two of eight-four first and second secretaries of industrialized obkomy and kraikomy in the RSFSR were industrial specialists (1969: 58, 68).

Writing five years after Khrushchev's ouster, Hough discerned only continuity in the cadres policy established by the erstwhile leader. "Even when there were changes in personnel after the removal of Khrushchev," he wrote, "the level of technical competence of the Party officials showed relatively little decline . . . " (p. 70).

However, Robert E. Blackwell, Jr. has challenged many findings in the literature on the regional party cadres' training and career patterns. While he admits that (a) the obkom elite is well educated, (b) the party leadership has tried to recruit a certain number of persons with technical educations, and (c) the degree of importance of political work vis-à-vis specialized training is declining, Blackwell is much more hesitant to join other scholars in emphasizing the consistent rise of the technocrat among the Soviet regional political elite.

Three important points speak directly to this issue. First, according to Blackwell's analysis, a sizable number of persons in the political elite "have no occupation other than politics, Soviet style" (1972b: 140). The leadership has *always* recruited into the elite strata a number of persons who have had experience in something other than party work. Second, Blackwell sees a clear relationship between the types of people recruited into responsible party positions and the period or regime during which they were recruited. "There was a steady increase in each period [until Brezhnev] in the number of persons with some form of agricultural or industrial experience" (1972b: 140). Finally, unlike Hough, Blackwell argues that in the post-Khrushchev period the policy of recruiting men with technical experience appears to have been reversed. "We find," he writes, "a noticeable increase in the number of obkom First Secretaries with political backgrounds" (1972b: 141).

Blackwell's more cautious appraisal of the generalist-specialist debate is as follows:

The party leadership after Khrushchev apparently has sensed a danger in making the apparatus the domain of a technocrat; yet it has not known how to deal with the situation adequately. It needs technocrats and at the same time fears them. It increases the importance of both specialized training *and* political education and decreases the importance of agricultural job experience while at the same time it seeks to maintain a certain level of technical competence within its ranks, particularly in the industrial center (1972b: 142).

Despite this caution, however, Blackwell's work must in the final analysis be seen as supportive of the general notion of the increased technical expertise among the regional party elite. "One could surmise from the data," he writes, "that the professional politician is likely to disappear from the political elite in future years" (1972b: 147). Blackwell, though, would likely place this date farther into the future than many of his research colleagues.

Elsewhere, Blackwell has continued to focus his energies on explicating career trends among the obkom elite. His work has revealed that (a) over 90 percent of the persons who eventually comprise the obkom leadership join the party prior to age thirty; (b) newly recruited obkom first secretaries achieve the various political levels at an increasingly older age; (c) the length of time required in political apprenticeship prior to achieving this obkom post is increasing; (d) the later one is appointed to this position, the less likely it is that he will advance in the hierarchical chain of command; (e) assignments to specific obkom posts are affected by background and training variables; and (f) there appears to be a timetable for the achievement of various career steps; if one is to achieve an obkom leadership position, he will in all likelihood (in more than nine of ten cases) do so before the age of fifty-one (1972b: 29–30; 1973b: 8). Blackwell also finds that, unlike the earlier trend, (g) co-optation of elites in the post-Khrushchev system is on the decline; (h) recruitment of specialists seems to have replaced their co-optation. Finally, he finds (i) very little difference between "co-opted" specialists and "recruited" specialists with regard to their career mobility patterns (Blackwell, 1973a).

As can be discerned from the above treatment, a sizable body of literature exists on the backgrounds and career types among the Soviet political and regional elite. Only a fragment of this corpus, however, speaks directly to the relationship between background variables and functional career types, on the one hand, and political elite mobility opportunities, on the other. Despite the fact that as far back as John A. Armstrong's 1959 study of the Ukrainian apparatus repeated references have been made to the connections between career backgrounds and career mobility patterns, very few systematic studies have been undertaken to examine the nature and degree of these relationships. While Armstrong's case study revealed that, at least within the Ukrainian party structure, "generalists" enjoyed the brightest career prospects (1959: 57), the level of generalization remained low. Indeed, despite this influential scholar's conclusions that the Soviet party and state elite "has undoubtedly been one of the most mobile political groups in modern history" (1959: 143), it was not until recent years that nomothetic treatments of these crucial relationships began to replace the idiographic case study.[1]

The first significant quantitative study of the nexus between the backgrounds of regional elite cadres and their respective political mobility opportunities was executed by Robert E. Blackwell, Jr. and William E. Hulbary. They examined the careers of 247 politically mobile obkom first secretaries during the 1950–1968 period. Data were collected on these individuals during a five-phase career sequence. These sequenced data linked social background variables with career development variables with a view toward explaining the variance in their measured mobility scores. Utilizing factor analysis and regression techniques, the analysis produced mixed results. On the one hand, the authors admit that the social background and career development variables they examined "appear to be less closely related to political mobility than actual performance prior to new assignment or the political contacts one has made during a career" (1973: 742). However, on the other hand, the analysis pointed to the fact that "how early one's career begins, the type of career affiliation one has, and the route one has used to achieve elite status can be important in explaining further career mobility" (1973: 742). As a prescription to other researchers in the area of political mobility, though, Blackwell and Hulbary advocated looking beyond social background and early career development variables. A more fruitful avenue of investigation, they argue, entailed an examination of career specialization and job performance (1973: 721).

John H. Miller (1977) focused his attention on the obkom elites of the non-Russian republics. His analysis included approximately 200 first and second secretaries in all the non-Russian union and autonomous republics between 1955 and 1975. Interested primarily in the ethnic determinants of mobility, Miller's analysis yielded several important findings: (a) dramatic promotion into Moscow all-union positions from the nationality areas is more likely for Russians than for non-Russians; (b) non-Russians tend to make their whole career in their home region, while Russians move from place to place with considerable versatility; (c) transfer into the Central Committee apparatus is more common for Russians than for non-Russians; (d) neither nationality nor the nature of the post renders the incumbent more vulnerable to demotion; and (e) Russian party officials who perform badly are more likely to be allowed to retreat into obscurity than are the poor-performing non-Russians, who are more liable to public disgrace (1977: 34–35). For Miller, the key to Russian power in non-Russian areas is control over local cadres. This goes far in explaining the now-regularized dyarchy of native first secretary and Russian second (cadres) secretary in the nationalities areas of the Soviet Union.

Perhaps the single most ambitious quantitative study of political mobility in the Soviet Union is Grey Hodnett's (1978). Like Miller, Hodnett focuses on leadership recruitment trends outside the R.S.F.S.R. He examines a variety of dimensions related to the mobility of over 1,100 republic-level elites, including individual backgrounds, early career variables, and career patterns, so as to establish trends in Soviet elite mobility for those cadres outside the Russian Republic.

Hodnett's results seem to corroborate Miller's findings. First, according to the analysis, only a small likelihood exists that the vast majority of republic elites will be transferred to another national republic, and only slightly greater chances exist for them to experience upward political mobility to a post in the R.S.F.S.R. Second, relating to the functional career specializations of these elites, Hodnett finds that the *kind* of work they engage in will have more to do with their next assignment than will the specific organization within which they are working. Third, party officials performing propaganda, or cultural or educational tasks tend, over time, to remain in these functional areas. Conversely, elites performing labor-oriented or personnel duties will in all likelihood *not* be involved in these areas in their next job assignment. Fourth, as they get older, Hodnett argues that occupants of party posts are increasingly less likely to be assigned another party post. The reverse seems to hold true for incumbents of leading state posts (1978: 341–344).

Hodnett's analysis seems to support best the so-called "role matching" explanation of elite recruitment (1978: 34–36). Defined as measuring the " 'fit' or lack of fit between the role a given politician is called upon to perform and his qualifications to do so," role matching is seen by Hodnett as "probably the explanation of recruitment practice with the broadest application" (1978: 394). The individual background characteristics of education, training, and substantive functional experience, then, offer the grounds for the most compelling explanation of mobility trends within the Soviet non-Russian republics.

Finally, Joel C. Moses' (1983) recent work on the functional career specializations among the Soviet regional elite speaks to the issue of their variance in political mobility opportunities. Moses examines the careers of some 614 members of 25 obkom bureaus between 1953 and 1979, specifically focusing on those 229 officials who were reassigned to at least one other post *outside* their base oblast. The analysis performed lends strong support to the conclusions cited by Hodnett. According to Moses,

46 percent of the variance in functional reassignment can be explained by differences in the career specialization of those reassigned. More simply, almost one out of every two times that officials have been transferred, the nature of their reassignment could be predicted on the basis of their functional type (1983: 50).

While these analyses do address the issue of functional "role matching" in mobility dyads, they fail to assess the relative vertical mobility chances likely to be experienced by these different career types. That is, while it has been established that the Soviet recruitment policy is at least partially based on matching job requirements and candidate skills, it has yet to be established whether and to what degree different backgrounds and/or functional career types are rewarded in the Soviet sociopolitical system. While the functional consistency of the cadres policy reveals the logic and centralized nature of the recruitment process, little analytical light has been shed in recent years on the relationship between backgrounds, career types, and political mobility opportunities in the Soviet Union. It is this gap in the literature that the present chapter seeks to address.

RESEARCH DESIGN AND DATA

Data on 255 persons who vacated the position of obkom first secretary between mid-1965 and mid-1987 were collected from a variety of sources.[2] Unlike the analysis in Chapter 2, where the focus was on discrete *positions* (individuals' data were added to the sample for *each* post held during the career), here the analysis focuses on the *individual* per se (that is, no matter how many obkom leadership posts were held by an individual, the data associated with his career were included in the sample only once). Personal background characteristics and career development variables were selected for the purpose of constructing for each obkom first secretary a complete personal and career history. In addition, through an examination and manipulation of the aggregated data, a number of general functional career types were sought. Both individual and aggregate data, then, are utilized in the analysis of the relationship between political elite mobility and individual background/career characteristics.

The selection and organization of pertinent data on these regional elites attempt to remain consistent with the efforts of the pioneering scholars listed in the previous section of this chapter. Blackwell (1973b) provides a list of seven individual characteristics which, he argues, constitute a person's "principal indicators of social background": (1) age at the assumption of the post, (2) year of birth, (3) ethnic origin, (4) social class of the parents, (5) level of education, (6) the type of higher educational specialization, and (7) the year higher education is completed (p. 11). The career development variables Blackwell selects as important are (1) the elite's structural affiliations, (2) his functional activities, and (3) the ages at which he attains certain posts or levels within the sociopolitical hierarchy. These ten characteristics, then, comprise for Blackwell, a solid data set for the categorization and analysis of Soviet elite career types.

Gehlen and McBride's (1968) analysis of the 1968 Central Committee examined the following personal background characteristics to ascertain trends in the composition of the Soviet elite: (1) age, (2) sex, (3) education, (4) occupation (learned), (5) occupation (practiced), (6) prior positions, (7) occupational changes, (8) place of residence, and (9) party status (Gehlen and McBride, 1968). Variances among these variables over time allowed the authors to postulate changes in the priorities of the leadership as well as the nature of the resultant elite itself.

John H. Miller's (1977) elite analysis further defines the list of significant personal characteristics that must be taken into account when engaging in this type of research. For each individual of his sample of approximately 200 republic elites outside the R.S.F.S.R., Miller noted their (1) nationality, (2) age, (3) length of service, (4) place of origin, (5) educational qualifications, (6) place of previous employment, (7) previous office held, (8) main thrust of the previous career, and (9) subsequent career. Most important, however, is his elaboration of the functional career specialization categories for an elite's career. Miller identifies seven functional "areas of substantial experience" for the elites in his sample (1977: 31): (a) agriculture, (b) youth affairs, (c) ideology, (d) industry, (e) control, (f) cadres or personnel, and (g) finance.

Using these and other studies as a guide, the present analysis incorporates 24 background/career variables in its analysis of the 255 regional elites of the sample. The biographical data for each elite was coded for (1) date of birth, (2) ethnicity, (3) social origins (class) of the parents, (4) level of education, (5) type of education, (6) Higher Party School education, (7) age at entrance to membership in the C.P.S.U., (8) age at assumption of the obkom first secretary post, (9) the apparatus affiliation of this post (for example, the Ukrainian SSR), (10) tenure in the first obkom first secretary post, (11) the leader's ethnic relationship to that oblast republic, (12) other obkom first secretaryships held, (13) the total tenure in these other obkom posts, (14) the regime under which the first obkom leadership post was attained, (15) age at entrance to candidate status in the C.P.S.U. Central Committee, (16) age at entrance to full membership in that Central Committee, (17) the type of any R.S.F.S.R. apparatus service, (18) the type of central party or all-union government apparatus service, (19) the post prior to the obkom post, (20) the post assumed after leaving the obkom post, (21) service in the Red Army, (22) Komsomol experience, (23) the functional focus of the career prior to the post of obkom first secretary, and (24) the functional focus after the obkom first secretary post (see Appendix V).

RESULTS

Background Characteristics and Elite Mobility

Analysis of the data on the 255 obkom first secretaries in the sample produces a rather complete profile of the backgrounds of these key elites. Although information on the social class of the parents is incomplete, the data reveal that almost 50 percent of those whose ethnicity was identified are Russian. This, of course, reflects the fact that 55 of the 129 oblasti under study lie within the confines of the R.S.F.S.R. However, Russian obkom first secretaries are not found only in the Russian Republic; thirty-six Russians in the sample headed an obkom outside the R.S.F.S.R. Indeed, twenty-seven of the thirty-eight first secretaries of Kazakh obkomy were Russian.

The typical future obkom first secretary gains entrance to the Communist Party of the Soviet Union at the age of twenty-five. The data reveal striking consistency in this regard. Less than 2 percent become party members in their teens, and 94 percent do so prior to their thirty-first birthday.

By the time of their admittance to the party, the vast majority of these future elites will have completed their higher education. Of the 194 individuals about whom educational attainment data are available, 154 (79.4 percent) graduated from an institution of higher learning. The obkom elite, generally speaking, is an educated elite. Only eight of the individuals under study had failed to complete at least their secondary education. This figure is more than compensated for by noting that thirteen obkom first secretaries attained the degree of Candidate of Sciences, the Soviet equivalent of the American Ph.D. degree. In sum, then, 146 of the 154 elites (94.8 percent) had completed their secondary education or, in most cases, better.

Most of those with university degrees specialized in substantive areas dealing with agriculture (n = 66), industry (n = 42), or engineering (n =

26). Only ten individuals graduated from pedagogical institutes, and even fewer in the fields of science, transport, economics, medicine, and law. Only approximately one-third of those identified possessed Higher Party School training. The great majority of obkom first secretaries in this sample, then, possess extensive technical training.

A variety of career paths lead to the post of regional first secretary, but most individuals enter this position from either a regional party position (for example, obkom second secretary) or a regional state position [for example, chairman of the oblast soviet executive committee (oblispolkom)]. Over two-thirds of the obkom first secretaries (38.0 percent and 29.8 percent, respectively) emerge from one of these two categories of positions.

By the time they are elevated to the obkom leadership post, these individuals have typically reached the age of forty-six. The data seem to indicate that if one is ever to attain this watershed position, he will do so before turning fifty-three. Over 90 percent of the elite sample became obkom first secretary by the age of fifty-two. Even more unlikely are the prospects of reaching this level of advancement before the age of thirty-seven; only six individuals (less than 3 percent) did so. The fact that over 90 percent of the elites in this sample attain the obkom first secretary post between the ages of thirty-seven and fifty-three indicates that the national leadership's cadres policy for regional party recruitment is attempting to ensure that these regional bosses have, by the time of their appointment, attained sufficient experience at other levels while not having passed through a certain phase in their career development.

The average first secretary will spend approximately eight years in his initial obkom leadership post. However, a wide range of observed tenures does exist: The minimum recorded tenure was one month, while the maximum tenure in the first obkom leadership post was 307 months (well over 25 years). This wide range (the standard deviation from the ninety-eight month mean is sixty-four months) seems to indicate that no set schedule or timetable for tenure in this "stepping stone" position has been established by the national leadership.[3] In any event, with such a range of variance, the mean tenure score tells us very little about individual cases.

Exiting the obkom first secretary post, the data indicate, usually offers the departing elite member an opportunity to move up the administrative ladder. Over 55 percent of those moving on to other assignments do so at a higher administrative level. Most (64.3 percent) of these elites assume positions in the republic or all-union government apparatus, while 35.7 percent continue to climb within the republic or central party structure. Many, however, remain in the same or similar jobs at the obkom tier. If the exiting obkom first secretary remains at the regional level, he is almost twelve times more likely to do so in a regional *party* post than in a regional government post. A sizable number of the obkom elites who left this post during the 1965–1987 period retired from active public service. Indeed, as many individuals retire from the obkom first secretary post as continue to move up the party hierarchy. Moreover, thirteen individuals are known to have died in office.

Finally, the evidence indicates that this regional elite post is a strong "feeder" for the national party decision-making bodies. Approximately 50 percent (125/255) of the elite sample attained full membership in the C.P.S.U. Central Committee. However, these key seats are disproportionately allotted to Russian (seventy-seven seats) and Ukrainian (twenty-eight seats) regional bosses.

A simple analysis of the background characteristics and career variables reveals several interesting findings about political mobility opportunities.

Ethnicity. Not surprisingly, certain advantages accrue to ethnic Russian elites in the Soviet Union. As a subgroup of elites, this pattern also holds for the obkom tier. First, the Russian elites who hold the position of obkom first secretary experience upward political mobility opportunities at a higher rate than any other ethnic group within the elite. The mean aggregate political mobility score for Russians is 7 percent above the national average, 4 percent above the Belorussian average, and over 7 percent above the Ukrainian elite average.

Second, ethnic Russians are the most overrepresented group of elites within the C.P.S.U. Central Committee. Fully 74.8 percent of all the Russian elites examined gained full membership in this important body. The comparative figures for even the other Slavic ethnic elites (Belorussians, 55.5 percent; Ukrainians, 52.8 percent) are significantly lower (see Table 4.2). Indeed, of the forty-six non-Slavic obkom first secretaries studied, only seven (15.2 percent) attained full membership in the Central Committee; this compares with a rate of 66.7 percent for ethnically Slavic obkom first secretaries.

Third, ethnic Russian first secretaries also seem to experience slightly longer tenures in their initial obkom leadership posts, as do Ukrainians. In addition, when examining the ethnicity of those elites who are placed in multiple obkom first secretaryships, we find a rather low percentage of Russians in this category. This latter point supports the notion of a generally upwardly mobile cohort of ethnically Russian elites who tend not to be placed in an equivalent lateral party post after a tenure in such a classic steppingstone position as the obkom first secretary. The two findings above combine to depict a situation, at least for the Russians, wherein the initial obkom leadership tenure is a trial period, after which the individual is either moved upward out of the obkom tier (if deemed successful or worthy) or left to govern his region for an extended time. Thus, those not moving up relatively rapidly would tend to inflate the mean tenure score or the group, while those who do move up would elevate the aggregate political mobility score.

Table 4.2
Ethnicity and Mobility among the Obkom Elite

Ethnicity	Mobility	Recruitment into Central Cmmtte (%)	Initial Tenure (Months)	Multiple ObSect Posts (%)
Russian (n=103)	12.39	74.8	114.8	22.3
Belorussian (n=9)	11.91	55.5	79.0	44.4
Ukrainian (n=53)	11.54	52.8	106.3	32.1
Kazakh (n=11)	11.42	45.5	76.3	63.6
Kirgiz (n=8)	11.29	0.0	63.5	0.0
Turkmen (n=4)	11.00	0.0	96.7	50.0
Uzbek (n=21)	10.48	9.5	75.8	28.6
Tadzhik (n=2)	9.66	0.0	191.0	50.0

Finally, the analysis reveals that those individuals who were ethnically alien to the obkom over which they exercised authority were neither significantly more nor less mobile than natives. The thirty-seven elites governing obkomy outside their native republics generated an aggregate mobility score of 11.22, while those elites identified as natives (n = 176) combined to produce a mobility score of 11.93. This finding runs counter to the expectation that Russians (thirty-six of the thirty-seven aliens were Russians outside the R.S.F.S.R.) entrusted to first secretaryships in the non-Russian republics of the USSR would tend to experience significantly higher mobility scores. This expectation, of course, is not confirmed when comparing the aggregate ethnic Russian score for all units (12.39) with that of those Russians holding these key posts outside the R.S.F.S.R. (11.93).

In all other respects, ethnicity does not seem to matter in the individual characteristics of these regional elites. Certainly very little about these party secretaries (other than the above) can be predicted on the basis of ethnicity (see Table 4.3).

Social Class. Only 10.9 percent (n = 28) of the elites in this sample could be categorized by the social class of their families. To the degree that any faith at all can be put in these numbers, though, certain findings present themselves. First, eighteen of the twenty-eight coded elite members grew up in kolkhoznik (collective farmer) families, six in blue-collar families, four in white-collar "employee" households, and none in households headed by a member of the intelligentsia. Second, compared with

Table 4.3
Ethnicity and Elite Step-level Progress

Ethnicity	Age at Entrance to: C.P.S.U.	Obkom First Secretary	CC CPSU (Candidate)	CC CPSU (Full)
Russian	25.2	46.4	49.6	51.8
Belorussian	24.6	45.2	52.7	55.6
Ukrainian	24.7	44.6	46.5	49.4
Kazakh	24.4	42.8	49.7	50.4
Kirgiz	25.0	44.3	55.0	—
Turkmen	24.3	47.2	—	—
Uzbek	25.6	44.6	48.2	57.5
Tadzhik	23.0	46.0	—	—

the other categories, obkom elites with a blue-collar background tend to (1) generate higher political mobility scores, (2) achieve the post of obkom first secretary some three years of age earlier, (3) remain in that post longer, and (4) hold this regional leadership post less often in the course of their respective careers (see Table 4.4).

However, the data on social class are far too unrepresentative to draw any generalizable conclusions. It may be worth noting, however, that among these successful elites (their social class backgrounds are known only because they have reached a certain high level in the system), those with agrarian roots perform the worst of the categories listed. A subsequent focus on educational content and functional career developments will seem to validate this particular inference.

Education. The obkom elite is an educated elite, with 86 percent of those coded in this category (n = 194) possessing at least a completed uni-

Table 4.4
Social Class and Mobility among the Obkom Elite

Social Class	Mobility	Age at Entrance to Obkom First Secretary	Initial Tenure (Months)	Multiple ObSect (%)
Worker (n=6)	14.06	41.3	150.0	16.7
Kolkhoznik (n=18)	13.30	44.3	115.9	44.4
Employee (n=4)	13.74	44.2	96.8	0.0
Intelligentsia (n=0)	—	—	—	—

Table 4.5
Level of Education and Mobility among the Obkom Elite

Level of Education	Mobility	Recruitment into Central Committee (%)	Initial Tenure (Months)	Multiple ObSect Posts (%)
Primary (n=0)	—	—	—	—
Incomplete Secondary (n=8)	10.83	12.5	87.7	50.0
Secondary (n=16)	11.48	68.7	106.0	56.2
Incomplete Higher (n=3)	11.33	33.3	36.0	66.7
Higher (n=154)	12.10	65.6	108.7	24.7
Candidate of Sciences (n=13)	11.56	38.5	106.7	23.1
Doctor of Sciences (n=0)	—	—	—	—

versity education. As Table 4.5 reveals, however, those obkom elites with the highest attained levels of education do not have appreciably higher political mobility scores than those with only a secondary or incomplete higher education. In fact, no significant correlation (.118) exists between the attained level of education and the political mobility scores of the obkom elite.

Nor, for that matter, does educational level speak to the incidence of C.P.S.U. Central Committee membership. While 65.6 percent of those who have a completed higher education attained full membership in the Central Committee, only 38.5 percent of the obkom first secretaries with the equivalent of the Ph.D. were full members. Finally, almost 69 percent of the elites with only a secondary education have been elevated to membership in this body—a higher rate than for those with university degrees. The data seems to indicate that while a completed university education might be a prerequisite for the attainment of the obkom first secretary post, it does not speak directly to the issue of recruitment into the Central Committee.

However, some variance in political mobility does appear when the focus of the analysis is shifted to the *content* of the education of the obkom first secretaries. Of the total number of elites about whom educational content data are available (n = 170), the vast majority falls into three categories: agriculture (38.8 percent), industry (24.7 percent), and

Table 4.6
Education Content and Mobility among the Obkom Elite

Education Content	Mobility	Recruitment into Central Committee (%)	Initial Tenure (Months)	Multiple ObSect Posts (%)
Legal (n=1)	17.33	100.0	104.0	0.0
Social Science (n=0)	—	—	—	—
Humanities (n=0)	—	—	—	—
Pedagogical (n=10)	11.18	40.0	120.0	20.0
Scientific (n=8)	12.13	62.5	101.6	37.5
Agricultural (n=66)	11.68	54.5	119.1	24.2
Engineering (n=26)	12.83	76.9	104.1	23.1
Industrial (n=42)	12.37	73.8	96.0	23.8
Transport (n=7)	12.50	85.7	95.0	0.0
Economic (n=6)	10.00	16.7	113.3	16.7
Medical (n=4)	10.03	25.0	66.2	50.0
Military (n=0)	—	—	—	—

engineering (15.3 percent). Somewhat surprising is the low number of elites with a pedagogical education (n = 10, 5.9 percent) (see Table 4.6).

Those regional elites with engineering educations have the highest political mobility, the agriculturalists, the lowest, and those with an industrial education fall in between. Almost 77 percent of the obkom secretaries trained in engineering eventually become full members of the C.P.S.U. Central Committee, and almost 74 percent of elites with industry-oriented educations do also. The figure is much lower (54.5 percent) for "agriculturalist" obkom first secretaries. In terms of the aggregate mobility scores generated by the members of these educational categories, the twenty-six "engineer" and forty-two "industrialist" obkom first secretaries produce scores of 12.83 and 12.37, respectively. The aggregate score for the sixty-six "agriculturalist" regional elites is 11.68. If Hodnett's "role matching" theory of recruitment policy is valid, these findings support the conclusions of the previous chapter that elites from the advanced industrial regions will experience relatively higher political mobility vis-à-vis those from agricultural regions.

The Higher Party Schools. Very frequently Soviet officials attend and graduate from either a Republic or C.P.S.U. Higher Party School. The training provided at these schools attempts to prepare individuals for the substantive tasks of managing party affairs. One might be tempted to assume that successful completion of the C.P.S.U. Higher Party School requirements would bode well for the career development of a Soviet party apparatchik. However, this assumption is not supported by the data examined here. In fact, those elites who have not attended a Higher Party School slightly outperform those who have (see Table 4.7).

Four points merit mention here. First, those with Higher Party School experience tend to have been recruited into the party at a slightly younger age than those who do not have such experience. Second, those elites who have not attended a Higher Party School gain entrance to the C.P.S.U. Central Committee at least as frequently as those who have attended. Third, the non-attendees seem to be recruited into the Central Committee at a younger age than the attendees. Those obkom first secretaries who have not attended either the C.P.S.U. Higher Party School or a Republic Higher Party School (n = 83) are, on average, 49.9 years old at the time of their elevation, while the comparable figure for the C.P.S.U. Higher Party School graduates (n = 35) was 54.3 years of age. In sum, then, it seems as though the attendance or lack of attendance of regional elites at party-directed Higher Schools makes little, if any, difference in the progress of elite careers. Indeed, it might well be true that only those aspiring elites who are considered by their superiors to be lacking in some fundamental skills will be recommended for course work in one or another of these Higher Party Schools.

Komsomol. The Komsomol organizations constitute a training ground for future members of the Communist Party of the Soviet Union. According to Ronald Hill and Peter Frank, the Komsomol is, in effect, "the junior section of the CPSU" (1986: 125). They cite Soviet statistics reporting that during the early 1980s, 72.5 percent of new recruits into the party ranks came from the Komsomol (1986: 25). One might expect, then, that those party elites who, like General Secretary Mikhail Gorbachev, have held substantive leadership posts in Komsomol organizations might experience greater mobility opportunities during their subsequent careers.

This expectation is also unsupported by the data (see Table 4.8). The age at entrance is slightly lower (by 2.6 years) for those who have held responsible Komsomol posts, yet in all other respects Komsomol administrative experience seems to make no substantive difference in the mobility and/or career development of these obkom elites. The mobility scores are almost identical (11.90, 11.83), as are the rates of recruitment into the C.P.S.U. Central Committee (56.1 percent, 57.7 percent), the

Table 4.7
Higher Party Schools and Mobility among the Obkom Elite

Higher Party School	Mobility	Recruitment into Central Committee (%)	Initial Tenure (Months)	Multiple ObSect Posts (%)
C. P. S. U. (n=58)	11.76	60.3	114.0	31.0
Republic (n=11)	10.84	18.2	121.5	36.4
No H. P. S. (n=135)	12.03	61.5	100.9	26.7

ages at elevation to the obkom post (44.5, 45.9) and to the Central Committee (51.5, 51.3), and virtually all other measured variables. Responsible posts in the Komsomol apparat, in a word, do not seem to affect the future career of elites either positively or negatively.

Military Experience. The biographical data on obkom first secretaries also coded their type of military experience. Three categories of experience were created: "wartime service," "peacetime service," and "no service." When one considers the time and energy given to exaggerating the roles of the Politburo elites in the Great Patriotic War, one might expect that actual military experience, especially during World War II, might provide some impetus to a rising elite's career. Once again, this premise is not supported by the data (see Table 4.9).

Hypothetically, one might anticipate some significant difference between the individual elites of the polar categories, yet none emerge. Veterans of "combat"[4] produce a mobility score virtually identical (11.85) to non-veterans (11.89). Looking at the important matter of recruitment into the C.P.S.U. Central Committee, no real difference can be seen.

Table 4.8
The Komsomol and Mobility among the Obkom Elite

Posts in Komsomol	Mobility	Age at Entrance to CPSU	Recruitment into Central Committee (%)	Initial Tenure (Months)	Multiple ObSect Posts (%)
YES (n=66)	11.90	23.1	56.1	100.2	30.3
NO (n=142)	11.83	25.8	57.7	108.0	26.1

Table 4.9
Military Service and Mobility among the Obkom Elite

Service in Red Army	Mobility	Recruitment into Central Committee (%)	Initial Tenure (Months)	Multiple ObSect Posts (%)
Wartime (n=67)	11.85	61.2	115.5	26.9
Peacetime (n=13)	11.32	38.5	100.8	30.8
No Service (n=119)	11.89	58.8	100.9	26.9

Sixty-one percent of war veteran obkom first secretaries were recruited, as opposed to 58.9 percent of the non-veterans. A brief look at Table 4.9 reveals little substantive variation between these two groups. When viewed from the perspective of career mobility, service during wartime is preferable to service during peacetime, but holds no real career advantage over non-service. Indeed, no service at all in the Soviet Army seems more helpful to the subsequent careers of regional elites than does service during peacetime. In general, though, military experience as an indirect indicator of career mobility and career development is insignificant.

Regime. If the data are analyzed by the regime during which the respective elites assumed their initial obkom first secretary post, several interesting findings present themselves (see Table 4.10). First, the obkom elite appointed by Khrushchev experienced the best opportunities for upward political mobility. These individuals (n = 91) generated the highest aggregate political mobility score (11.90) as well as the highest recruitment rate into the C.P.S.U. Central Committee (63.7 percent).

Second, given this fact, it seems surprising that the Khrushchev-appointed regional elite also possessed the longest mean tenure in this initial obkom leadership post, longer even than the "ossified" Brezhnev elite. Third, a clear aging trend exists within the obkom elite (as measured by their mean age at appointment). Stalin's regional elites were appointed, on average, at the age of 39.4. This figure rises steadily through the regimes of Khrushchev (44.7), Brezhnev (46.6), Andropov (50.6), and Gorbachev (56.0).[5] Of course, one must note the extremely low number of cases for the latter two regimes; in order to fix with more certainty the age structure of these elites named in the post-Brezhnev period, data on incumbents should be consulted.

Fourth, there is also a clear trend away from the previous pattern of appointing obkom first secretaries to a number of party leadership posts in different oblasti. Over time there are fewer and fewer "repeater" obkom

Table 4.10
The Effect of Regime on Mobility among the Obkom Elite

Regime	Mobility	Age at Entrance to ObSect	Recruitment into Central Committee (%)	Initial Tenure (Months)	Multiple ObSect Posts (%)
Stalin (n=11)	11.29	39.4	45.5	57.5	81.8
Khrushchev (n=91)	11.90	44.7	63.7	110.4	37.4
Brezhnev (n=141)	11.42	46.6	41.1	98.5	16.3
Andropov (n=8)	11.42	50.6	37.5	33.5	0.0
Chernenko (n=1)	10.00	n.a.	0.0	34.0	0.0
Gorbachev (n=3)	13.17	56.0	33.3	17.3	0.0

first secretaries; 81.8 percent of those regional elites appointed by Stalin held two or more obkom first secretaryships. The corresponding figures for those appointed by Khrushchev (37.4 percent) and Brezhnev (16.3 percent) decline precipitously. It is perhaps too early to judge the post-Brezhnev elite, but it is worth noting that of the twelve existing elites in the sample appointed by either Andropov, Chernenko, or Gorbachev, none to date has held more than one obkom first secretaryship.

Finally, a striking discrepancy exists between the mean tenure scores of the Khrushchev-Brezhnev regional elites and those of the post-Brezhnev period. Yet, these figures reflect the methodology employed. Since only exiting elites (non-incumbents) are included in the sample, and since it has been five years since Brezhnev's death, such a mean tenure discrepancy should be expected. Again, for certain categories of the data it is probably too soon to incorporate much of the post-Brezhnev data into a study of the exiting regional elites.

Career Development and Political Mobility

Having found, with a few notable exceptions, the personal background variables wanting in their explanatory power for political elite mobility, the analysis next examines career progression and functional career specialization.

Prior Position. Viewing the obkom leadership post as a "make or break" opportunity for elites, the analysis examines two dyads involving the obkom first secretary position. First, attention was focused on the post

Table 4.11
Prior Position and Mobility among the Obkom Elite

Post Prior to Obkom 1st Sect.	Mobility	Recruitment into Central Committee (%)	Initial Tenure (Months)	Multiple ObSect Posts (%)
Lower Party Level (n=16)	11.54	43.7	84.7	25.0
Lateral Party Level (n=92)	11.77	59.8	107.1	31.5
Higher Party Level (n=37)	12.12	51.4	103.9	18.9
Lower State Level (n=1)	10.00	0.0	60.0	0.0
Lateral State Level (n=72)	11.59	51.4	101.5	26.4
Higher State Level (n=21)	10.98	23.8	66.8	28.6
Komsomol (n=0)	—	—	—	—
Other (n=3)	11.56	66.7	108.0	0.0

prior to that of the obkom first secretary (see Table 4.11). At the most general level, the data reveal that if the elite member enters the obkom first secretaryship from another party post, that elite will experience greater subsequent mobility *from* to obkom seat than he would if he entered from an equivalent state/government post. The mean mobility score for regional elites of the former category (11.83) compares favorably with that of the latter category (11.44).

Moreover, a much higher percentage of obkom first secretaries whose prior post was a party post are recruited into the C.P.S.U. Central Committee at a much higher rate (55.9 percent) than those entering from a government post (44.7 percent).

Of course, *within* each category certain themes emerge. First, the vast majority (67.8 percent) of obkom leaders enter that post from another post at the oblast level. Second, a dyad consisting of a move from a government post at a lower level (for example, chairman of a raiispolkom or gorispolkom) to the obkom leadership position is extremely rare; of the

242 individuals on whom prior career data are available, only 1 individual experienced such a career move.

Third, no matter from what level an obkom first secretary comes before assuming that post, the data show that his prospects for *future* political mobility (beyond the obkom post) will be enhanced if that post was a party, not a government, post. Fourth, mirroring this trend, regardless of which level produces the obkom first secretary (lower, lateral, or higher), that secretary's future probability of being elevated into the C.P.S.U. Central Committee will be enhanced if that post was a party as opposed to a government post. Combined, 55.9 percent of the obkom elites whose prior position was a responsible party position were eventually elevated to the Central Committee. For elites whose prior post was a state/government post, the figure is 44.7 percent. Finally, those elites who go from a party post (at whatever level) to the obkom post will, on average, stay at that post slightly longer than those whose prior post was a state/government post. This is especially true if the prior post (party or state) was at a higher administrative level.

Subsequent Position. A very similar picture is produced when examining the post directly subsequent to that of the obkom first secretaryship (see Table 4.12). Again, the data reveal those dyads that remain consistently party dyads produce a better likelihood of upward political mobility for their incumbents. That is, if the elite exits the post of obkom first secretary to another party post, that elite will experience greater subsequent mobility than he would if he exited to a parallel state/government post. The mean mobility score for party-party dyads (12.37) is significantly higher than the score for the party-state dyads (11.52).

Second, obkom first secretaries who exit this post for another party post are much more likely (65.9 percent) to be recruited into the C.P.S.U. Central Committee than those who exit for a state/government post (46.1 percent). Combined with the political mobility scores, then, party-party dyads offer better overall mobility opportunities for regional party first secretaries.

Third, within each generic positional dyad, the data reveal an odd theme. Obkom first secretaries who leave their post for another party job are slightly more likely to stay at the obkom level (52.3 percent) than they are to go to the union republic or national party level (45.5 percent). Yet looking at the destinations of elites who experience a party-government dyad exiting the obkom first secretaryship, it is found that only 5.3 percent assume a government post at the oblast level, while 94.7 percent assume a government post at a higher level. Given the fact that a greater percentage of elites who *stay* at the regional party level after their first obkom leadership post attain full membership in the Central Committee (60.9 percent) than those who move to a *higher* government level (45.8 percent), it seems clear that the national leadership sees a relatively wide

Table 4.12
Subsequent Position and Mobility among the Obkom Elite

Post After Obkom First Secretary	Mobility	Recruitment into Central Committee (%)	Initial Tenure (Months)	Multiple ObSect Posts (%)
Lower Party Level (n=2)	10.50	0.0	36.0	50.0
Lateral Party Level (n=46)	11.94	60.9	69.1	93.5
Higher Party Level (n=40)	12.95	75.0	73.7	17.5
Lower State Level (n=0)	—	—	—	—
Lateral State Level (n=4)	10.85	50.0	33.0	100.0
Higher State Level (n=72)	11.56	45.8	96.2	12.5
Komsomol (n=0)	—	—	—	—
Other (n=19)	11.03	36.8	99.6	10.5
Retired (n=40)	11.27	52.5	169.7	0.0

discrepancy existing in the responsibilities of these different administrative structures. This sheds light on both the hierarchy of posts within the Soviet system (responsible party posts are in many ways equally as important as government posts at a higher administrative level) and the level of competition for advancement in the party apparatus.

"Crossover" Secretaries. The data show that those elites who hold more than one obkom first secretaryship in the course of their career do not measurably outperform those who do not. However, as a subset within the former category, special attention in the coding of the elite biographical data was paid to those individuals who have held obkom leadership posts in two different union republics. That is, those elites who "crossed over" republic lines to head oblast party committees were selected and examined comparatively with those elites with (a) non-crossover multiple obkom tenures, and (b) single obkom tenures. This attention is merited,

it is hypothesized, because the placement of an elite in multiple obkom leadership posts in different union republics must reveal that special faith has been placed by the national leadership in that elite's abilities to perform specified duties.

A case in point, perhaps, is Nikolai Vasilevich Bannikov, a Russian (like all the men in this group[6]), who, after serving almost two decades in the Kuibyshev oblast (R.S.F.S.R.) party organization, spent nine years in the Party apparatus of Karaganda oblast of Kazakhstan. He served first as second secretary (in charge of cadres) and then from 1964 to 1968 as obkom first secretary. Bannikov later returned to the Russian republic and served fifteen years as obkom first secretary in the important Irkutsk region.

In any event, the data reveal that those obkom first secretaries (n = 4) who have held this post in different union republics significantly outperform both (a) the non-crossover multiple obkom first secretaries and (b) the single tenure obkom first secretaries (see Table 4.13). In terms of political mobility, their score of 12.88 is 11.1 percent higher than the non-crossover multiple obkom elites and 10.8 percent higher than those with but a single obkom tenure. Moreover, they are recruited into the C.P.S.U. Central Committee much more frequently (75.0 percent) than either the former (50.8 percent) or latter (48.9 percent) group. These elites also tend (in three of four cases) to have short initial tenures in their *adopted* republic before being sent on to other assignments back in the R.S.F.S.R. Their mean initial tenure is thirty-six months—only 37 percent of the all-elites mean.

However, we cannot at this time rely on these figures due to the very small number of cases involved. Further research could include present incumbents in the sample of elites studied so as to decrease the obvious threats to any inferences drawn.

Functional Focus of Prior Career. The analysis assumed a much broader focus for the career development variables of each elite. Instead of looking at the prior and subsequent *posts* framing the obkom first secretaryship, each individual's prior and later *careers* were categorized into one of twenty-four functional categories. When analyzing the functional focus of the career prior to obkom first secretary, several points of interest emerge.

First, the most frequent prior career trend for these future obkom first secretaries is that of a mixed party-state generalist. This category of functional focus, borrowed from Joel C. Moses (1983), represents the careers of individuals who have held varied and responsible positions in both the party and state/government apparats. The diversity of these prior posts precludes the assignment to these men of a more specific functional label. They are, in a true sense, generalists.

Table 4.13
Crossover Careers and Mobility
among the Obkom Elite

Multiple Obkom First Secretaries	Mobility	Recruitment into Central Committee (%)	Initial Tenure (Months)	Subsequent ObSect Tenure (Months)
Crossover (n=4)	12.87	75.0	36.2	154.0
No Crossover (n=61)	11.58	50.8	62.0	116.2
Single Tenure	11.62	48.9	110.5	n.a.

Almost 30 percent of those individuals for whom a prior career history is available fall into this category (see Table 4.14). The mixed generalist is, however, in many respects similar to members of the other categories. He is moderately upwardly mobile (11.77), but is equaled by other functional career types. He is eventually recruited into the C.P.S.U. Central Committee in 55.6 percent of the cases. This figure is stronger than most other categories, but still not significantly more so than several others. He both enters the party and assumes the obkom leadership post not significantly sooner or later than any other type. The mixed generalist is, moreover, only slightly more likely than several other category elites to hold more than one obkom first secretaryship during his career.

The second most frequent career prior to an obkom first secretaryship is a regional party post. The entire prior career, of course, need not have been spent at oblast-level party posts (very few party officials begin their careers at this advanced level), but if the majority of the elite's responsible career is spent at this level, he would be included in this category.

One-fifth (20.3 percent) of the elite sample served in party posts at the oblast level before becoming obkom first secretaries. This functional career group's members exhibit subsequent career patterns that are almost identical to those of the mixed generalists. Their aggregate mobility score is virtually the same as that of the mixed generalist (11.73 and 11.77, respectively), and the same is true for mean initial obkom tenure (108.4 months, and 108.0 months), probability of holding multiple obkom first secretaryships (30.0 percent and 30.6 percent), and the rate of eventual recruitment into the C.P.S.U. Central Committee (54.0 percent and 55.6 percent). In a real sense, then, this distinction among men of these two functional categories is not useful in attempting to distinguish their respective career mobility.

Fifteen percent of the future obkom elites spent the majority of their prior careers in local party administration. A majority of the individuals

Table 4.14
Functional Focus of the Prior Career
and Mobility among the Obkom Elite

Focus of Prior Career	Mobility	Recruitment into Central Committee (%)	Initial Tenure (Months)	Multiple ObSect Posts (%)
Local Party (n=37)	11.82	59.5	108.8	27.0
Regional Party (n=50)	11.73	54.0	108.4	30.0
Republic Party (n=3)	11.00	0.0	45.3	33.3
Leading Party (n=2)	12.00	100.0	117.0	0.0
Military (n=1)	14.00	100.0	24.0	100.0
Punitive Organs (n=1)	13.00	100.0	66.0	100.0
Party Agriculture (n=9)	11.31	33.3	105.1	0.0
State Agriculture (n=18)	11.12	44.4	96.9	27.8
Cadres (n=7)	10.95	28.6	74.0	14.3
Youth Affairs (n=12)	11.06	41.7	76.0	25.0
Labor/T. U. C. (n=0)	—	—	—	—
AgitProp (n=0)	—	—	—	—
Foreign Affairs (n=0)	—	—	—	—
Industry/Constr. (n=23)	12.35	52.2	79.2	21.7
Local State (n=0)	—	—	—	—
Regional State (n=9)	10.46	22.2	64.1	22.2
Republic State (n=2)	10.50	0.0	82.5	50.0
Leading State (n=0)	—	—	—	—
Mixed Generalist (n=72)	11.77	55.6	108.0	30.6

in this category performed responsible duties in party posts below the ob-last level. While recalling that very few (6.6 percent) individuals enter the obkom leadership *directly* from a lower party level, about one in seven future first secretaries spent the bulk of their prior careers in party posts at the raion (district) or city level. These individuals possess relatively strong opportunities for upward political mobility (mobility score, 11.82;

Central Committee recruitment, 59.5 percent) and in most other respects resemble the majority of the remaining elite.

Those individuals whose prior careers were dominated primarily by agricultural pursuits constitute 11.0 percent of the sample. Two-thirds of this group (eighteen of the twenty-seven) held responsible agricultural posts in the government apparatus, but party agriculturalists and state agriculturalists are found to be, in most essential respects, identical. Two points, however, merit consideration.

First, individuals whose prior careers were in the agricultural area have, relative to the other major functional career categories, weaker prospects for upward political mobility. The aggregate mobility score (11.18) and likelihood of future recruitment into the C.P.S.U. Central Committee (40.7 percent) reveal again that brilliantly successful careers in the Soviet system are not probable in the functional area of agricultural affairs (party agriculturalists of this type are slightly more mobile, but this is offset by lower Central Committee recruitment).

Second, five of the eighteen (27.8 percent) obkom first secretaries whose prior careers were dominated by *state* agricultural posts later held more than one obkom first secretaryship. None of the nine obkom secretaries whose prior career was in *party* agriculture were appointed to a second obkom leadership position. With the relatively low mobility score and the genuinely weak Central Committee recruitment rate, rising Soviet party apparatchiki might be well advised in the interest of their future careers to attempt another functional avenue toward individual career success.

Twenty-three of the elites (9.3 percent) in our sample spent their careers leading up to the obkom first secretaryship in primarily industrial posts. These individuals clearly outperform those with prior careers in agriculture and can expect to experience better career opportunities subsequent to the obkom post. Their aggregate mobility score of 12.35 is 10.4 percent higher and their prospects of recruitment into the C.P.S.U. Central Committee (52.2 percent) are 28.3 percent brighter than for the agriculturalists.

No other single functional group constitutes even 5 percent of the prior careers of the obkom first secretaries in the sample. However, several points of interest should be cited. First, it seems clear (although the number of cases is low) that a predominant prior career in the oblast or union republic government apparatus severely weakens the chances of upward mobility for obkom first secretaries. Combined, their mean mobility score is a low 10.47 (lower than any other functional category), and these individuals have only an 18.2 percent chance of ever attaining full membership in the party Central Committee.

Second, a prior career in the functional area of cadres/personnel does not portend an overwhelmingly successful career beyond the post of obkom first secretary. Although not as dismal as for those from the regional or republic government administration, those whose prior career revolved around cadre affairs (for example, obkom second secretary, head of the Organizational-Party Works department in a republic party Central Committee) have relatively weak mobility prospects (10.95) and less than a three in ten chance of ever being among the party elite.

Finally, 4.9 percent (n = 12) of the elites spent most of their careers prior to the obkom first secretary post in responsible Komsomol positions. These individuals are noteworthy in that they seem to acquire the significant step-level assignments at a younger age than the other members of the elite. Their mean age at recruitment into the C.P.S.U. itself is a relatively low 21.5 years; they become obkom first secretary, on average, at 40.2 years of age; and, if they are to do so, they enter full status in the C.P.S.U. Central Committee at the age of 47.4 years. These numbers are 13.7, 12.9, and 7.5 percent below the all-elites means, respectively. This is not to say, of course, that they are significantly more mobile in an overall sense. Their scores in mobility of 11.06 and Central Committee recruitment rate of 41.7 percent are by no means extraordinary. In sum, they do not receive more or better posts than the other elites. They merely tend to be assigned to the posts, such as they are, at a younger age than the other elites.

Functional Focus of Later Career. When examining the functional focus of the careers of elites after leaving the post of obkom first secretary, the most notable finding is the large number of these elites who have *no* functional career having left the obkom post (see Table 4.15). Thirty-seven (16.7 percent) individuals retired from the obkom leadership post due to age or health problems. Another fourteen (6.3 percent) were removed from the post due to such problems as "serious shortcomings," "serious failings," or "serious deficiencies" in their performance as obkom first secretary. They were never assigned a substantial post again and no data are available on whatever subsequent employment they held. Still another thirteen individuals (5.9 percent) died in office. Combined, then, the data show that sixty-four obkom first secretaries (28.8 percent) either retire from, are forced to retire from, or die in this post. It is worth noting that, given the mean age at entry to the first obkom post (45.7 years), almost 30 percent of the regional party leaders who left this post between 1965 and 1987 never assumed a responsible public post again. It is clear that while the post of obkom first secretary is a significant "stepping stone" position to leading party and government jobs, for almost three in ten elites, it is the final post they will ever fill. Of course, by definition the higher one goes in the Soviet political hierarchy, the fewer available posts

Table 4.15
Functional Focus of the Later Career
and Mobility among the Obkom Elite

Focus of Later Career	Mobility	Recruitment into Central Committee (%)	Initial Tenure (Months)	Multiple ObSect Posts (%)
Local Party (n=0)	—	—	—	—
Regional Party (n=30)	11.26	46.7	67.7	93.3
Republic Party (n=16)	12.61	56.2	70.9	18.7
Leading Party (n=10)	13.79	90.0	83.5	10.0
Punitive Organs (n=13)	12.59	76.9	84.5	61.6
Party Agriculture (n=1)	9.00	0.0	67.0	0.0
State Agriculture (n=5)	10.70	40.0	76.8	20.0
Cadres (n=5)	11.77	60.0	69.6	0.0
Labor/T. U. C. (n=3)	11.22	33.3	120.7	33.3
Foreign Affairs (n=10)	12.52	80.0	109.1	0.0
Industry/Constr. (n=2)	14.83	100.0	120.0	100.0
Local State (n=0)	—	—	—	—
Regional State (n=2)	11.07	50.0	24.0	100.0
Republic State (n=34)	11.43	41.2	83.6	11.8
Leading State (n=23)	12.80	73.9	91.7	30.4
Mixed Generalist (n=4)	10.50	0.0	82.0	50.0
Retired (n=37)	11.28	54.5	167.7	10.8
Removed (n=14)	11.00	42.9	130.4	7.1
Died in Office (n=13)	11.00	50.5	78.2	23.1

one could expect to find. Competition for the important political positions above that of the obkom first secretary is more intense than the competition at lower levels.

Additional evidence reveals the special nature of the obkom first secretaryship. A wide discrepancy exists between those who *enter* the obkom post as a mixed generalist (29.3 percent of the sample) and those whose *later* career can be considered to be one of the mixed generalist type (1.8

percent). That is, while almost three in ten elites' *prior* careers are marked by a party-state generalist pattern, less than one in fifty elites' *subsequent* careers are so patterned. It is clear that after serving as an obkom first secretary, an elite's future career will tend to be much more narrowly focused than his prior career.

An almost equal number of elites stayed primarily at the regional party level (either retiring later from another obkom leadership post or assuming a lower post in the obkom apparatus) as left it for a post-career focus in the republic-level government structure. Thirty-four elites (15.3 percent) fell into the latter category, while thirty (13.5 percent) were categorized into the former. It is worth noting that evidence again indicates the power and prestige of the two competing career avenues: party and government. Those obkom first secretaries whose later careers focus at the union republic government level do *not* have greater upward mobility than those elites whose subsequent careers kept them at the regional party level. While those entering republic government posts have a slightly higher mean mobility score (11.43) than those remaining at the obkom level (11.26), the latter group experiences a higher recruitment rate into the C.P.S.U. Central Committee (46.7 percent) than the former (41.2 percent).

Comparing those whose subsequent careers were leading party (n = 10) and leading government (n = 23) posts, we see again that those associated with the party apparatus experience greater upward mobility (13.79) and Central Committee recruitment (90.0 percent) than those associated with the government apparatus (12.80, 73.9 percent). While both groups do well, ceteris paribus, those who go from the obkom party post to a subsequent career dominated by leading *party* posts tend to enjoy better career opportunities than those who go to a subsequent career primarily in the leading *government* apparatus. In fact, elites with later careers in state administration perform on a par, as in past cases, with the aggregate performance of those elites from the *next lowest* party level (12.60, 56.2 percent), although it seems that the phenomenon weakens in the higher levels of the Soviet political-administrative system.

Approximately 6 percent of the elites (n = 13) in the sample exited the obkom posts and engaged in a post-obkom career in the control organs. This category includes such apparats as those of the Committee of State Security (KGB), the Ministry of Internal Affairs (MVD), the party/state Control Committees, the procuracy, and so on. Elites of this group seem to have experienced rather strong career opportunities, as reflected in their mean mobility score (12.59) and their rate of admittance into the C.P.S.U. Central Committee (76.9 percent).

The present Soviet minister of internal affairs, Aleksandr Vladimirovich Vlasov, left his post of first secretary of the Rostov obkom in January 1986 to assume this key post. Vlasov's promotion was no doubt the result of his successful anti-corruption campaigns in the Northern Caucasus. As first secretary of the Chechen-Ingush autonomous republic (1975–1984) and of Rostov obkom (1984–1986), Vlasov's crackdowns reportedly resulted in the dismissal and initiation of criminal proceedings against several regional officials.

Several obkom secretaries during the 1965–1987 period left the obkom tier to take posts in the Soviet foreign ministry. In all cases (n = 10), these elites assumed the rank of USSR ambassador to a foreign country. Some commentators, such as Zhores A. Medvedev (1986), have cited this particular career transition as Brezhnev's favorite way of demoting leading cadres (see, for example, the career of Vitalii Vorotnikov). The evidence revealed herein casts some light on the nature of this career setback. The mobility scores of these ten elites averages 12.52 and eight of the ten have been elevated to full membership in the C.P.S.U. Central Committee. This later fact, however, must be taken in context. It would be odd indeed if a USSR ambassador to a major foreign state were *not* a voting member of the Central Committee. The elevation to this status seems pro forma. Since the mobility score to some extent will reflect membership in this body, the mobility scores of these individuals may be inflated. There is, to be sure, a pecking order among ambassadorial assignments (Western capitalist states top this list, and underdeveloped Third World outposts are likely at the bottom), but in all but a few cases, the move from an obkom first secretary (especially in the R.S.F.S.R.) to a USSR ambassador must be seen as a demotion.

Once again, the data reveal the poor prospects of those connected (by accident of birth, education, prior career, prior post, subsequent post, and now by later career) with agriculture. Only six individuals (2.7 percent) exited the obkom post for a decidedly agricultural career, and their prospects for an upwardly mobile post-obkom career seem rather dim. Their mean mobility score (10.42) is the lowest of any of the twenty-one categories, and only two of the six were elevated to full standing in the C.P.S.U. Central Committee. The notoriously poor performance of the agricultural sector of the Soviet economy as well as the structural characteristics of the agrarian regions of the Soviet Union evidently taint those elites associated with agriculture.

Only two individuals' subsequent careers were coded as mainly industrially oriented. As such, this category would not merit attention except for the fact that their combined mobility scores are quite high (14.83) and both became full members of the Central Committee. However, additional cases must be incorporated into the analysis before any valid inferences can be drawn. No other category garnered more than five individuals and, as such, cannot present enough cases for legitimate commentary.

Data Reduction and the Mobility Equation

In an attempt to subject the data to more rigorous methodological procedures, data reduction procedures were utilized as well. Because by their nature many of the categorical data discussed above do not lend themselves readily to multivariate analyses, it was necessary in evaluating the impact of individual background/career characteristics on political mobility to reformulate these variables as dummy variables. Creating dummy variables reduces a large number of categories into only two by aggregating any number of the categories into, in a sense, one in-group and one out-group. Although reducing the contextual richness of the variables themselves, the creation of new dummy variables has the advantage of permitting the utilization of multivariate analyses. In this way, then, one may assess the explanatory power of the individual background characteristics with respect to political elite mobility in the Soviet Union.

Based on the evidence found in the extant literature in this area (Blackwell, 1973b, 1972b; Fleron, 1973, 1970; Moses, 1983) as well as the suggestive analyses presented earlier in this chapter, certain background and/or career variables were included in an equation aimed at explaining the variance in mobility scores established in Chapter 2. These variables included (1) ethnicity, (2) level of education, (3) educational content, (4) military experience, (5) training in Higher Party Schools, (6) responsible post experience in Komsomol organizations, and (7) the post prior to the obkom first secretaryship. These seven variables, then, became the basis for the creation of seven background/career dummy variables that could be used together in a multiple regression analysis aimed at clarifying the degree to which this type of variable explains or can predict political mobility.

Because dummy variables are dichotomous representations of generally multi-category variables, the exact manner of creating these dummy variables will have an impact on the degree to which they can explain the dependent variable. As a result, a series of alternative dummy variable constructions for *each* of the seven background/career variables were tested and used in a multiple regression analysis in order to ascertain which dummy variable construction for each variable possessed the highest explanatory value with respect to the variance in political mobility scores. After determining the most fruitful construction of each of the seven variables, the analysis proceeded.

The multiple regression analysis indicated that, combined, these key individual background and career variables account for 25.6 percent of the variance in political mobility scores (see Table 4.16). This compares rather poorly with the structural explanation proffered in Chapter 3 that successfully accounted for 40.9 percent of that same variance (see Table 3.4), yet is substantially more promising than the results of previous research efforts (see, for example, Blackwell, 1973b; Blackwell and Hulbary, 1973) into the relationship between these types of variables and their collective impact on elite mobility.

Table 4.16 reveals that three of the seven dummy variables account for the bulk of the explanatory value of the equation. As shown in earlier sections of this chapter, ethnicity does have an impact on mobility although even this variable, the most salient of those background characteristics examined, does not constitute a reliable indicator of mobility. The level of education also distinguishes subsequent political mobility to some degree. Yet highly educated obkom first secretaries are only slightly more upwardly mobile than those not in this category. Finally, educational training (technical versus non-technical) can also aid to some degree the researcher interested in elite mobility.

This multivariate analysis supports the general themes developed in this chapter. Individual background and career variables are not powerful predictors of an elite's mobility from the post of obkom first secretary. Viewed in isolation, the seven key variables account for only one-quarter of the established variance in mobility scores. Yet, when juxtaposed with the bulk of the prior research into this specific relationship, the findings must be seen as encouraging.

CONCLUSION

Robert E. Blackwell, Jr., one of the most prominent contributors to the literature on Soviet regional elite mobility, wrote over fifteen years ago that "the prediction of career development beyond the obkom assignment is not greatly facilitated by knowing an individual's background, specialization or career development prior to the obkom assignment" (1973b: 9). The analysis produced herein must, in many ways, serve to corroborate this general assessment. However, the specific findings generated in this study do not warrant the adoption of such a pessimistic conclusion.

As the preceding pages have shown, the details of a person's background, training, and career development can aid the researcher in making meaningful statements about the political mobility opportunities that individual groups of elites will in all likelihood experience. Without subscribing to an ecological fallacy, certain factors (especially ethnicity and educational content) can be seen to influence individuals' subsequent political mobility. However, this reveals that we are forced to concur with Blackwell's contention when viewing many, if not most, of the variables. The individual's level of education, his age at the assumption of various posts (including the obkom first secretaryship), and his tenure(s) in the obkom leadership post are surprisingly not relevant to the issue of political mobility.[7]

Table 4.16
Relative Weights of Background/Career
Variables on Political Mobility

Variable	Beta Score*
Ethnicity	.27991
Level of Education	.22093
Educational Content	.17829
Komsomol Posts	.08589
Military Service	.07471
Prior Post	.06308
Higher Party School	-.04490

$$r^2 = .27682$$
$$\text{Adjusted } r^2 = .25632$$
$$F = 13.50653$$

*Significant at 0.05 level

One is left with the distinct impression that along most distinguishing personal characteristics, the obkom elite is a much more homogeneous elite group than was expected. A high degree of continuity marks the observed characteristics of this large elite sample. With this in mind, it is perhaps advisable to turn, in future efforts, to distinguishing the obkom elite as a group from other elite cohorts, rather than looking for intra-group variations. This statement, however, does not trivialize the differences regarding political mobility among the obkom elite. These differences are important as barometers of political changes not only among the regional leadership but, to the extent that the obkom elite of today is the national elite of tomorrow, among the national leadership as well. Cadre composition changes at the obkom tier reflect the decisions of the present national leadership and will effect changes in the future Soviet national leadership.

Because this chapter has necessarily focused on individuals who have *exited* the obkom leadership post, the analyses presented in these pages do not address the trends evident among the *incumbent* obkom elite. Most of the post-Brezhnev obkom secretaries have had insufficient time to experience mobility from their obkom assignments. Thus, the 129 men who currently constitute the Soviet prefectory escape the purview of this analysis. Yet this present elite cohort represents the regional elites of a "new era" in Soviet politics.

Since Brezhnev's death, the regional elite has been experiencing turnover at the rate of approximately one obkom first secretary every two weeks. The Brezhnev regional elite has been largely replaced by individuals named by Andropov and Gorbachev (turnover was very slow indeed under Chernenko). It is among this group that new patterns might be expected to become evident. The nature of the new regional elite is examined in the next, and final, chapter.

NOTES

1. To be sure, the case study remains a valid and valued method for the explication of knowledge in this area. The pedigree of important elite case studies extends back to Fainsod (1958) and runs through Armstrong (1959), Moses (1974), and Hill (1977).

2. See Chapter 2, note 4, for an extended list of the sources of biographical data on these 255 obkom elites.

3. Three-quarters of these obkom first secretaries will not be moved to another obkom leadership post. Only 65 of the 255 elites (25.5 percent) held 2 or more regional first secretaryships.

4. It is difficult to ascertain whether a given individual actually saw combat during the war. An elite was so coded if he was in the Red Army and/or partisan movement at any time during the 1941–1945 period.

5. It is important to keep in mind that the elites under study are those who have *exited* the obkom post. As such, these age figures are in all likelihood somewhat unrepresentative of the total population appointed by Gorbachev since only three of the seventy or so obkom elites he has appointed to date have vacated these posts. Chapter 5 focuses more directly on the incumbent regional elite.

6. The other men in this small group are (1) Vasilii Yefremovich Chernyshev [Brest obkom (CPBelo) 1946–1948; Minsk obkom (CPBelo) 1948–1950; Kaliningrad obkom (CPSU) 1951–1959], (2) Mikhail Sergeevich Solomentsev [Karaganda obkom (CPKaz) 1959–1962; Rostov (CPSU) 1964–1966], and (3) Aleksandr Konstantinovich Protozanov [Tiumen obkom (CPSU) 1963–1964; East Kazakhstan obkom (CPKaz) 1969–1983].

7. Indeed, it is striking just how little these career development variables speak to the issue of political elite mobility. A simple regression analysis was performed on the following variables and shows the weakness of their explanatory power:

Variable	Correlation with Mobility Score
Level of Education	.118
Age at Entrance to C.P.S.U.	.039
Age at Assumption of Obkom First Secretary Post	-.015
Tenure in Initial Obkom First Secretaryship	.135
Tenure in Other Obkom First Secretaryships	.027
Total Tenure as Obkom First Secretary	.008
Age at Elevation to Central Committee (Candidate)	-.038
Age at Elevation to Central Committee (Full)	-.121

In addition, these variables were included in a factor analysis that produced the following rotated factor matrix:

Variable	F1	F2	F3
Level of Education	−.67580	−.34345	.53351
Age at Entrance to C.P.S.U	−.19032	.71695	−.00190
Age at Obkom First Secretary	.23142	.23166	.87216
Initial Tenure	.17231	.69573	.18383
Other Tenures	−.20132	−.62416	−.58339
Age at Cand. Central Committee	.93639	−.15086	.25746
Age at Full Central Committee	.92193	.06883	.18724

These factor scores for each of the 255 cases were then used in a regression run with the political mobility scores as the dependent variable. This analysis produced equally weak correlation coefficients to which the following figures attest:

Variable	Correlation with Mobility Score
Factor 1	.039
Factor 2	.138
Factor 3	.272

REFERENCES

Armstrong, John A. *The Soviet Bureaucratic Elite: A Case Study of the Ukrainian Apparatus.* New York: Praeger, 1959.

Blackwell, Robert E., Jr. "Cadres Policy in the Brezhnev Era," *Problems of Communism* (March–April 1979): 29–42.

_____ . "The Soviet Political Elite—Alternative Recruitment Policies at the Obkom Level," *Comparative Politics* 6, no. 1 (October 1973a): 99–121.

_____ . "The Relationship between Social Background Characteristics, Career Specialization, Political Attitudes, and Political Behavior among Soviet Elites: A Research Design." Paper presented at the annual meeting of the

American Political Science Association, New Orleans, LA, September 4–8, 1973b.

—— . "Career Development in the Soviet Obkom Elite: A Conservative Trend," *Soviet Studies* 24 (July 1972a): 26–39.

—— . "Elite Recruitment and Functional Change: An Analysis of the Soviet Obkom Elite, 1950–1968," *Journal of Politics* 34 (1972b): 124–152.

Blackwell, Robert E., Jr. and William Hulbary. "Political Mobility among Soviet Obkom Elites: The Effects of Regime, Social Backgrounds and Career Development," *American Journal of Political Science* 17 no. 4 (1973): 721–743.

Cleary, J. W. "Elite Career Patterns in a Soviet Republic," *British Journal of Political Science* 4 (1974): 323–344.

Daniels, Robert V. "Soviet Politics Since Khrushchev," in John W. Strong, ed. *The Soviet Union Under Brezhnev and Kosygin.* New York: Van Nostrand, Reinhold, 1971.

Fainsod, Merle. *Smolensk Under Soviet Rule.* New York: Random House, 1958.

Farrell, R. Barry, ed. *Political Leadership in Eastern Europe and the Soviet Union.* Chicago: Aldine Publishing Co., 1970.

Fleron, Frederic. 1973. "System Attributes and Career Attributes: The Soviet Leadership System, 1952 to 1965," in Carl Beck et al. *Comparative Communist Political Leadership.* New York: David McKay Co., Inc..

—— . "Representation of Career Types in the Soviet Political Leadership," pp. 108–139 in R. Barry Farrell, ed. *Political Leadership in Eastern Europe and the Soviet Union.* Chicago: Aldine Publishing Co., 1970.

—— . *Communist Studies and the Social Sciences: Essays on Methodology and Empirical Theory.* Chicago: Rand McNally, 1969.

Gehlen, Michael P. "The Soviet Apparatchiki," pp. 140–156 in R. Barry Farrell, ed. *Political Leadership in Eastern Europe and the Soviet Union.* Chicago: Aldine Publishing Co., 1970.

Gehlen, Michael P., and Michael McBride. "The Soviet Central Committee: An Elite Analysis," *American Political Science Review* 62, no. 4 (December 1968): 1232–1241.

Hammer, Darrell P. *USSR: The Politics of Oligarchy.* Hinsdale, IL: Dryden Press, 1974.

Harasymiw, Bohdan. *Political Elite Recruitment in the Soviet Union.* New York: St. Martin's Press, 1984.

Hill, Ronald J. *Soviet Political Elites: The Case of Tiraspol.* New York: St. Martin's Press, 1977

Hodnett, Grey. *Leadership in the Soviet National Republics: A Quantitative Study of Recruitment Policy.* Oakville, Ont.: Mosaic Press, 1978.

—— . "The Obkom First Secretaries," *Slavic Review* 24, no. 4 (December 1965): 636–652.

Hough, Jerry F. *The Soviet Union and Social Science Theory.* Cambridge, Mass.: Harvard University Press, 1977.

—— . *The Soviet Prefects: The Local Party Organs in Industrial Decision-Making.* Cambridge, MA: Harvard University Press, 1969.

Kress, John H. "Representation of Positions on the CPSU Politburo," *Slavic*

Review 39, no. 2 (June 1980): 218–238.

Lodge, Milton. " 'Groupism' in the Post-Stalin Period," *Midwest Journal of Political Science* 12, no. 3 (August 1968): 330–351.

Medvedev, Zhores A. *Gorbachev.* New York: W. W. Norton, 1986.

Miller, John H. "Cadres Policy in Nationality Areas: Recruitment of CPSU First and Second Secretaries in non-Russian Republics of the USSR," *Soviet Studies* 29 (January 1977): 3–36.

Moore, Barrington. *Terror and Progress USSR: Some Sources of Change and Stability in the Soviet Dictatorship.* Cambridge, Mass.: Harvard University Press, 1954.

Moses, Joel C. 1983. "Functional Career Specialization in Soviet Regional Elite Recruitment," in T. H. Rigby and Bohdan Harasymiw, eds. *Leadership Selection and Patron-Client Relations in the USSR and Yugoslavia.* London: George Allen and Unwin, 1963.

————. *Regional Party Leadership and Policy-Making in the USSR.* New York: Praeger, 1974.

Rigby, T. H., and Bohdan Harasymiw, eds. *Leadership Selection and Patron-Client Relations in the USSR and Yugoslavia.* London: George Allen and Unwin, 1983.

Skilling, H. Gordon and Franklyn Griffiths. *Interest Groups in Soviet Politics.* Princeton, N.J.: Princeton University Press, 1971.

Stewart, Philip D. *Political Power in the Soviet Union: A Study of Decision-Making in Stalingrad.* New York: Bobbs-Merrill, 1968.

Stewart, Philip D., and Kenneth Town. "The Career-Attitude Linkage among Soviet Regional Elites: An Exploration of its Nature and Magnitude." Paper presented at the annual meeting of the American Political Science Association, Chicago, August 29–September 2, 1974.

5

REGIONAL CADRES POLICY AFTER BREZHNEV: CHANGES IN THE OBKOM ELITE

INTRODUCTION

Writing in the last years of the Brezhnev era, Thomas H. Rigby hypothesized that "tomorrow's top leadership will probably be drawn in large part from today's obkom secretaries. . . . They will have spent more of their careers under the calmer rule of Brezhnev than under the murderous rule of Stalin and the turbulent rule of Khrushchev" (1980: 62–63). Indeed, Rigby's hypothesis about the regional party elite is based upon a practice rather well established in the brief history of the Soviet Union. The obkom first secretary tier has consistently had within it the individuals who would go on to comprise the next generation of national political elites.

Ever since Stalin's regional cadres policy produced such future notables as Andrei Kirilenko, Nikolai Podgorny, Mikhail Suslov, Demian Korotchenko, as well as Nikita Khrushchev and Leonid Brezhnev, Soviet leaders have felt compelled for a variety of reasons to utilize their control over the party personnel nomenklatura to stock the Soviet oblasti with their own regional cohort.[1] Many of these regional prefects have risen over the years to occupy the leading responsible party and government posts in the Soviet political system.

Evaluating Rigby's statement almost eight years after it was written, it is clear that the basis upon which it was made has remained fundamental to Soviet leadership maintenance. No fewer than eleven of the top party figures of the Gorbachev leadership were, at one point in their respective careers, an obkom first secretary. This list includes Mikhail Gorbachev himself, Second Secretary Yegor Ligachev, and many others.[2]

After the many years of rather conservative personnel turnover at the obkom tier that marked the Brezhnev period, Brezhnev's successors have been engaged in a rigorous cadres replenishment. The new leaders have, with the exception of Konstantin Chernenko, grasped the opportunity to replace regional elites of the Brezhnev mold with a cohort more consistent with their own ideas and ideals for the Soviet future. Indeed, well over 90 percent of the regional party first secretaries now in place in the Soviet Union have been moved into their posts since the death of Leonid Brezhnev in November 1982. At a rate approaching the hectic years of the Khrushchev era, regional party leaders have been replaced with new first secretaries roughly at the rate of one every two weeks for almost seven years. It is safe to say that the regional party leadership has been purged of its Brezhnevite character. The present cohort of Soviet prefects is clearly the product of Yurii Andropov and, more importantly, Mikhail Gorbachev.

This chapter provides a comprehensive overview of the post-Brezhnev Soviet regional cadres policy. Recalling Rigby's speculative remarks, as well as the character of Soviet national leadership replenishment, it is clear that from this regional cohort will emerge not only Gorbachev's successive leadership coalitions, but also the leaders of the post-Gorbachev era. Indeed, what was said of Brezhnev holds equally well for Gorbachev—that is, that the cadres policy pursued in the present "will thus be a crucial determinant of the near-future of the Soviet political system" (Mitchell, 1982: 593). In a fundamental sense, then, Soviet leaders *have* chosen their successors; Gorbachev has already gone a long way in selecting his. An understanding of the nature of this new regional leadership group, the future national leaders of the Soviet Union, is crucial, therefore, for a sophisticated understanding of Soviet politics—present and future.

BREZHNEV'S "STABILITY OF CADRES"

The cadres policy of Brezhnev's successors can certainly be seen as a response to the policies pursued in the area of personnel during the 1965–1982 period. Likewise, in reviewing Brezhnev's disposition of personnel questions, a policy position variously labeled "Stability of Cadres," "Trust in Cadres," "Respect for Cadres," or "Faith in Cadres," one must assuredly view it as a calculated response to the erratic cadres policy of his immediate predecessor Nikita Khrushchev. Indeed, Khrushchev's mismanagement of the regional party and state cadres was prominent among the causes of the coup of October 1964 (Rigby, 1970: 173).

The origins of the Brezhnev cadres policy lie in the "hare-brained" organizational schemes of Khrushchev. The Brezhnev-Kosygin leadership quickly replaced the free-wheeling cadres policy of Khrushchev with a far less politicized approach to making personnel decisions. The immediacy of the problem is revealed by the fact that within two weeks of the ouster of Khrushchev, the erstwhile leader's approach to personnel selection had been reversed. In the first edition of the C.P.S.U.'s theoretical journal, *Partiinaia Zhizn,* to appear after the coup, the first of a two-pronged attack on the reversed policy was articulated:

Without according assistance to lower-level officials, without knowledge of [their] circumstances, a demanding attitude can easily boil down to leadership "in general," which often leads to the unjustified reshuffling of cadres . . . Indisputedly, bad officials must be replaced. The renewal of cadres is a natural phenomenon. Not infrequently, however, there are still efforts to represent frequent changes of them as a virtue (*Partiinaia Zhizn,* 1964, no. 20, p. 6).

The second overt criticism of Khrushchev's policy of limited tenures, constant reshuffling, and "systematic renewal" of cadres was voiced in the first post-coup edition of the important journal *Kommunist:*

Recently, however, work with cadres and the rational employment of them has been subjected to artificial complications. The frequent restructurings and reorganizations have entailed repeated mass reallocation of officials. This switching around of cadres has not allowed them to concentrate on the decision of long-term questions of economic development of the oblast, krai, or raion, and has imbued officials with a feeling of lack of self-confidence which hinders them from working calmly and fruitfully (*Kommunist,* 1964, no. 16: 7–8).

Brezhnev's first act as general secretary of the Communist party of the Soviet Union, then, was to reassure the party *apparatchiki* that their jobs, their influence, and their perquisites would not be touched (Ford, 1984: 1133). In his first major public speech to the party members, at the 23d Party Congress in March 1966, Brezhnev was quick to state his policy in explicit terms:

The frequent restructurings and reorganizations of Party, Soviet and economic bodies that were carried out in recent years had a negative effect on the selection, promotion, and training of cadres. As a rule, they were attended by an unwarranted shuffling and replacement of cadres, which engendered a lack of self-assurance in officials, prevented them from demonstrating their abilities to the full and created the soil in which irresponsibility could sprout . . . We are pleased to be able to remind the Congress that the November, 1964, plenary session of the C.P.S.U. reunited the province industrial and rural Party organizations into single entities, thereby restoring the Leninist principle of Party structure and eliminating the serious errors that have been committed in this matter. (*Applause.*) Also reinstated were the rural district Party committees, which in a short time have firmly reasserted their status as militant and authoritative propagators of Party policy in the countryside. (*Applause.*) . . . The development of the principle of democratic centralism has found expression in the further strengthening of the principle of collective leadership at the center and in the localities, in the enhancement of the role of the plenary sessions of the C.P.S.U. Central Committee and also of plenary sessions of local Party organs, in the manifestation of complete trust in cadres and in the improvement of inner-Party channels of information (*Pravda* and *Izvestia,* March 30, 1966).

Thus, Brezhnev by early 1966 had reinforced the earlier comments of Aleksei Kosygin, who six months earlier had spoken at the September 1965 plenary session of the C.P.S.U. Central Committee. Kosygin had assured the audience that "stability of cadres" would govern his attitude toward government personnel as well:

Many thousands of able and competent organizers of socialist production have grown up in the country during the years of Soviet rule. At present more than 2,000,000 specialists with a higher or specialized secondary education are employed in industrial enterprises. More then 4,000,000 Communists are working in them. This is an immense force, by relying on which we can resolve the most complex tasks. The Party and the people hold the cadres of specialists and production organizers in high esteem, place great confidence in them and give them all possible support in their complex and socially useful work (*Pravda* and *Izvestia,* September 28, 1965).

Thus, within months of the mid-October removal of the first secretary, the Brezhnev-Kosygin leadership had stated in no uncertain terms its policy toward cadres. For almost twenty years after the fall of Khrushchev the resultant leadership, even after the decline of its initial collective nature, maintained a rather consistent personnel policy marked by the extremely slow turnover of elites at all levels of the Soviet system. Both the genesis of the "stability of cadres" policy and its subsequent effects on the Soviet system, however, merit specific consideration as they directly impinge upon the prerogatives and the necessities of the post-Brezhnev Soviet leadership.

Western analysts' characterizations of the roots of Brezhnev's "stability of cadres" policy revolve around two basic and related themes. First, and perhaps the more standard of the two explanations, stresses Nikita Khrushchev's treatment of the party and state cadres, especially those in the C.P.S.U. Central Committee, and point to Brezhnev's reversal of that cadres policy as evidence of his attempt to appease the powerful national and regional officialdom. The adopted "stability of cadres" policy was, seen in this light, a necessary policy, almost dictated from below, for Brezhnev to adopt if he wished to build personal authority (Breslauer, 1982).

Robert A. D. Ford's (1984) depiction of the events surrounding the adoption of this policy can be seen as a classic example of this first type of explanation:

Khrushchev's reforms were tolerated until he began to tinker with the structure of the Party and introduced changes that would have reduced the power of the thousands of small Party bosses all over the country (p. 1133).

Throughout 1960–1961 a "bloodless purge" of the majority of the regional party bosses revealed that even that group of officials who, in effect, had salvaged Khrushchev's career during the 1957 Anti-Party Group coup attempt, could not count on Khrushchev for personal job security (Hough, 1979: 2). Indeed, by the early 1960s, approximately two-thirds of the R.S.F.S.R. obkom first secretaries installed by Khrushchev in the mid-1950s had been replaced (Rigby, 1978a: 5). According to this school of thought, the rapid pace of regional elite turnover created a sense of frustration and insecurity which would eventually contribute greatly to Khrushchev's removal from power in 1964.

These frustrations and their sense of career instability were only intensified by further actions taken by Khrushchev in the first three years of the new decade. In October 1961, the Party Rules were changed and Khrushchev, for the first time, instituted minimum turnover quotas as well as limited office tenures for party committee members at virtually all levels of the system. Following these cadres policy changes was perhaps the most self-damaging of all Khrushchev's schemes. In November 1962, the C.P.S.U. first secretary initiated a sweeping administrative reorganization which

split a large proportion of the regional party organizations into two, one for industry and one for agriculture, each with its own regional committee (obkom), executive bureau, and secretariat. This not only created further administrative confusion, but struck directly at the incumbent obkom first secretaries by duplicating the offices and thus sharply reducing their individual power and status (Rigby, 1978a: 6).

This series of attacks on the powerful regional party elite, according to this explanation of the fall of Khrushchev and the genesis of "stability of cadres," had gone too far. The new leadership quickly reunified the party apparatus, restoring, in 75 percent of the cases, the erstwhile obkom first secretary to his former leadership post. Scholars stressing these events in their analyses argue that Brezhnev "apparently concluded that his own political fortunes [were] best served by identifying his administration with cadres stability" (Blackwell, 1979: 29), which without doubt would "foster support for [the] regime within this crucial elite group" (Rigby, 1978: 8; Hough, 1979: 3; Mitchell, 1982: 592).

A second slant on the origins of Brezhnev's "stability of cadres" policy views it less as a policy dictated from below and more as the result of a Politburo-level compact entered into by the main actors of the October 1964 coup. Seen from this perspective, the conservative cadres policy instituted by Khrushchev's successors was primarily an instrument aimed at facilitating the reintroduction and preservation of oligarchic, or collective, leadership patterns at the apex of the Soviet system. Khrushchev was ousted by his lieutenants in the Politburo "because the strains between the lesser oligarchs and the predominant leader had finally become intolerable. The coup was designed to restore rule by 'pure' oligarchy" (Rigby, 1970: 173).

Several scholars have pointed to the existence among the so-called Brezhnev-Kosygin team of a conscious compact about the proper nature of decision making (Rigby, 1970; Hodnett, 1975; Lapidus, 1977; Blackwell, 1979). Rigby himself was the first to proffer the theory of the leadership compact and articulates most explicitly the probable contents of the agreement:

Whatever private reservations individual leaders may have entertained, it seems likely that, at the least, an implicit compact of this kind [i.e., one aimed at collective leadership and "mutual control"] was at the basis of the agreement and conspiracy to remove Khrushchev, and that this compact probably envisaged the following practical devices to this end:
1) Keeping the two top posts in different hands. 2) Reducing opportunities for patronage. 3) Distributing among leaders seats in the Party Presidium, Presidium of the Council of Ministers, and Central Committee Secretariat in such a way as to avoid dangerous patterns of overlap. 4) Maintaining countervailing power between topmost leaders (Rigby, 1970: 175).

The "stability of cadres" policy, from this perspective, was adopted as a means of ensuring the integrity of this collective compact. It improved the Soviet leadership style through much of the Brezhnev era because it effectively depoliticized the personnel selection process, thereby limiting much of the intra-elite power struggle. As Gail Lapidus argues, the curtailing of the high elite turnover rates associated with Khrushchev's leadership had "the immediate virtues of preserving stability at the apex and of limiting a potentially destabilizing competition over power and patronage among the elite" (1977: 35). Robert Blackwell describes in perhaps the clearest terms just how the Brezhnev cadres policy fits into the overall attitude of the post-Khrushchev Soviet leadership:

Following N. S. Khrushchev's overthrow, his heirs replaced their patron's freewheeling cadres policy with a far less politicized approach in making personnel decisions. These changes—perhaps one should call them reforms—have considerably narrowed the tactical options in the leadership struggle and thereby strengthened the institutional restraints against abuses of power by the more ambitious members of the Politburo (1979: 29).

These two foci on the genesis of "stability of cadres," of course, are not at all antithetical. Indeed, they serve to highlight the significant degree of support that the policy must have engendered at the time. Whatever the exact impetus for its adoption, the "stability of cadres," implemented rather evenly for almost twenty years, had a profound impact on the nature of Soviet politics and society; its effects have been extremely far-reaching.

Brezhnev's cadres policy, in a word, entailed the extremely slow turnover of elites at virtually all levels of the Soviet system. This aspect of Brezhnev's "trust" in the party and government cadres revealed itself in a multitude of ways. At the highest political level, change in the composition of the Politburo slowed considerably. Over the first six and a half years after the removal of Khrushchev, only two individuals (Kirill Mazurov and Arvid Pelshe) were promoted to full Politburo membership (Hodnett, 1975: 8). Changes at this level remained relatively low throughout the Brezhnev period and by the early 1980s the inner core of the Politburo averaged almost 75 years of age. The average age of the full voting members of the Politburo continued to rise throughout the period, going from fifty-eight in 1966, to sixty-two in 1972, and to over seventy in 1980 (Hough, 1980: 61). When Brezhnev died in November 1982, twelve full Politburo members remained (at least temporarily); seven were over seventy years of age (Brown, 1983: 26).

Similarly low turnover rates, as well as parallel aging patterns, emerged at lower levels as a result of "stability of cadres." In the C.P.S.U. Central Committee, membership in which defines the true power elite in the Soviet Union, low replacement rates provided further evidence of the "faith" Brezhnev placed in these individuals. The rates of reelection for the living full members of the Central Committee at each of the C.P.S.U. Congresses during the Brezhnev era attest to the nature of the policy. As Table 5.1 reveals, Brezhnev's Central Committees retained a much higher degree of continuity than either Khrushchev's or Gorbachev's. The 1971 Central Committee membership reflected an 81 percent reelection rate of members of the 1966 Central Committee. Indeed, a full 61 percent of the voting members elected into Khrushchev's final Central Committee in 1961 still alive in 1971 were reelected into Brezhnev's second "reconstructed" Central Committee (Hough, 1976: 3).[3] This trend continued: The 1976 Central Committee reelected 89 percent of the living full members of the 1971 Central Committee, and 89 percent of these members, if still alive five years later, were reelected in 1981. Indeed, if one controls for the "automatic" turnover of the worker and peasant representatives, these figures would be even higher.

As a result of these extremely high reelection rates, the age structure of the Central Committee followed that of the Politburo. The average Central Committee member elected at Khrushchev's last Party Congress in

Table 5.1
Central Committee Reelection Rates, 1961–1986

Congress	(Year)	Living Full Members Reelected (%)
22nd	(1961)	54
23rd	(1966)	76
24th	(1971)	81
25th	(1976)	89
26th	(1981)	89
27th	(1986)	60

1961 was fifty-two years of age. Those identical elite elected at Brezhnev's final Congress (26th) in 1981 averaged sixty-two years of age. These phenomena have led Jerry F. Hough to remark, "one could say that Central Committee membership in the Brezhnev era almost became a near-life peerage—something that one would normally retain until one died or was forced to retire for reasons of health" (1982b: 47).

The continuance of such a personnel policy for almost two decades has had dramatic implications on the governance of the Soviet Union. In reviewing briefly below the impact that "stability of cadres" has had on Soviet political life, it becomes clear that the cadres policy of Brezhnev's successors must be viewed, first and foremost, as a series of responses to the problems it created. That is, just as Brezhnev's personnel policy was a conservative reaction to the radical policy of his predecessor Khrushchev, those of Andropov and Gorbachev must be seen as a more bold response to *their* predecessor, Brezhnev.

The "stability of cadres" policy engendered both positive and negative effects for the Soviet system. In fact, much of the negative aspect of the policy can be seen as the long-term consequences of its short-term benefits.

"Stability of cadres" enhanced the stability of the Soviet national leadership in a variety of ways. First, it limited the "potentially destabilizing competition over power and patronage within the elite" (Lapidus, 1977: 35). In effect, it depoliticized cadres policy to such an extent that, according to Robert Blackwell, "cadres policy has not been a major weapon of political combat since Khrushchev . . ." (1979: 38).

This depoliticization of Soviet personnel policy, moreover, spilled over into other areas as well. "Stability of cadres" can be seen as an instrumental aspect of a more general and consistent leadership approach:

[The Brezhnev leadership's] deliberate use of depoliticization as a strategy for the management of economic and social change . . . , the effort to play down, if not remove from public view altogether, the ideological and conflict-provoking aspects of policy-formation and intra-elite relations contrasts sharply with what was a quintessential feature of Soviet political life until recently (Lapidus, 1977: 26).

Because of the extended tenures of most responsible positions during "stability of cadres," the Brezhnev period witnessed an increase in the functional specialization of its party and state cadres. Since movement among a variety of functional posts was, by design, curtailed by the cadres policy, the development of more "generalist" skills was discouraged. Cadres' functional skills, as a result, became more compartmentalized and, to a degree, more stable and rational in the process (Mitchell, 1982: 592–94; Rigby, 1978a: 22).

A third positive effect of the cadres policy adopted by Brezhnev concerns the regularization of local mobility patterns. While Khrushchev was implementing a policy of increased geographic "circulation" of elites, Brezhnev very early in his tenure advocated the regularized, if more lethargic, mobility patterns. More officials were promoted locally, from within the same organization or geographic region (Rigby, 1978: 13). As Brezhnev himself stated at the 1971 24th Party Congress, "the Central Committee has pursued a consistent policy of promoting local personnel; people have been promoted to these posts [Republic party secretaries, obkom and kraikom first secretaries] from the centre only in exceptional circumstances" (*XXIV S"ezd, stenograficheskii otchet,* vol. I, p. 124). Again, Brezhnev's goal was to establish continuity in leadership, sensitivity to local conditions, and increased regularization of the patterns of cadre mobility—all relatively lacking under Khrushchev where various elites were "parachuted" into posts from without.

Despite these significant benefits of "stability of cadres," the Brezhnev cadres policy, after eighteen years of rather consistent application, seriously jeopardized the long-term interests of the Soviet system. Many of its negative aspects combined to emasculate the Soviet leadership at all levels and engendered the general economic and social malaise that was inherited by Brezhnev's successors.

The most obvious problem caused by Brezhnev's conservative cadres policy, and one chronicled above, was the consistent aging of the elite. By the early 1980s and especially at the higher echelons of the party and government apparatuses, the Soviet leadership resembled a "gerontocracy" that lacked not only the will but the physical wherewithal to implement the needed reforms in the system. Soviet society became moribund as the inner core of the Soviet leadership became feeble, hospitalized, and died one by one. While these key officials experienced their extended illnesses, the apparatuses that they governed became even more immobilized and demoralized. The society came to reflect its leaders—during the last half-decade of the Brezhnev era the entire Soviet system lost whatever dynamic element it theretofore possessed.

The elite aging phenomenon infected other aspects of the political system. The inhibition upon cadre advancement not only divided the elite into distinct and competing age cohorts—the "generation gap" in the elite (Hough, 1980)—but engendered the significant resentment of lower-level cadres who, despite extended experience and advancing age, could not move up the political-administrative ladder (Rigby, 1978a: 5). The regional party bosses, once considered to be in "stepping stone" positions ready for promotion to the center, found themselves instead in dead-end jobs. Some 30 percent of the regional party first secretaries of the Brezhnev generation either died in that post, or retired from it out of active political life (see Chapter 4). Life in the Soviet republics as a result became increasingly isolated from national politics as the influx of personnel (especially non-Russians) into central leadership posts became increasingly restricted (Mitchell, 1982; John H. Miller, 1977).

At the systemic level, the Brezhnev leadership, at least implicitly, accepted and paid the price of system immobilism for the achievement and advancement of depoliticization (Mitchell, 1982: 591). As Thomas H. Rigby has put it:

A "normal" Soviet rate of turnover in senior posts would place extreme strains on an oligarchy concerned to ensure that such appointments do not allow one of their number to acquire too much patronage strength. The solution adopted by the oligarchy has been to cut back turnover well below the "normal" Soviet level, indeed to a level that appears exceptionally modest by any standard. . . . For [this] attempt to stabilize the oligarchy by a system of "mutual control," and certain of the particular devices employed to this end, produce—perhaps inevitably—some serious side-effects, which of their nature seem bound to become more acute as time goes on (1970: 179, 190–191).

At this level of analysis, these "serious side-effects" predicted by Rigby took the form of the ossification of the policies governing the Soviet system. The institutionally-entrenched and aging elite of the late Brezhnev period were unable to alter policy to confront the contemporary problems of state. While the tradeoff agreed to back in the mid-sixties produced the leadership consensus that marked the Brezhnev period, the dictates of the actuarial tables ensured that as the long-time leaders died off, the carefully-built consensus would break down. Thus, while the "stability of cadres" policy was successful as a strategy of consensus-building through the enlistment and maintenance of key political support systems, it must be regarded as a failure as a strategy for long-term policy innovations and creative and flexible governance. Indeed, this lack of policy innovation and general systemic immobilism must be considered the main legacy of the Brezhnev era. It is against this inheritance that Brezhnev's heirs have been inveighing.

REGIONAL CADRES POLICY IN THE POST-BREZHNEV PERIOD

Regional cadres policy in the post-Brezhnev Soviet Union more closely resembles that of the Khrushchev period than that of the 1965–1982 period. In the first 53 months after the death of Brezhnev in November 1982, 107 obkom first secretaries were replaced—a rate of one every two weeks. By the end of March 1987, only thirty-five (27.1 percent) obkom first secretaries named by Brezhnev were still in that office. This pace of elite turnover at the obkom tier is roughly double the turnover rate associated with Brezhnev's "Stability of Cadres," which produced only one replacement per month in this elite category (Blackwell, 1979: 34). Indeed, the overall trend since Brezhnev's death is only slightly below the frantic cadres policy established by Khrushchev; in fact, Gorbachev's pace of replenishing the tier of obkom first secretaries has to date significantly outpaced even Khrushchev's effort. Table 5.2 provides a comparison of elite turnover rates within this important party tier.

The data indicate the rigorous approach to cadres policy adopted by both Andropov (thirty-two first secretaries replaced in sixteen months) and Gorbachev (sixty-five first secretaries replaced in his first twenty-five months as general secretary), as well as the cadres policy reversal under Brezhnev's ally Chernenko. Only ten obkom first secretaries were replaced in the twelve months during which Chernenko was general secretary. It is worth noting, moreover, that eight of these ten changes occurred in January and February 1985, when Chernenko was effectively removed from his leadership post during the final stages of his terminal illness. Almost certainly these changes were effected by Gorbachev, already running the day-to-day affairs of the party. Accepting this premise, Chernenko's cadres policy was, in effect, to do as little as possible to the obkom leadership posts. If we attribute these changes to Gorbachev, his regional cadres replacement rate rises somewhat, to 2.81 changes per month.

However, a word of caution must be raised against the assumption that changing people has changed expectations. The "stability of cadres" policy created an expectation among the elites at all levels that they had the right to a post for life unless they committed a serious blunder. It is far from clear whether Gorbachev's cadres policy has been able to weaken this expectation in any real sense. Indeed, the evidence of certain Central

Table 5.2
Elite Turnover among Obkom First Secretaries
by Regime

Regime	Mean Changes/Month	Mean Changes/Year
Khrushchev	2.25	27
Brezhnev	1.08	13
Andropov	2.00	24
Chernenko	0.83	10
Gorbachev	2.60	31

Committee members maintaining their seats even after losing the substantive post that merited their election seems to indicate that this elite expectation is still quite strong.

Regional cadres policy under Brezhnev's heirs has been, with one possible exception, rather evenly applied through each of the eight union republics and the oblast structure. Proportionally, each republic has experienced a rather appropriate number of replacements among their obkom first secretaries. Only the regional party bosses of the Ukrainian party apparatus have seemingly experienced disproportionately fewer changes at this tier. Table 5.3 reveals that, when comparing the pace of elite turnover with the number of party organizations within these eight republics, the cadres policy of the post-Brezhnev period has been, with the possible exception of the Ukrainian SSR, evenly distributed throughout the system.

Table 5.3
Regional Elite Turnover by Republic

SSR	Obkomy (#)	% of Total	Turnover (#)	% of Total
RSFSR	55	42.6	46	42.9
Ukrainian	25	19.4	15	14.0
Kazakh	19	14.7	16	15.0
Uzbek	12	9.3	12	11.2
Belorussian	6	4.7	6	5.6
Turkmen	5	3.9	4	3.7
Kirgiz	4	3.1	4	3.7
Tadzhik	3	2.3	4	3.7
	129		107	

Examined from a different perspective, under Gorbachev the Ukrainian republic has experienced disproportionately fewer personnel changes, defined in terms of the number of Ukrainian elites replaced as a percentage of the total number of elites replaced, than was the case under Andropov. Table 5.4 reveals that less than 10 percent of the sixty-five changes in the obkom elite effected by Gorbachev through the first quarter of 1987 involved elites governing Ukrainian regional party units. Even if it is assumed that Gorbachev was responsible for the rash of obkom changes during the final two months of the Chernenko interregnum (January–February 1985), during which time eight obkom first secretaries were replaced (only two of whom were from the Ukrainian party apparatus), Gorbachev's cadres policy attention toward the Ukraine would still be low, at less than 11 percent of the total. The Ukrainian party apparatus, then, has received approximately half the cadres policy attention than it did under Andropov and Chernenko. As a result, there has been a less significant turnover among the regional elites of the Ukrainian party structure. Indeed, of the twenty-five Ukrainian obkom first secretary incumbents in early April 1987 (fifty-three months after Brezhnev's death), thirteen were holdover Brezhnev appointees.[4]

Despite the overall rapid pace of regional elite turnover established by Brezhnev's heirs, the mean age of newly appointed first secretaries continues to be quite high. Indeed, as Table 5.5 shows, the post-Brezhnev leaders have continued the established trend of appointing increasingly older cadres to this regional party leadership position. The mean age at the time of appointment for obkom first secretaries of the post-Brezhnev era is 52.6 years, 4.5 years older than the Brezhnev regional elite, and almost six full years older than those placed by Khrushchev.

Viewed from another perspective, this increasing entry age of the regional party elite is even more striking. Stalin's obkom first secretaries were, in 98 percent of the cases, less than fifty years old at the time of their appointment. Presently, this figure is approximately 12 percent of the cases. Indeed, even in the "reformist" post-Brezhnev era, over three-quarters (77.8 percent) of the newly-appointed obkom first secretaries entered their posts beyond their fiftieth birthdays. However, this trend may be, and has been since the death of Brezhnev, counteracted to some degree by the maintenance of relatively shorter obkom tenures. As noted above, both Andropov and Gorbachev have employed Khrushchevian turnover rates in their respective regional cadres policies.

Miller (1983) examined 208 transfer dyads involving the naming of new obkom first secretaries during the Khrushchev and Brezhnev periods. His research established that in 40.4 percent (n = 84) of these cases, the new obkom first secretary left a previously-held obkom first secretaryship in a different oblast in order to assume his new obkom posi-

Table 5.4
Regional Cadres Policy Attention
by Republic and Regime

SSR	Andropov #	(%)	Chernenko #	(%)	Gorbachev #	(%)
RSFSR	14	(43.7)	3	(30.0)	29	(44.6)
Ukrainian	7	(21.9)	2	(20.0)	6	(9.2)
Kazakh	3	(9.4)	4	(40.0)	9	(13.8)
Uzbek	4	(12.5)	1	(10.0)	7	(10.8)
Belorussian	2	(6.2)	0	(0.0)	4	(6.2)
Turkmen	0	(0.0)	0	(0.0)	4	(6.2)
Kirgiz	0	(0.0)	0	(0.0)	4	(6.2)
Tadzhik	2	(6.2)	0	(0.0)	2	(3.1)
	32		10		65	

tion. That is, the primary feeder of individuals into obkom first secretaryships during this time frame was that of a different obkom first secretaryship. Table 5.6 reveals the most frequent transfers[5] involving the naming of new obkom leadership incumbents during these two regimes. The evidence indicates the top seven feeder posts into the regional first secretary slot and reveals the likelihood of these dyadic transfers.

Under Khrushchev and Brezhnev, of the seven most frequent transfer dyads, 82.7 percent were a transfer from the regional level, either from the party or the government apparatus. The remaining frequent transfers were individuals whose prior responsibilities were at the union republic level (17.3 percent). Appointments from the central party apparatus were

Table 5.5
Mean Age at Appointment of
Obkom First Secretaries by Regime

Regime	Mean Age at Appointment	% of Appointees 50 Years or Older
Stalin (n=139)	40.8	2.1
Khrushchev (n=245)	46.5	32.6
Brezhnev (n=186)	48.1	39.8
Andropov (n=29)	51.7	69.0
Chernenko (n=8)	53.6	87.5
Gorbachev (n=17)	53.5	88.2

Table 5.6
Most Frequent Feeder Posts to Obkom First Secretaryships
under Khrushchev and Brezhnev

Feeder Post	#	%	Cumulative %
1. Obkom First Secretary	84	40.4	40.4
2. Obkom Second Secretary	37	17.8	58.2
3. Oblispolkom Chairman	28	13.5	71.7
4. Obkom Secretary	23	11.0	82.7
5. Republic CC Secretary	14	6.7	89.4
6. Republic CC Dept. Head	12	5.8	95.2
7. Republic Minister	10	4.8	100.0

relatively rare, as were those involving the all-union government apparatus.

Of the 107 transfers to the post of obkom first secretary between December 1982 and March 1987, the prior position of the new incumbent is identifiable in ninety-three cases. The data indicate that some significant changes in the feeder positions into the obkom first secretaryship have taken place since the death of Brezhnev. Table 5.7 shows the obkom leadership feeder posts of the post-Brezhnev period and reveals several new transfer dyads of significance.

The likelihood of the obkom first secretary-obkom first secretary transfer, once quite prevalent, has been less frequent in the post-Brezhnev period. In the prior period, this dyad was, by more than two to one over the second-most frequent dyad, easily the most likely transfer pattern. In the later period, it ranks as the fourth most likely dyad, constituting less than 10 percent of the total transfers.

Over the past five years or so, three transfer dyads have become more predominant in the naming of new obkom first secretaries. First, the oblispolkom chairman-obkom first secretary dyad has been the most prevalent, constituting almost one in five transfers. Interestingly, in eight of the eighteen dyads of this type, the new obkom first secretary was named from a *different* oblast altogether. Ten regional government chairmen stayed in their original oblast for their new party boss assignment.

A second rather significant transfer dyad involves the feeder position of C.P.S.U. central committee inspector. The second-most frequent transfer feeder (n = 16) accounts for approximately 17 percent of the new obkom first secretaries. This feeder post was not among the top seven such posts listed by Miller for the Khrushchev and Brezhnev periods, but it has been quite significant since 1983. Indeed, Table 5.8 shows that this

Table 5.7
Feeder Posts to Obkom First Secretaryships
in the Post-Brezhnev Period (n = 93)

Feeder Post	#	%	Cumulative %
1. Oblispolkom Chairman	18	19.4	19.4
2. Inspector, CC CPSU	16	17.2	36.6
3. Obkom Second Secretary	15	16.1	52.7
4. Obkom First Secretary	9	9.7	62.4
5. Secretary, Union Republic CC	5	5.4	67.8
Minister, Union Republic CofM	5	5.4	73.2
7. Obkom Secretary	3	3.2	76.4
Raikom First Secretary	3	3.2	79.6
Dep Head of CPSU CC Dept.	3	3.2	82.8
Oblispolkom First Deputy Chairman	3	3.2	86.0
11. Minister, USSR CofM	2	2.1	88.1
Gorkom First Secretary	2	2.1	90.2
13. Head of Union Republic CC Dept.	1	1.1	91.3
Head of USSR CofM Dept.	1	1.1	92.4
Head of Union Republic CofM Dept.	1	1.1	93.5
Gorispolkom Chairman	1	1.1	94.6
Secretary, Union Republic Komsomol	1	1.1	95.7
Deputy Minister, USSR CofM	1	1.1	96.8
Head of CC CPSU Section	1	1.1	97.9
Chairman, Union Republic People's Control Committee	1	1.1	99.0
First Deputy Head of CC CPSU Dept.	1	1.1	100.1

transfer dyad has been a favorite of Mikhail Gorbachev, who accounts for thirteen of the sixteen such dyads.

The third significant feeder post to the obkom first secretaryship in the post-Brezhnev period has been the traditionally strong feeder of the obkom second secretary. In fifteen of the ninety-three identifiable transfer dyads, the new obkom first secretary was previously an obkom second secretary. In 60 percent of these fifteen cases, the transfer was from within the same oblast party committee; in six cases, the transfer involved two different obkomy. Each of these three major transfer feeder posts (oblispolkom chairman, C.P.S.U. Central Committee inspector, and obkom second secretary) account for over 10 percent of the total transfers involving new obkom first secretaries. Combined, they constitute almost 53 percent of the total. Each dyad, moreover, is more likely to occur than the once most frequent dyad of the Khrushchev and Brezhnev periods.

Several other transfers merit separate consideration. Six promotions to the obkom first secretaryship came from significantly lower levels. In three cases, a raikom first secretary was elevated to the regional party leadership post, twice a gorkom first secretary was so moved, and finally

Table 5.8
Feeder Posts to Obkom First Secretaryships
in the Post-Brezhnev Period by Regime (n = 93)

Feeder Post	#	Andr.	Chern.	Gorb.
1. Oblispolkom Chairman	18	4	2	12
2. Inspector, CC CPSU	16	2	1	13
3. Obkom Second Secretary	15	9	1	5
4. Obkom First Secretary	9	1	4	4
5. Secretary, Union Republic CC	5	1	1	3
Minister, Union Republic CofM	5	3	1	1
7. Obkom Secretary	3	2	–	1
Raikom First Secretary	3	–	–	3
Dep Head of CPSU CC Dept.	3	–	–	3
Oblispolkom First Deputy Chairman	3	–	–	3
11. Minister, USSR CofM	2	–	–	2
Gorkom First Secretary	2	1	–	1
13. Head of Union Republic CC Dept.	1	–	–	1
Head of USSR CofM Dept.	1	1	–	–
Head of Union Republic CofM Dept.	1	–	–	1
Gorispolkom Chairman	1	1	–	–
Secretary, Union Republic Komsomol	1	1	–	–
Deputy Minister, USSR CofM	1	–	–	1
Head of CC CPSU Section	1	–	–	1
Chairman, Union Republic People's Control Committee	1	1	–	–
First Deputy Head of CC CPSU Dept.	1	–	–	1
	93	27	10	56

a gorispolkom chairman was elevated. Interestingly, five of these six transfers were effected by Gorbachev, and all recipient obkomy were within non-Slavic republics. The Kazakh capital city Alma Ata lost both its party boss and its chief government official to Kazakh obkom posts. A third transfer is noteworthy because it involved the naming of a Russian raikom first secretary from Leningrad oblast to an obkom first secretaryship in Uzbekistan. The specific importance of the region involved (Navoi), noted for its newly discovered natural gas reserves, may account for this interest on the part of the central leadership.[6]

Miller in addition categorized 147 transfer dyads involving the transfer of incumbent obkom first secretaries out of their posts and into a different position during the Khrushchev and Brezhnev regimes (1983: 68–72). He identified six primary recipient posts of these individuals leaving the obkom post. In eighty-four cases (57.1 percent) the recipient post of an exiting obkom first secretary during this time was that of a different obkom first secretaryship. This transfer dyad is by far the most ubiquitous dyad of those identified (see Table 5.9).

Table 5.9
**Most Frequent Recipient Posts from Obkom First Secretaryships
under Khrushchev and Brezhnev**

Recipient Post	#	%	Cumulative %
1. Obkom First Secretary	84	57.1	57.1
2. Secretary, Union Republic CC	23	15.7	72.8
3. Minister, Union Republic CofM	12	8.2	81.0
4. Oblispolkom Chairman	10	6.8	87.8
5. Secretary, CC CPSU	9	6.1	93.9
6. Chairman, Union Republic CofM	9	6.1	100.0

In twenty-three of the observed cases (15.7 percent) the recipient post was a union republic-level Central Committee secretaryship. Approximately half again as many (n = 12) were elevated to a union republic-level minister post. Three even rarer recipient posts identified by Miller were (1) chairman of an oblispolkom, (2) C.P.S.U. Central Committee secretary, and (3) chairman of a union republic council of ministers.

Interestingly, Miller found a close approximation of government-based *feeder* posts (18.3 percent of the observed cases) and government-based *recipient* posts (21.1 percent). In other words, in looking at both feeder and recipient posts revolving around the obkom first secretaryship, Miller found that in over 80 percent of the total cases, the dyads entailed party-to-party transfers. Finally, only 6.1 percent (n = 9) of the observed cases in the Miller study involved obkom first secretary elevations to the Center; the overwhelming majority were intra-Republic transfers.

Of the 107 transfers that removed an obkom first secretary between December 1982 and March 1987, the recipient post of the departing regional elite is identifiable in ninety-one cases. The evidence indicates several substantive trends that distinguish the post-Brezhnev years from those of the prior periods. Table 5.10 shows the recipient posts of transferred obkom first secretaries in the post-Brezhnev period.

The most frequent result of a transfer out of the post of obkom first secretary in the post-Brezhnev period has been retirement from active political life. Forty-three holders of the ninety-one (47.2 percent) identifiable recipient positions were retired; if one adds the single instance of the obkom first secretary dying in office, it is found that approximately half of the obkom first secretaries who have left this post since the death of Brezhnev have not received other substantive political posts. Indeed, this percentage might be somewhat greater if all 107 transfer results were known. It stands to reason that if substantive posts were assigned to these sixteen transferred obkom first secretaries, these posts would be known. The fact that no subsequent post assignment was mentioned in the Soviet

Table 5.10
Recipient Posts from Obkom First Secretaryships
in the Post-Brezhnev Period (n = 91)

Recipient Post	#	%	Cumulative %
1. Retired	43	47.2	47.2
2. Obkom First Secretary	9	9.9	57.1
3. Secretary, CC CPSU	4	4.4	61.5
4. Secretary, Union Republic CC	3	3.3	64.8
Chairman, Union Republic CofM	3	3.3	68.1
6. First Secretary, Union Republic CC	2	2.2	70.3
First Dep Chairman, Union Republic CofM	2	2.2	72.5
Minister, USSR CofM	2	2.2	74.7
Dep Chairman, USSR State Committee	2	2.2	76.9
Dep Chairman, USSR People's Control Cmtte	2	2.2	79.1
Head, CC CPSU Department	2	2.2	81.3
Head, Union Republic CC Department	2	2.2	83.5
USSR Ambassador	2	2.2	85.7
14. Dep Chairman, Union Republic CofM	1	1.1	86.8
Dep Chairman, USSR CofM	1	1.1	87.9
First Dep Chairman, USSR CofM	1	1.1	89.0
Member, Oblispolkom	1	1.1	90.1
First Dep Chairman, USSR State Committee	1	1.1	91.2
Member, CPSU Party Control Committee	1	1.1	92.3
First Dep Head, Union Republic Department	1	1.1	93.4
Chairman, USSR People's Control Committee	1	1.1	94.5
Chair, Union Republic Supreme Soviet	1	1.1	95.6
First Deputy Minister, USSR CofM	1	1.1	96.7
Inspector, CPSU CC	1	1.1	97.8
Chairman, Union Republic State Committee	1	1.1	98.9
Deceased	1	1.1	100.0

press for the sixteen erstwhile regional bosses, and that no assignments were found to have been given subsequent to the date of "transfer," seems to indicate that the center had no prearranged transfer in mind, save that the incumbent obkom first secretary be removed.

The likelihood of party-government crossover in post transfers differs somewhat from the expectations raised by Miller's analysis. Whereas in the cases cited by Miller government-party (18.3 percent) and party-government (21.1 percent) transfers involving the obkom post were of relatively modest probability, the data show that in the post-Brezhnev period a greater probability exists for these two transfers. Thirty-two of the ninety-three feeder posts (34.4 percent) were government posts and nineteen of the recipient posts (40.4 percent, if indeed there *was* a recipient post) were in the government apparatus. In a word, the post-Brezhnev Soviet leadership has employed a regional cadres policy that has entailed a greater degree of apparatus crossover than its predecessor regimes.

Miller identifies only nine of the observed transfers (6.1 percent) of the

Khrushchev/Brezhnev era where an obkom first secretary was moved to a post in the all-union center apparatuses. By any measure, the probability of regional elites being moved to the center is significantly higher in the post-Brezhnev Soviet Union. Of the ninety-one identified recipient posts, twenty-one (23.1 percent) have been in either the central government or party structure. If the analysis controls for the retirement and death of obkom first secretaries, then a full 44.7 percent of these obkom first secretaries who were given substantive assignments after their obkom tenures were given these assignments in the central apparatuses.

Table 5.11 reveals that these three major trends have been applied rather consistently throughout the post-Brezhnev period by its three C.P.S.U. general secretaries. First, the data with respect to the rate of retirement indicate that for each of the three general secretaries, approximately half of the replaced obkom first secretaries were retired. The actual rates under Andropov, Chernenko, and Gorbachev (47.8, 50.0, and 46.6 percent, respectively) reveal not only the relative lack of variance in this aspect of the cadres policy, but also attest to the generalized aging pattern of the regional elite.

Second, the dyadic party-government crossover rates that are revealed by the transfer data also depict an impressive level of consistency. Of the thirty-nine transfer dyads effected by Andropov, 35.9 percent involved apparatus crossover. The comparable figures for Chernenko (26.7 percent) and Gorbachev (38.4 percent) reflect this general consistency. This pattern seems even more established when separately analyzing the feeder crossovers (33.3, 30.0, and 35.7 percent, respectively) and recipient crossovers (41.7, 20.0, and 43.4 percent, respectively) for General Secretaries Andropov, Chernenko, and Gorbachev. If the relatively unreliable (due to a small number of cases) figures representing the Chernenko regime are controlled for, the level of consistency is further heightened. The feeder dyad crossovers tend to occur less frequently (33.3, 35.7 percent) than do the recipient dyad crossovers (41.7, 43.3 percent), but little variance exists *within* the categories under Andropov and Gorbachev.

Third, somewhat less consistency has marked the probability of post-Brezhnev recipient posts of obkom first secretaries being at the all-union government or central party levels. The probabilities of receiving a position at the center (assuming a subsequent substantive post *was* assigned) under Andropov (58.3 percent), Chernenko (20.0 percent), and Gorbachev (43.3 percent) show some significant variance. However, for the post-Brezhnev period as a whole, this figure (44.7 percent) or the related figure that includes those retired out of the obkom tier (23.1 percent) still outdistances the comparable phenomena of the prior period, as detailed by Miller (1983).

Table 5.11
Recipient Posts from Obkom First Secretaryships
in the Post-Brezhnev Period by Regime (n = 91)

Recipient Post	#	Andr.	Chern.	Gorb.
1. Retired	43	11	5	27
2. Obkom First Secretary	9	1	4	4
3. Secretary, CC CPSU	4	2	–	2
4. Secretary, Union Republic CC	3	–	–	3
Chairman, Union Republic CofM	3	1	–	2
6. First Secretary, Union Republic CC	2	–	–	2
First Dep Chairman, Union Republic CofM	2	1	–	1
Minister, USSR CofM	2	–	–	2
Dep Chairman, USSR State Committee	2	–	–	2
Dep Chairman, USSR People's Control Cmtte	2	2	–	–
Head, CC CPSU Department	2	–	–	2
Head, Union Republic CC Department	2	–	–	2
USSR Ambassador	2	1	1	–
14. Dep Chairman, Union Republic CofM	1	–	–	1
Dep Chairman, USSR CofM	1	–	–	1
First Dep Chairman, USSR CofM	1	–	–	1
Member, Oblispolkom	1	1	–	–
First Dep Chairman, USSR State Committee	1	1	–	–
Member, CPSU Party Control Committee	1	1	–	–
First Dep Head, Union Republic Department	1	1	–	–
Chairman, USSR People's Control Committee	1	–	–	1
Chair, Union Republic Supreme Soviet	1	–	–	1
First Deputy Minister, USSR CofM	1	–	–	1
Inspector, CPSU CC	1	–	–	1
Chairman, Union Republic State Committee	1	–	–	1
Deceased	1	–	–	1
	91	23	10	58

Finally, two other figures highlighted by the data deserve mention. First, while it was found that (especially for Gorbachev) the post of C.P.S.U. Central Committee inspector was a primary feeder of the post of obkom first secretary (17.2 percent of all incoming obkom party leaders in the post-Brezhnev period), the likelihood of the reverse transfer dyad, with the Central Committee post being a recipient post, is extremely rare. In only one of the ninety-one observed cases (Absamat Masaliev of Issyk-Kul' obkom, Kirgizia) was an obkom first secretary moved into the post of C.P.S.U. Central Committee inspector.

Second, the obkom elite, despite a high percentage of retirees, has produced regional representatives in several key republic and national political posts in both the government and the party (see Appendix VI). Three union republic premiers, two union republic party first secretaries, two USSR ministers, the first deputy and a deputy chairman of the USSR Council of Ministers, two C.P.S.U. Central Committee department heads, a chairman of the USSR People's Control Committee, and, most impressively, four C.P.S.U. Central Committee secretaries have emerged directly from the obkom tier to these posts in the post-Brezhnev period. This final figure is especially impressive when it is recalled that only seven regional first secretaries entered this politically powerful tier (Politburo or Secretariat) in the entire 1965–1982 period.

It is worth noting in conclusion that thirteen of these sixteen significant transfers were effected by Gorbachev, perhaps signaling a return for the obkom party post of its traditional "stepping-stone to the Center" character—a quality not evident during much of Brezhnev's final years in power.

CONCLUSION

Assessing the prerequisites for reform in the Soviet Union in the Gorbachev era, George W. Breslauer argues that the general secretary

must bring in people who are not only beholden to him for their new jobs but also share his general orientation, who agree with his view that what is needed now is to get the country moving again. He needs people who agree that the country cannot afford to continue a relaxed style of political administration. In many instances these will be individuals with whom Gorbachev has worked in the past and with whom he therefore shares experiences and old-boy ties, and, partly for that reason, shares a common orientation as well. In other instances, he may bring in people whom he knows, through reports of trusted associates, shares his general outlook (1986a: 18).

Clearly at the root of Breslauer's conception of reform's necessities is Gorbachev's cadres policy. Only to the degree that Gorbachev is capable of consolidating his personal authority through this personnel replenishment can his already articulated reform policies of *perestroika* and *glasnost'* take hold.

In like mind, Robert A. D. Ford has identified two major obstacles to serious reform in the Soviet Union. The first barrier is "the immense power of the middle-level and provincial Party officials to resist change." The second obstacle facing Gorbachev is the "strong doubts on the part of the Party leaders about the ideological and political consequences of effective reform" (1984: 1138–1139). Both of these obstacles to reform may be overcome by a rigorous cadres policy that not only replaces the regional party officialdom, but also goes a long way in reconstituting the top political leadership in Moscow. This chapter has chronicled just such a cadres policy.

Yet, it is important to keep in mind that Gorbachev's success in "restructuring" Soviet society will not in the final analysis depend on his cadres policy. While the latter is necessary for the enthusiastic implementation of new policies, it is by no means sufficient for *policy* success. Indeed, the completely successful replenishment of middle-level and national elites, which Gorbachev has to date gone a long way in achieving (Colton, 1986: 82–97), will only provide a relatively objective setting within which Gorbachev's substantive policies might be judged. His own cohorts in key political positions throughout the Soviet system will only allow his policy program for the Soviet future to succeed or fail on its own grounds. Cadres policy is, in a word, an instrumental means to a policy end.

While we may at the present point in history highlight Gorbachev's success in reversing both the stagnation among the Soviet elite and the psychological malaise in Soviet society generally, we are not yet in a position to assess the post-Brezhnev leadership's ability to restructure the Soviet polity and economy along more efficient and more appropriate lines. Given the dictates of the Soviet structure and the relatively narrow range of acceptable alternatives, Gorbachev's success in achieving this "restructuring" of Soviet society will certainly be much more difficult than his success to date in raising societal expectations. While this climate of expectations in many segments of Soviet society seem to support Gorbachev's gambit, it must be remembered that in the past equally powerful forces have proved unable to overcome the rather dominant inertia that governs Soviet politics.

NOTES

1. Other notable members of the Stalin regional cohort are Sergei Kirov, Gennadii Voronov, Petr Shelest, Andrei Zhdanov, and Nikolai Ignatov.

2. The ex-first secretaries who have helped constitute Gorbachev's leadership group (either in the Politburo or the Secretariat) are Gorbachev, Ligachev, Vitalii Vorotnikov, Lev Zaikov, Mikhail Solomentsev, Vladimir Shcherbitskii, Petr Demichev, Vladimir Dolgikh, Boris Yeltsin (forced from the leadership in November 1987), Yurii Solovev, and Vsevolod Murakhovskii.

3. Compare this fact to the following: The 1961 22d Party Congress, convened eight years after the death of Stalin, elected a Central Committee with only two "leftovers" from Stalin's final Central Committee of 1952.

4. Despite the large *number* of changes made, in the early spring of 1987, thirty-five Brezhnev holdovers remained (27.1 percent of the incumbent posts): two in Uzbekistan, two in Turkmenistan, one in Kirgizia, one in Belorussia, three in Kazakhstan, thirteen in the Ukraine, and thirteen in the R.S.F.S.R. As a result, while 107 *secretaries* were replaced, only 94 *obkomy* experienced a change in leadership. Several obkomy, then, experienced multiple leadership turnover since December 1982.

5. Not every transfer involving the naming of a new obkom first secretary is listed by Miller. Only the "most frequent transfers" are listed.

6. See Appendix VI for the list of all transfer dyads in the post-Brezhnev period.

REFERENCES

Blackwell, Robert E., Jr. 1979. "Cadres Policy in the Brezhnev Era," *Problems of Communism* (March–April 1979): 29–42.

Breslauer, George W. "The Nature of Soviet Politics and the Gorbachev Leadership," pp. 11–30 in Alexander Dallin and Condoleeza Rice, eds. *The Gorbachev Era*. Stanford, Cal.: Stanford Alumni Association, 1986.

———. *Khrushchev and Brezhnev as Leaders: Building Authority in Soviet Politics*. London: George Allen and Unwin, 1982.

Brown, Archie. "Andropov: Discipline *and* Reform?", *Problems of Communism*, (January–February 1983): 18–31.

Colton, Timothy J. *The Dilemma of Reform in the Soviet Union*, rev. and enlarged ed. New York: Council on Foreign Relations, 1986.

Dallin, Alexander, and Condoleeza Rice, eds. *The Gorbachev Era*. Stanford, Cal.: Stanford Alumni Association, 1986.

Ford, Robert A. D. "The Soviet Union: The Next Decade," *Foreign Affairs* 62, no. 5 (Summer 1984): 1132–1144.

Harasymiw, Bohdan. *Political Elite Recruitment in the Soviet Union*. New York: St. Martin's Press, 1984.

———. "Conclusion: Some Theoretical Considerations on Advancement within the Political Elite in Soviet-style Systems, pp. 229–242 in T. H. Rigby and Bohdan Harasymiw, eds. *Leadership Selection and Patron-Client Relations in the USSR and Yugoslavia*. London: George Allen and Unwin, 1983.

Hill, Ronald J., and Peter Frank. *The Soviet Communist Party*, 3d ed. Boston: Allen and Unwin, 1986.

Hodnett, Grey. "Succession Contingencies in the Soviet Union," *Problems of Communism* (March–April 1975): 1–21.

Hough, Jerry F. "Soviet Succession: Issues and Personalities," *Problems of Communism* (September–October 1982): 20–40.

———. "Changes in Soviet Elite Composition," pp. 39–64 in Seweryn Bialer and Thane Gustafson, eds. *Russia at the Crossroads: The 26th Congress of the CPSU*. London: George Allen and Unwin, 1982.

———. "The Generation Gap and the Soviet Succession," *Problems of Communism* (July–August 1979): 1–16.

———. "The Brezhnev Era: The Man and the System," *Problems of Communism* (March–April 1976): 1–17.

Lapidus, Gail Warshofsky. "The Brezhnev Regime and Directed Social Change: Depoliticization as Political Strategy," pp. 26–38 in Alexander Dallin, ed., *The Twenty-fifth Congress of the CPSU: Assessment and Context*. Stanford, Cal.: Hoover Institution Press, 1977.

Miller, John. "Nomenklatura: Check on Localism?," pp. 62–97 in T. H. Rigby and Bohdan Harasymiw, eds. *Leadership Selection and Patron–Client Rela-*

tions in the USSR and Yugoslavia. London: George Allen and Unwin, 1983.

Miller, John H. "Cadres Policy in the Nationality Areas: Recruitment of CPSU First and Second Secretaries in Non-Russian Republics of the USSR," *Soviet Studies* 29, no. 1 (January 1977): 3–36.

Mitchell, R. Judson. "Immobilism, Depoliticization, and the Emerging Soviet Elite," *Orbis* (Fall 1982): 591–610.

Moses, Joel C. "Functional Career Specialization in Soviet Regional Elite Recruitment," pp. 15–61 in T. H. Rigby and Bohdan Harasymiw, eds. *Leadership Selection and Patron-Client Relations in the USSR and Yugoslavia.* London: George Allen and Unwin, 1983.

Rigby, T. H. "How the Obkom Secretary was Tempered," *Problems of Communism* (March–April 1980): 57–63.

_____. "The Soviet Regional Leadership: The Brezhnev Generation," *Slavic Review* 37, no. 1 (March 1978): 1–24.

_____. "The Soviet Leadership: Towards a Self-Stabilizing Oligarchy?" *Soviet Studies* 22, no. 2 (October 1970): 167–191.

Rigby, T. H., and Bohdan Harasymiw, eds. *Leadership Selection and Patron-Client Relations in the USSR and Yugoslavia.* London: George Allen and Unwin, 1983.

Rush, Myron. "Succeeding Brezhnev," *Problems of Communism* (January–February 1983): 2–7.

Schapiro, Leonard. *The Communist Party of the Soviet Union.* New York: Random House, 1959.

Urban, Michael E. "The Structure of Elite Circulation in the Belorussian Republic: Centralization, Regionalism and Patronage." Paper presented to the eighteenth national convention of the American Association for the Advancement of Slavic Studies, New Orleans, Lou., November 20–23, 1986.

SUMMARY AND CONCLUSIONS

It is necessary at the end of this study to reemphasize the philosophical orientation that supports the executed research. The approach that has been embraced is decidedly structural in its focus on the phenomenon under study; that is, it seeks to explain elite mobility patterns in the Soviet Union by reference to the structure of the Soviet political system that supports that elite stratum.

Such an approach presupposes that a society and economy with the size and sophistication of the Soviet Union will support a political system that meets what Barrington Moore called the system's "minimum technical requirements." He writes, "some degree of clarity and regularity in the allocation of rights, duties, and functions is necessary for the continuation of any administrative system"—even that of the Soviet Union (Moore, 1954: 12, 188). The decline of totalitarianism in the USSR and the maintenance of a complex political system in a technocratic age by definition implies "a heavy reduction of emphasis on the power of the dictator and its replacement by rational and technical criteria of behavior and organization" (Moore, 1954: 189).

This set of assumptions provides the foundation for the approach to political elite mobility utilized in this study. Elite movement in even a minimumly technocratic social system will be based less on arbitrary forces and more on the rational-technical dictates of the system. There will exist, in a word, a *structure* of opportunity based more or less on rational systemic forces. This study has attempted to explicate key elements of that opportunity structure. That such an approach to the study of Soviet elite mobility is fruitful seems clear. While this effort might best be considered a kind of "exploratory surgery," the results of these efforts surely instill confidence in expanding still further the scope of the study.

The results of the project point clearly to the facts that (a) significant variance exists in the political mobility opportunities Soviet regional party units offer their indigenous elite; (b) this variance of political mobility opportunities is not random or arbitrary, but represents a real "structure" of opportunities; (3) a Soviet regional elite's subsequent career success is *not* greatly determined by an individual background/career characteristic (or set of them); and (4) the single best predictor of career success for a Soviet regional elite is the *structural* characteristic of his base region.

The socioeconomic development variables that are examined in Chapter 3 provide statistically significant indicators of political elite mobility within the Soviet political-administrative system. Indeed, the results of this effort reveal that over 40 percent of the variance in the observed unit mobility scores can be explained by looking at these structural measures. The structural characteristics of the units governed by the elite members under study go a long way in determining the subsequent career mobility patterns of these elites.

Such results should encourage further research into the structure of political opportunities in the Soviet Union. Despite being ignored relative to other approaches in research into Soviet elite mobility, investigations into the more structural aspects of the Soviet system certainly seem warranted. Indeed, investigation into the exact nature of the linkages between Soviet structural characteristics and more general systemic attributes (elite mobility is but one of these attributes) is called for. If the results of this elite mobility study are at all indicative, much can be learned about the nature of the Soviet political system by examining the structural forces that determine that system to a sizable extent.

Chapter 4's examination of individual background and career characteristics of the elite sample reveals the relatively low impact of these variables on political elite mobility. Only approximately 26 percent of the variance in political mobility scores could be explained by reference to these variables. With few exceptions, very little about the subsequent career prospects of obkom first secretaries can be determined by knowing the individual and/or career characteristics of the elite member leading up to the assumption of that regional post. These results serve in effect to emphasize the significance of the structural explanation.

Examined in bivariate and multivariate analyses, several variables that might intuitively seem determinative of elite career patterns are found to be weak in their explanatory power. Statistically insignificant correlations are found to exist between political mobility and such background variables as level of education, age at the assumption of various offices, and tenures in regional party posts. Generally, these findings support the extant literature in this area which speaks to the nature and strength of the linkages between individual and career characteristics, on the one hand, and political mobility patterns, on the other.

Robert Blackwell's conclusion that the prediction of career mobility beyond the obkom post "is not greatly facilitated" (1973b: 9) by knowing these background characteristics finds support in the results of this study. In a word, this study lends further support to the notion that research into such background/career variables is as yet unable to provide very useful knowledge in the area of elite mobility in the Soviet Union. Yet the results encourage further research into this relationship. The results attained in this section of the study exceeded all expectations, such as they were, gleaned from the prior research. To the degree that individual background and career variables can be of use in explicating mobility patterns, their relationship to the level of success in *reaching* the obkom tier in the first place might provide a more fruitful avenue of further research.

Other approaches to the study of mobility, of course, merit attention as well. First among these alternative explanations for the variance in mobility opportunities in the USSR is the so-called performance school. As an approach based on rational-technical criteria for political mobility, the performance school looks to the regional elite's level of success in governing the oblast's social, political, and economic activities as a basis for evaluating (promoting, demoting, and so on) responsible cadres. Moreover, the rational criterion of job performance in evaluating cadres will in all likelihood increase under Gorbachev as the general secretary looks to restructure Soviet society along more rational lines. Unlike the Brezhnev era, when the performance criterion was not universally applied to leading cadres (see Chapter 5), Gorbachev's success in implementing his reform agenda will in large part be determined by the elevation of capable (defined in performance terms) personnel into leading posts. In a sense, the standards for elite mobility in the Soviet Union have changed since the death of Brezhnev; scholarly approaches to the study of elite mobility, therefore, should focus increasing attention on performance variables.

The study of patron–client relations has been a traditional approach to the study of elite movement in many societies, including the Soviet Union. In times of personal regime consolidation, patronage provides a mechanism for the general secretary and the new national leadership group to staff important posts throughout the political-administrative hierarchy with like-minded and loyal followers. The examination of clientelism, therefore, might be called for so as to identify the members of these new political cohorts. However, by their very nature, individual patron–client cohorts are limited in size and tend to be the basis of political mobility patterns only during specific periods. Moreover, in the new Gorbachev era, it is perhaps likely that the performance criterion discussed above will be superimposed upon these patronage networks.

As time passes after the original regime consolidation period (usually marked by rather high turnover rates among elite groups below the Kremlin), idiosyncratic explanations such as those based on clientelism promise to provide increasingly less and the rational-technical explanations promise to provide ever more insight into political elite mobility in the Soviet Union.

The results of this study of regional elite mobility in the Soviet Union point to the necessity of further research into the forces conditioning elite mobility in the USSR. While the results of this investigation are encouraging, they in no way exhaust the topic. If the structural explanation successfully accounts for approximately 40 percent of the variance in measured political mobility scores of a certain number of elites at a certain level of the political-administrative hierarchy of the Soviet Union, then it is obvious that such an explanation fails to account for the majority of this phenomenon even at this particular level of analysis. That the results of this study may be considered significant and novel, despite this seeming weakness, attests to the difficulties and complexities that inhere in the investigation of political elite mobility in the Soviet Union.

APPENDIX I
STEWART'S
POSITIONS, CODES,
AND MOBILITY INDEX

CODE = 9

- *All-Union Party Posts:*
  1st Secretary
  Full Member of Politburo (Presidium)
  Chairman Central Committee Bureau for the RSFSR
- *All-Union Government Posts:*
  President, Chairman of the Presidium of USSR Supreme Soviet
  Chairman of All-Union Council of Ministers

CODE = 8

- *All-Union Party Posts:*
  2nd Secretary and Secretaries of the CPSU
  Candidate Member of Politburo
  Chairman, Party Control Commission
- *All-Union Government Posts:*
  1st Deputy Chairman of All-Union Council of Ministers

CODE = 7

- *All-Union Party Posts:*
  Deputy Chairman Party Control Commission
- *Union-Republic Party Posts:*
  1st Secretary
  1st Deputy Chairman Central Committee Bureau for RSFSR
  Deputy Chairman Central Committee Bureau for RSFSR
- *All-Union Government Posts:*
  Deputy Chairman All-Union Council of Ministers
  Minister of the USSR
  Chairman USSR State Committee or Commission

CODE = 6

- *All-Union Party Posts:*
  Central Committee Department Head
  Editor, Central Party Press Organ

- *Union-Republic Party Posts:*
  2nd Secretary of Republic Central Committee
  Full Member Central Committee Bureau for RSFSR
  Chairman Republic Party-State Control Committee

- *All-Union Government Positions:*
  USSR Ambassador
  Deputy USSR Minister
  Deputy Chairman USSR State Committee or Commission

- *Union-Republic Government Posts:*
  Chairman Presidium Republic Supreme Soviet
  Chairman, First Deputy Chairman RSFSR Council of Ministers
  Chairman, First Deputy Chairman, Ukraine Council of Ministers
  Member, RSFSR or Ukraine Council of Ministers Presidium
  "Significant" RSFSR Minister

CODE = 5

- *Oblast* Party Committee First Secretary

CODE = 4

- *All-Union Party Posts:*
  Chairman Central Auditing Commission
  Central Committee "official" (title not known)
  CC Party Organizer, CC instructor
  "Executive Party Worker"

- *Union-Republic Party Posts:*
  Candidate Member Presidium
  Department Head, Official, Party Organizer,
  Instructor, "Executive Party Worker"
  Deputy Chairman Party-State Control Commission

- *Lower Party Organs Posts:*
  Secretary *oblast* party committee
  Gorkom, Autonomous *oblast, Okrug* first secretary
  Executive Party Worker (level not known)

- *All-Union Government Posts:*
  All not listed above

- *Union-Republic Government Posts:*
  All not listed above
  Oblast Soviet Executive Committee Chairman
  Chairman Council of the National Economy (oblast) (1957–64)

CODE = 3

- 1st Secretary City or Rural District Party Committee
  2nd Secretary, City Party Committee, Autonomous *Oblast,* or Autonomous
      Okrug Party Committee
- *Local Government Posts:*
  Other *oblast* Executive Committee Post
  Chairman City, etc. Soviet Executive Committee Administrative Post
      in Education
  Higher Party School Student
  Director, Head, Chief of Enterprise, *Kombinant,* etc.
  Other *Sovnarkhoz* position not listed above

CODE = 2

- Other Party Post not listed above except in Primary Party Organization
  First Secretary Primary Party Organization
- *Local Government Posts:*
  Chairman City or Rural District Soviet Executive Committee
  Teacher: Elementary through Higher Education

CODE = 1

  Other Primary Party Organization Post
  Other Urban or Rural District Executive Committee Post
  Student

CODE = 0

  Position following *oblast* Party Committee First Secretaryship is Unknown,
      or *obkom* First Secretary removed by retirement, illness, or death.

APPENDIX II
POSITIONS AND CODES AS SCORED ON MOBILITY INDEX

CODE = 18

- *All-Union Party Posts:*
  1st Secretary CC CPSU
  Full Member of Politburo CC CPSU
  Chairman, Bureau for the RSFSR (CC CPSU)
- *All-Union Government Posts:*
  Chairman, Presidium of USSR Supreme Soviet
  Chairman, USSR Council of Ministers

CODE = 16

- *All-Union Party Posts:*
  2nd Secretary/Secretaries of CC CPSU
  Candidate Member of Politburo CC CPSU
  Chairman, Party Control Commission (CC CPSU)
- *All-Union Government Posts:*
  1st Deputy Chairman of USSR Council of Ministers

CODE = 14

- *All-Union Party Posts:*
  Deputy Chairman, Party Control Commission (CC CPSU)
- *Union-Republic Party Posts:*
  1st Secretary (UR CC)
  1st Deputy Chairman, Bureau for RSFSR (UR CC)
  Deputy Chairman, Bureau for RSFSR (UR CC)
- *All-Union Government Posts:*
  Deputy Chairman, USSR Council of Ministers
  Minister of the USSR
  Chairman, USSR State Committee/Commission

CODE = 12

- *All-Union Party Posts:*
  Head of Department, CC CPSU
  Editor, Central Party Press Organ

- *Union-Republic Party Posts:*
  2nd Secretary/Secretaries of CC CP of UR
  Full Member, Bureau for RSFSR (UR CC)
  Full Member, UR Central Committee Politburo
  Chairman, Party-State Control Committee (UR CC)

- *All-Union Government Positions:*
  USSR Ambassador
  Deputy USSR Minister
  Deputy Chairman, USSR State Committee/Commission

- *Union-Republic Government Posts:*
  Chairman, Presidium UR Supreme Soviet
  Chairman, Union Republic Council of Ministers
  Chairman, RSFSR Council of Ministers
  1st Deputy Chairman, RSFSR Council of Ministers
  Chairman, Ukrainian SSR Council of Ministers
  1st Deputy Chairman, Ukrainian SSR Council of Ministers
  Member, Presidium of RSFSR Council of Ministers
  Member, Presidium of Ukrainian SSR Council of Ministers
  "Significant" RSFSR Minister

CODE = 10

- *Regional Party Posts:*
  1st Secretary *oblast* party committee *(obkom)*
  1st Secretary *krai* party committee *(Kraikom)*
  1st Secretary Autonomous Republic (ASSR)

CODE = 8

- *All-Union Party Posts:*
  Chairman, Central Auditing Commission CC CPSU
  Party Organizer, CPSU Central Committee
  Instructor, CPSU Central Committee
  Inspector, CPSU Central Committee
  "Official," CPSU Central Committee
  "Executive Party Worker," CPSU Central Committee

- *Union-Republic Party Posts:*
  Candidate Member, UR Central Committee Politburo
  Head of Department, UR Central Committee
  Party Organizer, UR Central Committee
  Instructor, UR Central Committee
  Inspector, UR Central Committee
  "Official," UR Central Committee

"Executive Party Worker," UR Central Committee
Deputy Chairman, UR Party-State Control Commission

- *Lower Party Organs Posts:*
Secretary, *oblast* party committee *(obkom)*
1st Secretary, *gorod* party committee *(Gorkom)*
1st Secretary, Autonomous *oblast* party committee
1st Secretary, *okrug* party committee
"Executive Party Worker" (level not known)

- *All-Union Government Posts:*
All those not listed above

- *Union-Republic Government Posts:*
Chairman, *oblast* soviet executive committee *(Oblispolkom)*
Chairman, *oblast* Council of the National Economy *(Sovnarkhoz)*

CODE = 6

- *Local Party Posts:*
1st Secretary, *raion* party committee *(Raikom)*
2nd Secretary, *gorod* party committee *(Gorkom)*
2nd Secretary, Autonomous *Oblast* party committee
2nd Secretary, Autonomous *Okrug* party committee

- *Local Government Posts:*
Other *oblast* soviet executive committee posts
Chairman, *gorod* soviet executive committee (Gorispolkom)
Student at Party Higher School
Director (Head/Chief) of enterprise, *kombinant,* etc.
Other *Sovnarkhoz* posts not listed above

CODE = 4

- *Local Party Posts:*
1st Secretary, Primary Party Organization
Other Party posts (above PPO level) not listed above

- *Local Government Posts:*
Chairman, *raion* soviet executive committee *(Raiispolkom)*
Teacher: Elementary through Higher Education

CODE = 2

- *Party/Government Posts:*
Other Primary Party Posts not listed above
Other *raiispolkom* posts not listed above
Student

CODE = 0

- Position following 1st Secretary of *oblast* party committee is
a) unknown

b) retired
c) dismissed
d) removed
e) death

SUPPLEMENTAL SCORES

CODE = 4

- *Party Organs Affiliation:*
  Full Member of Politburo CC CPSU (SIMULTANEOUS)

CODE = 3

- *Party Organs Affiliation:*
  Candidate Member of Politburo CC CPSU (SIMULTANEOUS)

CODE = 2

- *Party Organs Affiliation:*
  Full Member, Central Committee CPSU
  Full Member of Politburo CC CP of Union Republic (SIMULTANEOUS)

- *Government Organs Affiliation:*
  Member, Presidium USSR Supreme Soviet

CODE = 1

- *Party Organs Affiliation:*
  Candidate Member, Central Committee CPSU
  Candidate Member of Politburo CC CP of Union Republic
       (SIMULTANEOUS)

- *Government Organs Affiliation:*
  Member, Presidium Union Republic Supreme Soviet

- These supplemental scores for *party organs* affiliations are normally to be assigned as such:
  1. CC CPSU status is evaluated and assigned *twice*, once at the end of the tenure as *obkom* 1st Secretary, and once at the end of the individual's career. If the subject ends his career as an *obkom* 1st Secretary, the score is assigned only once.
  2. Politburo status (CC CPSU and CC CPUR) which occurs *simultaneous* with another substantive post (e.g., *obkom* 1st Secretary, Chair of UR Council of Ministers, Secretary of CC CPSU, Minister of USSR Council of Ministers, etc.) are treated as supplemental. They will be scored once, as they arise.

- These supplemental scores for *government organs* affiliations are to be assigned only once, as they arise.

- These supplemental scores are *not* to be considered separate posts in any averaging calculations that may be performed to determine individual or unit mobility scores. They function to distinguish *oblast* party committee posts that carry with them varying memberships in the above party organs. Thus, they reflect the variations of importance among different *oblast* party committees.

APPENDIX III-A
SELECTED DATA ON REGIONAL UNITS OF THE SOVIET UNION

OBLAST (SSR#)	AREA	POP.	POP. CHANGE	POP. DENSITY	PERCENT URBAN
Aktiubinsk (7)	2987	671	212	.22	50
Alma Ata (7)	1047	1897	265	1.81	63
Altai krai (1)	2617	2712	-101	1.04	54
Amur (1)	3637	1007	274	.28	66
Andizhan (3)	42	1481	44	35.26	32
Arkhangelsk (1)	5874	1504	168	.26	74
Ashkhabad (6)	954	778	121⁻	.82	61
Astrakhan (6)	441	941	191	2.13	68
Belgorod (1)	271	1319	72	4.87	57
Brest (8)	323	1991	175	4.31	50
Briansk (1)	349	1481	- 83	4.24	62
Bukhara (3)	394	969	296	2.46	33
Chardzhou (6)	938	638	85⁻	.68	46
Cheliabinsk (1)	879	3512	365	4.00	82
Cherkassy (2)	209	1533	57	7.33	47
Chernovosty (2)	319	1459	-103	4.57	48
Chernigov (2)	81	905	96	11.17	39
Chimkent (7)	1163	1637	766	1.41	41
Chita (1)	4315	1298	242	.30	63
Crimea (1)	270	1914	569	7.09	64
Dnepropetrovsk (2)	319	3747	846	11.75	82
Donetsk (2)	265	5252	780	19.82	89
Dzhambul (7)	1446	976	356	.67	47
Dzhezkazgan (7)	3134	463	1⁻	.15	81
Dzhizak (3)	205	584	158⁻	2.85	27
East Kazakhstan (7)	973	902	86	.93	62
Fergana (3)	71	1858	762	26.17	33
Gomel (8)	404	1646	234	4.07	56
Gorkii (1)	748	3680	9	4.92	75
Grodno (8)	250	1142	50	4.57	49
Gurev (7)	1120	382	57	.34	60
Irkutsk (1)	7679	2676	553	.35	79
Issyk-Kul (4)	435	369	20⁻	.85	31
Ivanovo (1)	239	1316	-26	5.51	81
Ivano-Frankovsk (2)	139	1360	201	9.78	39
Kalinin (1)	841	1642	-141	1.95	69
Kaliningrad (1)	151	824	180	5.46	78
Kaluga (1)	299	1020	68	3.41	65
Kamchatka (1)	4723	415	176	.09	82
Karaganda (7)	854	1310	22	1.53	86
Kashka-Daria (3)	284	1285	313⁻	4.52	25
Kemerovo (1)	955	3047	101	3.19	87

OBLAST (SSR#)	AREA	POP.	POP. CHANGE	POP. DENSITY	PERCENT URBAN
Khabarovsk krai (1)	8246	1663	475	.20	79
Kharkov (2)	314	3110	524	9.90	76
Kherson (2)	285	1194	319	4.10	59
Khmelnitskii (2)	206	1537	−88	7.46	40
Khorezm (3)	63	840	423	13.33	24
Kiev (2)	289	4279	1300	14.81	77
Kirov (1)	1208	1660	−175	1.37	55
Kirovograd (2)	246	1238	−3	5.03	67
Kokchetav (7)	781	634	45	.81	36
Kostroma (1)	601	796	−112	1.32	66
Krasnodar krai (1)	836	4924	949	5.89	53
Krasnoiarsk krai (1)	24016	3343	589	.14	71
Krasnovodsk (6)	1385	332	37˜	.24	81
Kuibyshev (1)	536	3166	757	5.91	79
Kuliab (5)	120	497	51˜	4.14	26
Kurgan (1)	710	1095	48	1.54	52
Kurgan-Tuibe (5)	126	851	n.a.	6.75	18
Kursk (1)	298	1354	−153	4.54	52
Kustanai (7)	1145	987	84	.86	49
Kzyl-Orda (7)	2281	595	242	.26	65
Leninabad (5)	261	1326	210˜	5.08	35
Leningrad (1)	859	5943	1512	6.80	90
Lipetsk (1)	241	1219	46	5.06	60
Lvov (2)	218	2622	386	12.03	55
Magadan (1)	11911	510	247	.04	80
Mangyshlak (7)	1666	288	49˜	.17	90
Mary (6)	868	695	107˜	.80	31
Minsk (8)	408	2954	852	7.24	68
Mogilev (8)	290	1264	74	4.36	61
Moscow (1)	470	14737	3411	31.36	90
Murmansk (1)	1449	1043	418	.72	92
Namangan (3)	79	1232	208˜	15.59	36
Naryn (4)	511	247	33˜	.48	18
Navoi (3)	1108	556	n.a.	.50	42
Nikolaev (2)	246	1268	227	5.15	62
North Kazakhstan (7)	443	592	74	1.34	44
Novgorod (1)	553	736	6	1.33	68
Novosibirsk (1)	1782	2696	274	1.51	72
Odessa (2)	333	2588	478	7.77	64
Omsk (1)	1397	2010	276	1.44	64
Orel (1)	247	875	−66	3.54	59
Orenburg (1)	1240	2126	171	1.71	62
Osh (1)	595	1600	636	2.69	29
Pavlodar (7)	1275	867	299	.68	61
Penza (1)	432	1496	− 36	3.46	58
Perm (1)	1606	3007	− 62	1.87	75
Poltava (2)	288	1727	74	6.00	53

OBLAST (SSR#)	AREA	POP.	POP. CHANGE	POP. DENSITY	PERCENT URBAN
Primore krai (1)	1659	2079	647	1.25	77
Pskov (1)	553	839	- 76	1.52	58
Rostov (1)	1008	4187	675	4.15	70
Rovno (2)	201	1149	172	5.72	40
Riazan (1)	396	1328	-128	3.35	61
Sakhalin (1)	871	679	50	.78	82
Samarkand (3)	164	1837	699	11.20	40
Saratov (1)	1002	2596	344	2.59	73
Semipalatinsk (7)	1796	792	198	.44	49
Smolensk (1)	498	1134	22	2.28	64
Syr-Daria (3)	51	494	- 82	9.69	30
Stavropol krai (1)	806	2647	645	3.28	52
Sumy (2)	238	1444	- 79	6.07	56
Surkhan-Daria (3)	208	1020	- 14	4.90	19
Sverdlovsk (1)	1948	4557	350	2.34	85
Talass (4)	257	272	n.a.	1.06	24
Taldy-Kurgan (7)	1185	689	18⁻	.58	41
Tambov (1)	343	1338	-206	3.90	52
Tashauz (6)	736	595	107⁻	.81	30
Tashkent (3)	156	3869	1637	24.80	71
Ternopol (2)	138	1162	30	8.42	34
Tomsk (1)	3169	921	163	.29	67
Transcarpathia (2)	128	1188	203	9.28	38
Tselinograd (7)	1246	837	53	.67	59
Tula (1)	257	1878	- 43	7.31	79
Turgai (7)	1119	298	36⁻	.27	33
Tiumen (1)	14352	2293	1143	.16	69
Ulianovsk (1)	373	1289	154	3.46	67
Urals (7)	1512	603	169	.40	40
Vinnitsa (2)	265	1997	-161	7.54	38
Vitebsk (8)	401	1392	88	3.47	59
Vladimir (1)	290	1603	154	5.53	77
Volgograd (1)	1141	2499	527	2.19	73
Volyn (2)	202	1032	98	5.11	43
Vologda (1)	1457	1326	13	.91	62
Voronezh (1)	524	2461	30	4.70	57
Voroshilovgrad (2)	267	2808	207	10.52	85
Yaroslavl (1)	364	1441	49	3.96	79
Zaporozhe (2)	272	2008	457	7.38	73
Zhitomir (2)	299	1570	- 26	5.25	47

APPENDIX III-B
SELECTED DATA ON REGIONAL UNITS OF THE SOVIET UNION

OBLAST (SSR#)	RUSSIAN (%)	NATIVE (%)	URBAN: NATIVE (%)	WORKERS (%)	KOLKHOZ-NIKI (%)
Aktiubinsk (7)	26	48	26	65	10
Alma Ata (7)	53	24	12	60	10
Altai krai (1)	87	13	9	66	15
Amur (1)	91	9	8	67	8
Andizhan (3)	5	82	64	32	52
Arkhangelsk (1)	92	8	8	71	5
Ashkhabad (6)	n.a.	n.a.	n.a.	n.a.	n.a.
Astrakhan (6)	76	24	16	57	17
Belgorod (1)	95	5	5	40	45
Brest (8)	8	86	70	44	39
Briansk (1)	97	3	5	57	25
Bukhara (3)	11	72	41	38	44
Chardzhou (6)	12	69	42	38	41
Cheliabinsk (1)	81	19	16	74	3
Cherkassy (2)	6	93	83	36	49
Chernovosty (2)	5	94	85	32	53
Chernigov (2)	6	69	60	36	49
Chimkent (7)	22	47	26	63	15
Chita (1)	90	10	8	61	15
Crimea (1)	67	33	21	59	14
Dnepropetrovsk (2	21	75	70	61	16
Donetsk (2)	41	53	50	72	7
Dzhambul (7)	32	41	18	59	19
Dzhezkazgan (7)	n.a.	n.a.	n.a.	n.a.	n.a.
Dzhizak (3)	n.a.	n.a.	n.a.	n.a.	n.a.
East Kazakhstan (7)	69	23	8	72	6
Fergana (3)	9	75	49	53	28
Gomel (8)	9	84	70	58	24
Gorkii (1)	94	6	5	62	16
Grodno (8)	8	65	57	43	40
Gurev (7)	27	62	48	69	4
Irkutsk (1)	87	13	11	70	6
Issyk-Kul (4)	32	57	24	45	38
Ivanovo (1)	97	3	4	71	8
Ivano-Frankovsk (2)	39	5	85	47	37
Kalinin (1)	95	5	5	60	18
Kaliningrad (1)	77	23	22	n.a.	n.a.
Kaluga (1)	95	5	7	62	15
Kamchatka (1)	83	17	15	57	4
Karaganda (7)	51	19	11	75	5
Kashka-Daria (3)	4	85	63	48	34
Kemerovo (1)	89	11	11	76	3

OBLAST (SSR#)	RUSSIAN (%)	NATIVE (%)	URBAN: NATIVE (%)	WORKERS (%)	KOLKHOZ- NIKI (%)
Khabarovsk krai (1)	85	15	13	68	2
Kharkov (2)	29	66	60	57	17
Kherson (2)	18	78	71	58	23
Khmelnitskii (2)	4	91	77	28	58
Khorezm (3)	2	92	77	47	36
Kiev (2)	14	79	70	48	18
Kirov (1)	91	9	6	62	19
Kirovograd (2)	9	88	82	39	45
Kokchetav (7)	40	23	13	73	6
Kostroma (1)	97	3	4	63	16
Krasnodar krai (1)	88	12	12	55	26
Krasnoiarsk krai (1)	86	14	11	71	6
Krasnovodsk (6)	n.a.	n.a.	n.a.	n.a.	n.a.
Kuibyshev (1)	94	6	12	63	12
Kuliab (5)	n.a.	n.a.	n.a.	n.a.	n.a.
Kurgan (1)	92	8	5	58	23
Kurgan-Tuibe (5)	n.a.	n.a.	n.a.	n.a.	n.a.
Kursk (1)	98	2	5	39	46
Kustanai (7)	46	16	5	76	2
Kzyl-Orda (7)	19	70	51	63	8
Leninabad (5)	11	53	42	42	41
Leningrad (1)	90	10	10	73	3
Lipetsk (1)	98	2	3	63	19
Lvov (2)	8	88	77	50	29
Magadan (1)	76	24	21	65	2
Mangyshlak (7)	n.a.	n.a.	n.a.	n.a.	n.a.
Mary (6)	9	79	52	33	47
Minsk (8)	13	80	69	55	20
Mogilev (8)	10	86	74	55	27
Moscow (1)	91	9	9	60	1
Murmansk (1)	85	15	14	64	1
Namangan (3)	4	81	65	36	48
Naryn (4)	4	94	79	33	48
Navoi (3)	n.a.	n.a.	n.a.	n.a.	n.a.
Nikolaev (2)	16	79	69	65	29
North Kazakhstan (7)	64	15	6	76	12
Novgorod (1)	97	3	4	65	15
Novosibirsk (1)	91	9	7	66	8
Odessa (2)	24	55	48	44	32
Omsk (1)	80	20	13	66	11
Orel (1)	98	2	3	48	34
Orenburg (1)	72	28	20	57	23
Osh (1)	12	52	18	54	29
Pavlodar (7)	44	25	12	72	6
Penza (1)	86	14	7	65	17
Perm (1)	82	18	13	66	12

Appendix III-B (continued)

OBLAST (SSR#)	RUSSIAN (%)	NATIVE (%)	URBAN: NATIVE (%)	WORKERS (%)	KOLKHOZ-NIKI (%)
Poltava (2)	7	91	82	40	43
Primore krai (1)	86	14	12	67	2
Pskov (1)	97	3	5	53	27
Rostov (1)	91	9	9	62	15
Rovno (2)	4	94	83	40	46
Riazan (1)	98	2	3	57	23
Sakhalin (1)	80	20	19	69	2
Samarkand (3)	8	77	43	43	38
Saratov (1)	88	12	9	59	17
Semipalatinsk (7)	41	44	23	65	12
Smolensk (1)	97	3	5	63	17
Syr-Daria (3)	14	58	29	57	22
Stavropol krai (1)	83	17	13	58	22
Sumy (2)	12	87	82	41	44
Surkhan-Daria (3)	7	73	36	38	47
Sverdlovsk (1)	89	11	11	73	31
Talass (4)	n.a.	n.a.	n.a.	n.a.	n.a.
Taldy-Kurgan (7)	41	41	17	60	21
Tambov (1)	98	2	3	56	27
Tashauz (6)	2	59	34	29	53
Tashkent (3)	30	40	33	55	15
Ternopol (2)	2	96	88	27	60
Tomsk (1)	89	11	9	64	9
Transcarpathia (2)	3	76	65	49	35
Tselinograd (7)	46	19	13	74	2
Tula (1)	96	4	5	69	9
Turgai (7)	34	33	14	73	2
Tiumen (1)	81	19	14	67	11
Ulianovsk (1)	76	24	15	59	22
Urals (7)	38	49	12	67	11
Vinnitsa (2)	5	92	76	33	53
Vitebsk (8)	12	83	72	54	28
Vladimir (1)	97	3	4	73	6
Volgograd (1)	90	10	7	63	15
Volyn (2)	4	95	86	36	49
Vologda (1)	98	2	3	61	19
Voronezh (1)	93	7	6	48	33
Voroshilovgrad (2)	45	55	51	72	9
Yaroslavl (1)	98	2	3	64	13
Zaporozhe (2)	29	66	60	55	24
Zhitomir (2)	6	85	71	38	46

APPENDIX III-C
SELECTED DATA ON REGIONAL UNITS OF THE SOVIET UNION

OBLAST (SSR#)	INCREASE IN LIVING SPACE	RETAIL SALES	DOCTORS PER CAPITA	HOSPITAL BEDS PER CAPITA	COLLEGE STUDENTS
Aktiubinsk (7)	297	611	375	125	74
Alma Ata (7)	633	2091	549	133	946
Altai krai (1)	6024	2561	305	137	398
Amur (1)	2077	1134	414	146	149
Andizhan (3)	n.a.	n.a.	n.a.	n.a.	n.a.
Arkhangelsk (1)	3186	1746	375	142	151
Ashkhabad (6)	1097	733	n.a.	n.a.	304
Astrakhan (6)	1602	892	566	157	142
Belgorod (1)	3085	1098	261	128	120
Brest (8)	4436	989	277	118	1822
Briansk (1)	2484	1317	274	118	169
Bukhara (3)	n.a.	n.a.	n.a.	n.a.	n.a.
Chardzhou (6)	1161	463	n.a.	n.a.	72
Cheliabinsk (1)	6816	3501	334	137	631
Cherkassy (2)	2665	1399	325	131	98
Chernovosty (2)	1336	788	389	124	127
Chernigov (2)	2125	1246	301	132	86
Chimkent (7)	425	1195	226	111	156
Chita (1)	1697	1124	312	124	145
Crimea (1)	404	2983	593	126	234
Dnepropetrovsk (2)	8781	3939	403	134	807
Donetsk (2)	9558	5766	387	136	663
Dzhambul (7)	275	795	245	126	174
Dzhezkazgan (7)	137	417	355	142	60
Dzhizak (3)	n.a.	n.a.	n.a.	n.a.	n.a.
East Kazakhstan (7)	302	841	304	132	123
Fergana (3)	n.a.	n.a.	n.a.	n.a.	n.a.
Gomel (8)	794	983	287	127	240
Gorkii (1)	7314	3727	355	121	680
Grodno (8)	480	956	338	131	99
Gurev (7)	172	333	347	151	43
Irkutsk (1)	6137	2720	353	137	656
Issyk-Kul (4)	n.a.	20	278	108	n.a.
Ivanovo (1)	2535	1337	407	144	299
Ivano-Frankovsk (2)	1866	1149	344	120	140
Kalinin (1)	3366	1665	346	139	240
Kaliningrad (1)	1388	884	406	132	155
Kaluga (1)	2121	882	494	128	89
Kamchatka (1)	1019	639	526	148	21
Karaganda (7)	431	1355	457	151	332
Kashka-Daria (3)	n.a.	n.a.	n.a.	n.a.	n.a.

OBLAST (SSR#)	INCREASE IN LIVING SPACE	RETAIL SALES	DOCTORS PER CAPITA	HOSPITAL BEDS PER CAPITA	COLLEGE STUDENTS
Kemerovo (1)	5687	3214	372	152	424
Khabarovsk Krai (1)	3860	1957	449	147	488
Kharkov (2)	6931	3316	448	127	1324
Kherson (2)	2733	1227	331	125	140
Khmelnitskii (2)	2465	1295	296	126	162
Khorezm (3)	n.a.	n.a.	n.a.	n.a.	n.a.
Kiev (2)	9969	5338	592	129	1546
Kirov (1)	3464	1635	283	145	183
Kirovograd (2)	1913	1109	347	143	114
Kokchetav (7)	287	617	269	132	35
Kostroma (1)	1683	842	308	143	133
Krasnodar krai (1)	8557	4843	389	120	556
Krasnoiarsk krai (1)	8647	3763	351	137	661
Krasnovodsk (6)	404	272	n.a.	n.a.	11
Kuibyshev (1)	7166	3024	406	123	725
Kuliab (5)	n.a.	n.a.	147	93	n.a.
Kurgan (1)	1986	1049	258	138	152
Kurgan-Tuibe (5)	n.a.	n.a.	140	83	n.a.
Kursk (1)	2240	1145	298	126	152
Kustanai (7)	597	1023	253	131	98
Kzyl-Orda (7)	178	366	309	132	57
Leninabad (5)	n.a.	n.a.	216	101	n.a.
Leningrad (1)	4823	8769	731	131	2803
Lipetsk (1)	2471	1092	278	119	113
Lvov (2)	3883	259	422	120	718
Magadan (1)	1102	896	497	159	28
Mangyshlak (7)	66	163	248	104	5
Mary (6)	1228	499	n.a.	n.a.	n.a.
Minsk (8)	1424	2393	462	120	973
Mogilev (8)	562	1010	287	137	243
Moscow (1)	4664	24898	702	127	7119
Murmansk (1)	2559	1223	472	116	63
Namangan (3)	n.a.	n.a.	n.a.	n.a.	n.a.
Naryn (4)	n.a.	8	229	99	n.a.
Navoi (3)	n.a.	n.a.	n.a.	n.a.	n.a.
Nikolaev (2)	2213	1334	326	128	130
North Kazakhstan (7)	314	598	281	132	135
Novgorod (1)	1708	771	337	145	68
Novosibirsk (1)	5497	2623	406	131	845
Odessa (2)	3418	2649	491	123	841
Omsk (1)	5020	1961	425	128	511
Orel (1)	1769	796	284	125	99
Orenburg (1)	4660	1968	317	129	226
Osh (1)	n.a.	71	204	112	n.a.
Pavlodar (7)	460	876	285	136	107

OBLAST (SSR#)	INCREASE IN LIVING SPACE	RETAIL SALES	DOCTORS PER CAPITA	HOSPITAL BEDS PER CAPITA	COLLEGE STUDENTS
Penza (1)	2978	1311	251	119	257
Perm (1)	5876	3039	350	137	500
Poltava (2)	3320	1621	349	131	219
Primore Krai (1)	4741	2841	418	129	501
Pskov (1)	1782	834	322	141	106
Rostov (1)	7702	4004	347	120	1073
Rovno (2)	2187	939	299	119	151
Riazan (1)	2383	1259	392	133	204
Sakhalin (1)	1514	1081	471	175	26
Samarkand (3)	n.a.	n.a.	n.a.	n.a.	n.a.
Saratov (1)	6468	2383	406	121	633
Semipalatinsk (7)	313	673	378	131	135
Smolensk (1)	2704	1101	402	135	154
Syr-Daria (3)	4480	n.a.	n.a.	n.a.	n.a.
Stavropol krai (1)	2442	2572	391	115	375
Sumy (2)	n.a.	1276	295	132	94
Surkhan-Daria (3)	n.a.	n.a.	n.a.	n.a.	n.a.
Sverdlovsk (1)	9596	4698	338	141	915
Talass (4)	n.a.	91	1839	467	n.a.
Taldy-Kurgan (7)	213	567	256	120	32
Tambov (1)	2178	1121	250	123	165
Tashauz (6)	1213	317	n.a.	n.a.	n.a.
Tashkent (3)	n.a.	n.a.	n.a.	n.a.	n.a.
Ternopol (2)	1763	913	345	125	137
Tomsk (1)	2320	988	438	143	458
Transcarpathia (2)	1745	1131	330	115	92
Tselinograd (7)	314	748	326	137	204
Tula (1)	3351	1844	312	134	233
Turgai (7)	194	280	305	147	22
Tiumen (1)	6777	2736	328	123	289
Ulianovsk (1)	2523	1138	261	122	177
Urals (7)	222	530	292	133	99
Vinnitsa (2)	2813	1678	345	138	170
Vitebsk (8)	602	1062	348	139	93
Vladimir (1)	3363	1549	315	130	178
Volgograd (1)	4698	2344	375	126	405
Volyn (2)	1766	859	313	130	65
Vologda (1)	3243	1362	282	136	187
Voronezh (1)	3807	2144	351	120	600
Voroshilovgrad (2)	4316	3065	341	139	366
Yaroslavl (1)	3312	1455	417	137	227
Zaporozhe (2)	3851	2208	393	127	301
Zhitomir (2)	2320	1277	306	124	84

Appendix III-C (continued)

<u>TABLE KEY</u>

* SSR # : 1 = R.S.F.S.R.
          2 = Ukrainian S.S.R.
          3 = Uzbek S.S.R.
          4 = Kirgiz S.S.R.
          5 = Tadzhik S.S.R.
          6 = Turkmen S.S.R.
          7 = Kazakh S.S.R.
          8 = Belorussian S.S.R.

* AREA : (x 100 km^2)
* POPULATION : 1983 data; (x 1,000)
* POPULATION CHANGE : 1963 -- 1983; (x 1,000)
          ‾ : 1976 -- 1983
* POPULATION DENSITY : (x 1,000/km^2)
* PERCENT URBAN : 1983 data
* PERCENT RUSSIAN : 1970 data
* PERCENT NATIVE : 1970 data; for units inside the
      R.S.F.S.R., "native" connotes all non-Russians;
      outside the R.S.F.S.R., "native" connotes the titular
      ethnic group of the respective Union Republics.
* URBAN : PERCENT NATIVE : 1970 data
* WORKFORCE PERCENTAGES : 1970 data
* INCREASE IN LIVING SPACE : 1980 data (x 1,000 $meters^2$)
* RETAIL SALES : 1980 data (x 1,000,000 rubles)
* DOCTORS PER CAPITA : 1980 data (# per 100,000 pop.)
* HOSPITAL BEDS PER CAPITA : 1980 data (# per 10,000 pop.)
* COLLEGE STUDENTS : 1980 data (x 100 students)

APPENDIX IV
ROTATED FACTOR SCORES FOR OBLAST DEVELOPMENTAL VARIABLES

OBLAST (SSR#)	FACTOR 1	FACTOR 2	FACTOR 3
Aktiubinsk (7)	-.56932	-.05016	.25229
Alma Ata (7)	..	..	..
Altai krai (1)	.18268	-.92744	-.81933
Amur (1)	-.47465	-.53752	1.05129
Andizhan (3)	..	..	..
Arkhangelsk (1)	-.33570	-.88366	.73616
Ashkhabad (6)	..	..	..
Astrakhan (6)	-.67585	.42143	2.21633
Belgorod (1)	-.25656	-.18161	-1.58159
Brest (8)	.16459	1.12307	-1.06784
Briansk (1)	-.22609	-.77680	-1.42139
Bukhara (3)	..	..	..
Chardzhou (6)	..	..	..
Cheliabinsk (1)	.62971	-1.06791	.08567
Cherkassy (2)	-.10321	1.92328	-.50896
Chernovtsy (2)	-.14635	1.58642	-.88119
Chernigov (2)	-.38110	2.07915	-.41717
Chimkent (7)	-.22803	-.33369	-1.18356
Chita (1)	-.21801	-.77101	-.47204
Crimea (1)	.47307	.14460	.92696
Dnepropetrovsk (2)	1.26467	.69731	.52135
Donetsk (2)	1.88945	.08984	.19736
Dzhambul (7)	-.47048	-.22623	-.67405
Dzhezkazgan (7)	..	..	..
Dzhizak (3)	..	..	..
East Kazakhstan- (7)	-.74928	-.72832	.16438
Fergana (3)	..	..	..
Gomel (8)	-.35877	.93819	-.09201
Gorkii (1)	.91251	-1.08692	-1.05535
Grodno (8)	-.54182	1.20338	-.28156
Gurev (7)	-1.20972	.42644	1.84003
Irkutsk (1)	.41803	-1.04331	.21818
Issyk-Kul (4)	..	..	..
Ivanovo (1)	-.36040	-.71674	.75893
Ivano-Frankovsk (2)	-.04433	1.73623	-.71117
Kalinin (1)	-.40875	-.66670	.01911
Kaliningrad (1)	..	..	..
Kaluga (1)	-.45710	-.76046	-.34600
Kamchatka (1)	-.93723	.04428	2.89366
Karaganda (7)	-.73566	-.46415	1.93828
Kashkadaria (3)	..	..	..
Kemerovo (1)	.19614	-.96031	.78274

OBLAST (SSR#)	FACTOR 1	FACTOR 2	FACTOR 3
Khabarovsk krai (1)	-.10369	-.56461	1.63545
Kharkov (2)	.96481	.69563	.64284
Kherson (2)	-.24992	.85266	.01892
Khmelnitskii (2)	-.10773	1.98201	-1.14931
Khorezm (3)	..	..	..
Kiev (2)	1.92365	1.36651	1.28806
Kirov (1)	-.32385	-.72797	-.20884
Kirovograd (2)	-.45562	1.88307	.32145
Kokchetav (7)	-.89433	-.68723	-.44780
Kostroma (1)	-.76632	-.70507	.12609
Krasnodar krai (1)	1.74343	-.65769	-1.66729
Krasnoiarsk krai (1)	.66835	-1.19167	-.23443
Krasnovodsk (6)	..	..	..
Kuibyshev (1)	.90108	-.86018	-.29441
Kuliab (5)	..	..	..
Kurgan (1)	-.59125	-.58507	-.64433
Kurgan-Tuibe (5)	..	..	..
Kursk (1)	-.30883	-.10079	-1.56012
Kustanai (7)	-.73128	-1.04025	-.35597
Kzyl-Orda (7)	-.92419	.41281	1.18201
Leninabad (5)	..	..	..
Leningrad (1)	2.30260	-.38589	1.52103
Lipetsk (1)	-.27979	-.91612	-1.30562
Lvov (2)	.64337	1.51205	-.05210
Magadan (1)	-.97381	.06223	2.97088
Mangyshlak (7)	..	..	..
Mary (6)	..	..	..
Minsk (8)	.58256	1.15800	.77704
Mogilev (8)	-.60784	1.19459	.45131
Moscow (1)	7.24723	.31595	1.46169
Murmansk (1)	-.22862	-.69868	1.22680
Namangan (3)	..	..	..
Naryn (4)	..	..	..
Navoi (3)	..	..	..
Nikolaev (2)	-.25423	1.07619	.12933
North Kazakhstan (7)	-.87014	-.90587	-.31302
Novgorod (1)	-.81204	-.65456	.41013
Novosibirsk (1)	.19565	-.90778	.19914
Odessa (2)	.61072	.99053	.29446
Omsk (1)	.00417	-.65404	.02078
Orel (1)	-.49996	-.43650	-1.18572
Orenburg (1)	.00600	-.38905	-.61282
Osh (1)	..	..	..
Pavlodar (7)	-.73306	-.66923	.22889
Penza (1)	-.22558	-.92874	-1.34184
Perm (1)	.35903	-.85552	-.11083
Poltava (2)	-.08129	1.70240	-.18368
Primore krai (1)	.30560	-.81855	.75895

Appendix IV (continued)

OBLAST (SSR#)	FACTOR 1	FACTOR 2	FACTOR 3
Pskov (1)	-.70896	-.37642	-.22969
Rostov (1)	1.27889	-1.05041	-1.12934
Rovno (2)	-.25180	1.68146	-1.05456
Riazan (1)	-.37516	-.46395	-.26376
Sakhalin (1)	-1.07694	.01324	3.15803
Samarkand (3)	..	..	..
Saratov (1)	.54896	-.78762	-.51339
Semipalatinsk (7)	-.59804	-.02929	.30997
Smolensk (1)	-.50728	-.59703	-.31302
Syr-Daria (3)	..	..	..
Stavropol krai (1)	.40766	-.53459	-1.09474
Sumy (2)	-.25087	1.60469	-.36752
Surkhan-Daria (3)	..	..	..
Sverdlovsk (1)	1.10348	-1.37840	-.03790
Talass (4)	..	..	..
Taldy-Kurgan (7)	..	..	..
Tambov (1)	-.26446	-.72807	-1.58190
Tashauz (6)	..	..	..
Tashkent (3)	..	..	..
Ternopol (2)	-.19569	2.36568	-.95133
Tomsk (1)	-.64254	-.43522	1.19294
Transcarpathia (2)	-.01866	1.17855	-1.11142
Tselinograd (7)	-.79231	-.70333	.46642
Tula (1)	-.08008	-.90774	-.08696
Turgai (7)	..	..	..
Tiumen (1)	.54947	-1.01105	-.65955
Ulianovsk (1)	-.27326	-.52542	-.89450
Urals (7)	-.89090	-.23300	-.06531
Vinnitsa (2)	-.02415	2.03866	-.54760
Vitebsk (8)	-.59703	1.27925	.64849
Vladimir (1)	-.15370	-1.09648	-.18563
Volgograd (1)	.37097	-.84136	-.35890
Volyn (2)	-.42771	1.97027	-.45948
Vologda (1)	-.39920	-.87623	-.55195
Voronezh (1)	.29753	-.39843	-1.32335
Vorochilovgrad (2)	.43374	.15231	.58624
Yaroslavl (1)	-.25571	-.67635	.49466
Zaporozhe (2)	.23358	.76922	.32856
Zhitomir (2)	-.11715	1.50285	-.85238

APPENDIX V
CAREER TYPES OF OBKOM FIRST SECRETARIES: A CODEBOOK

Var #	Variable Name	Column Number
1	NAME (First 8 characters of ObSec's surname)	1-8
2	DATE OF BIRTH (Year)	10-13
3	ETHNICITY 01=Russian 02=Ukrainian 03=Belorussian 04=Kazakh 05=Uzbek 06=Kirgiz 07=Tadzhik 08=Turkmen 09=Armenian 10=Georgian 11=Estonian 12=Latvian 13=Lithuanian 14=Moldavian 15=Azeri 16=Other 00=Unknown	15-16
4	SOCIAL ORIGIN 1=Worker 2=Peasant 3=Employee 4=Intelligentsia 0=Unknown	18

Appendix V (continued)

Var #	Variable Name	Column Number
5	EDUCATIONAL LEVEL	20

  1=Primary
  2=Incompleted Secondary
  3=Completed Secondary
  4=Incompleted Higher
  5=Completed Higher
  6=Candidate of Sciences
  7=Doctor of Sciences
  0=Unknown

| 6 | EDUCATION: HIGHER PARTY SCHOOL | 22 |

  1=CPSU Higher Party School
  2=SSR Higher Party School
  3=No Higher Party School

| 7 | EDUCATION: CONTENT | 24-25 |

  01=Legal
  02=Social Sciences
  03=Humanities
  04=Pedagogical
  05=Scientific
  06=Agricultural (Agronomy, etc.)
  07=Engineering (Shipbuilding, etc.)
  08=Industrial (Metallurgy, etc.)
  09=Transport/Communications
  10=Economic
  11=Medical
  12=Military
  13=Other
  00=Unknown/n.a.

| 8 | AGE AT ENTRANCE TO CPSU | 27-28 |

| 9 | AGE AT ASSUMPTION OF 1ST OBSEC POST | 30-31 |

Var #	Variable Name	Column Number
10	APPARATUS AFFILIATION OF ABOVE POST	33

      1=RSFSR
      2=Ukrainian SSR
      3=Belorussian SSR
      4=Kazakh SSR
      5=Uzbek SSR
      6=Kirgiz SSR
      7=Tadzhik SSR
      8=Turkmen SSR

| 11 | TENURE IN 1ST OBSEC POST | 35-37 |

    (Months in office)

| 12 | OBSEC ETHNIC NATIVE OF OBLAST SSR? | 39 |

      1=Yes
      2=No
      0=Unknown

| 13 | MULTIPLE OBSEC POSTS HELD IN CAREER? | 41 |

      1=Same SSR
      2=Different SSRs
      3=No

| 14 | TENURE IN OTHER OBSEC POSTS | 43-45 |

    (Months in office)

| 15 | MOVED INTO OBSEC TIER UNDER: | 47 |

      1=Stalin
      2=Khrushchev
      3=Brezhnev
      4=Andropov
      5=Chernenko
      6=Gorbachev

| 16 | AGE AT ENTRANCE TO CAND. CC CPSU | 49-50 |

    00=Unknown/n.a.

Var #	Variable Name	Column Number
17	AGE AT ENTRANCE TO FULL CC CPSU	52-53
	00=Unknown/n.a.	
18	RSFSR APPARATUS SERVICE	55
	1=Party	
	2=State	
	3=Party and State	
	4=Other	
	5=None	
19	MOSCOW APPARATUS SERVICE	57
	1=Party	
	2=State	
	3=Party and State	
	4=Other	
	5=None	
20	POST PRIOR TO 1ST OBSEC	59
	1=Lower Party Level	
	2=Lateral Party Level	
	3=Higher Party Level	
	4=Lower State Level	
	5=Lateral State Level	
	6=Higher State Level	
	7=Komsomol	
	8=Other	
	9=Retired	
	0=Unknown	
21	POST AFTER 1ST OBSEC	61
	(see above var 20 for codes)	
22	SERVICE IN RED ARMY	63
	1=Wartime	
	2=Peacetime	
	3=No	
	0=Unknown/n.a.	

Var #	Variable Name	Column Number
23	<u>KOMSOMOL POSTS</u>	65

1=Yes
2=No
0=Unknown/n.a.

| 24 | <u>FUNCTIONAL FOCUS: PRE-OBSEC CAREER</u> | 67-68 |

01=Local Party Administration
02=Regional Party Administration
03=Republic Party Administration
04=Leading Party Administration
05=Military
06=Punitive Organs (KGB, MVD, Control Cmttees)
07=Party Agriculture
08=State Agriculture
09=Personnel/Cadres/Organizational-Party Work
10=Youth Affairs
11=Labor/T.U.C. Affairs
12=Propaganda/Culture/Education
13=Foreign Affairs
14=Industry/Construction/Transport
15=Local State Administration
16=Regional State Adminstration
17=Republic State Adminstration
18=Leading State Adminstration (AU)
19=Mixed Party-State Generalist
20=Retired (Health/Age)
21=Retired (Removed/Ousted/Scandal)
22=Died in Office
00=Unknown

| 25 | <u>FUNCTIONAL FOCUS: POST-OBSEC CAREER</u> | 70-71 |
| | (see above var 24 for codes) | |

| 26 | <u>MOBILITY SCORE</u> | 73-77 |

APPENDIX VI
CHANGES IN OBKOM
FIRST SECRETARIES
IN THE
POST-BREZHNEV
PERIOD

CHANGES UNDER ANDROPOV

I. **RSFSR** (N = 14)

1. **Krasnodar Krai** (6/27/83)
   OUT: Vitalii Vorotnikov   IN: Georgii Razumovskii
   TO: Chair RSFSR C of M   FROM: Head Dept USSR CofM
                                    (Agro-Ind Complex)

2. **Arkhangelsk obkom** (11/21/83)
   OUT: Boris V. Popov   IN: Petr Telepnev
   TO: Retired   FROM: Inspector CC CPSU
                                    2nd Sect. Tiumen obkom

3. **Belgorod obkom** (2/9/83)
   OUT: Mikhail Trunov   IN: Aleksei Ponomarev
   TO: Chair of Board of   FROM: Chair Belgorod oblispolkom
   Tsentrosouyuz of
   Belgorod oblast

4. **Briansk obkom** (1/28/84)
   OUT: Yevgenii Sizenko   IN: Anatolii Voistrochenko
   TO: 1st Dep Chair USSR   FROM: Unknown
   State Cmtte (Agro-Ind)
   [11/20/85 --]

5. **Chelyabinsk obkom** (1/7/84)
   OUT: Mikhail Voropaev   IN: Gennadii Verednikov
   TO: Dep Chair Party Cntrl   FROM: Inspector CC CPSU
   Cmtte (CC CPSU)

6. **Irkutsk obkom** (3/28/83)
   OUT: Nikolai Bannikov   IN: Vasilii Sitnikov
   TO: Retired   FROM: 2nd Sect. Kemerovo obkom

7. **Kaliningrad obkom** (1/1984)
   OUT: Nikolai Konovalov   IN: Dmitrii V. Romanin
   TO: Memb. Party Cntrl   FROM: 2nd Sect. Kaliningrad
   Cmtte (CC CPSU)   obkom

8. **Kaluga obkom** (12/9/83)
   OUT: Andrei Kandrenkov   IN: Gennadii I. Ulanov
   TO: Retired   FROM: Sect. Kaluga obkom

Appendix VI (continued)

9. **Leningrad obkom** (6/21/83)
   OUT: Grigorii Romanov
   TO: Sect. CC CPSU

   IN: Lev Zaikov
   FROM: Chair Leningrad gorispolkom

10. **Lipetsk obkom** (1/14/84)
    OUT: Grigorii Pavlov
    TO: Retired

    IN: Yurii Manaenkov
    FROM: 2nd Sect. Tambov obkom

11. **Tomsk obkom** (4/29/83)
    OUT: Yegor K. Ligachev
    TO: Sect. CC CPSU
        (Cadres)

    IN: Aleksandr G. Melnikov
    FROM: 2nd Sect. Tomsk obkom

12. **Ulianovsk obkom** (12/1983)
    OUT: Ivan M. Kuznetsov
    TO: Unknown

    IN: Gennadii V. Kolbin
    FROM: 2nd Sect. CC CPGeorgia

13. **Vladimir obkom** (12/16/83)
    OUT: Mikhail Ponomarev
    TO: Dep Chair Party Cntrl
        Cmtte (CC CPSU)

    IN: Ratmir S. Bobovikov
    FROM: Chair Leningrad oblispolkom
          Cand. CC CPSU

14. **Volgograd obkom** (1/24/84)
    OUT: Leonid S. Kulichenko
    TO: Retired

    IN: Vladimir I. Kalashnikov
    FROM: RSFSR Min of Land
          Reclamation & Water Economy

II. **UKRAINIAN SSR** (N = 7)

1. **Chernigov obkom** (1/7/84)
   OUT: Nikolai V. Umanets
   TO: Retired

   IN: Leonid I. Palazhchenko
   FROM: 1st Sect. Volin obkom

2. **Dnepropetrovsk obkom** (2/4/83)
   OUT: Yevgenii Kachalovskii
   TO: 1st Dep Chair UkSSR
       C of M

   IN: Viktor G. Boiko
   FROM: Chair Dnepropetrovsk
         Oblispolkom

3. **Odessa obkom** (10/12/83)
   OUT: Nikolai Kirichenko
   TO: Retired

   IN: Anatolii P. Nochevkin
   FROM: 2nd Sect. Odessa obkom

4. **Volyn obkom** (1/9/84)
   OUT: Leonid Palazhchenko
   TO: 1st Sect. Chernigov
       obkom

   IN: Zinovii S. Kovalchuk
   FROM: Sevt. Volyn obkom

5. **Ternopol obkom** (2/25/83)
   OUT: Ivan M. Yarkovoi
   TO: "Transfer to another
       job"

   IN: Anatolii Kornienko
   FROM: 1st Sect. Komsomol
         UkSSR

6. **Ivano-Frankovsk** (12/22/83)
    OUT: Ivan I. Skyba   IN: Ivan A. Liakhov
    TO: 1st Dep Head Dept   FROM: 2nd Sect. Iv-Fra obkom
    CC CPUk (Ag & Food Ind)

7. **Vinnitsa obkom** (3/3/83)
    OUT: Vasilii N. Taratuta   IN: Leontii L. Krivoruchko
    TO: USSR Ambassador to   FROM: 2nd Sect. Vinnitsa obkom
    Algeria

III. **KAZAKH SSR** (N = 3)

1. **Dzhambul obkom** (2/26/83)
    OUT: Khasan Bekturganov   IN: Anuar K. Zhakupov
    TO: Retired   FROM: 1st Sect. Alma Ata gorkom

2. **East Kazakh obkom** (12/19/83)
    OUT: Aleksandr Protozanov IN: Anatolii V. Milkin
    TO: Retired   FROM: Chair KazSSR Peoples
                                   Control Committee

3. **Dzhezkazgan obkom** (11/1982)
    OUT: Konstantin S. Losev   IN: Nikolai G. Davydov
    TO: Retired   FROM: 2nd Sect. Chimkent obkom

IV. **BELORUSSIAN SSR** (N = 2)

1. **Vitebsk obkom** (10/13/83)
    OUT: Sergei M. Shabashov   IN: Sergei T. Kabiak
    TO: Retired   FROM: Chair Grodno oblispolkom

2. **Mogilev obkom** (5/25/83)
    OUT: Vitali Prishchepchik   IN: Vasilii S. Leonov
    TO: Unknown   FROM: Unknown

V. **KIRGHIZ SSR** (N = 0)

VI. **TURKMEN SSR** (N = 0)

VII. **TADZHIK SSR** (N = 2)

1. **Kurgan-Tuibe obkom** (2/1984)
    OUT: Gaibnazar P. Pallaev   IN: Abdukharim K. Kasimov
    TO: Unknown   FROM: Unknown

2. **Kuliab obkom** (12/22/83)
    OUT: Akhmed. Khisamutdinov IN: Izatullo Khaeev
    TO: Unknown   FROM: TadSSR Min of Meat &
                                   Dairy Industry

Appendix VI (continued)

VIII. UZBEK SSR (N = 4)

   1. **Bukhara obkom** (1/4/84)
       OUT: Abduvakhid Karimov   IN: Ismail D. Dzhabbarov
       TO: "transfer to other   FROM: 2nd Sect. Navoi obkom
       work"

   2. **Dzhizak obkom** (2/1983)
       OUT: Tukhtamysh Baimirov   IN: Khabibulla A. Shagazatov
       TO: "reassignment. ."   FROM: UzSSR Min of Instal &
                                       Special Construc Work

   3. **Namangan obkom** (1/19/84)
       OUT: Makhkam K. Kamalov   IN: Nazir R. Radzhabov
       TO: Unknown   FROM: Unknown

   4. **Kashkadaria obkom** (2/1984)
       OUT: Ruzmet G. Gaipov   IN: Nurmumin T. Turapov
       TO: Unknown   FROM: Unknown

CHRONOLOGY OF OBKOM PERSONNEL CHANGES
UNDER ANDROPOV

Month/Year	Oblast	Republic
November 1982 (1)	Dzhezkazgan	Kazakh SSR
December 1982 (0)	-----	-----
January 1983 (0)	-----	-----
February 1983 (5)	Belgorod	RSFSR
	Dnepropetrovsk	Ukrainian SSR
	Ternopol'	Ukrainian SSR
	Dzhambul	Kazakh SSR
	Dzhizak	Uzbek SSR
March 1983 (2)	Irkutsk	RSFSR
	Vinnitsa	Ukrainian SSR
April 1983 (1)	Tomsk	RSFSR
May 1983 (1)	Mogilev	Belorussian SSR
June 1983 (2)	Krasnodar Krai	RSFSR
	Leningrad	RSFSR
July 1983 (0)	-----	-----
August 1983 (0)	-----	-----
September 1983 (0)	-----	-----
October 1983 (2)	Odessa	Ukrainian SSR
	Vitebsk	Belorussian SSR
November 1983 (1)	Arkhangelsk	RSFSR
December 1983 (6)	Kaluga	RSFSR
	Ulianovsk	RSFSR
	Vladimir	RSFSR
	Ivano-Frankovsk	Ukrainian SSR

	East Kazakh	Kazakh SSR
	Kuliab	Tadzhik SSR
January 1984 (9)	Briansk	RSFSR
	Chelyabinsk	RSFSR
	Kaliningrad	RSFSR
	Lipetsk	RSFSR
	Volgograd	RSFSR
	Chernigov	Ukrainian SSR
	Volyn	Ukrainian SSR
	Bukhara	Uzbek SSR
	Namangan	Uzbek SSR
February 1984 (2)	Kurgan-Tuibe	Tadzhik SSR
	Kashka-Daria	UzbekSSR

Appendix VI (continued)

CHANGES UNDER CHERNENKO

I. RSFSR (N = 3)

   1. **Altai Krai** (2/18/85)
     OUT: Nikolai F. Aksenov   IN: Filipp V. Popov
     TO: Unknown   FROM: RSFSR Min of Housing/
                              Local Economy

   2. **Primore Krai** (4/9/84)
     OUT: Viktor P. Lomakin   IN: Dmitrii N. Gagarov
     TO: USSR Ambassador to   FROM: Inspector CC CPSU
         Czechoslovakia

   3. **Rostov obkom** (7/25/84)
     OUT: Ivan A. Bondarenko   IN: Aleksandr V. Vlasov
     TO: Retired   FROM: 1st Sect. Chechen-
                              Ingush ASSR

II. UKRAINIAN SSR (N = 2)

   1. **Khmelnitskii obkom** (1/4/85)
     OUT: Timofei G. Lisovoi   IN: Vladimir G. Dikusarov
     TO: Retired   FROM: 1st Sect. Chernovtsy obkom

   2. **Chernovtsy obkom** (1/8/85)
     OUT: Vladimir G. Dikusarov IN: Nikolai N. Nivalov
     TO: 1st Sect. Khmelnitskii FROM: 2nd Sect. Dnepropetrovsk
        obkom   obkom

III. KAZAKH SSR (N = 4)

   1. **Kokchetav obkom** (1/29/85)
     OUT: Orazbek Kuanyshev   IN: Makhtai R. Sagdiev
     TO: 1st Sect. Turgai obkom FROM: Chair Kustanai oblispolkom

   2. **Kzyl-Orda obkom** (1/23/85)
     OUT: Takei Ye. Yesetov   IN: Yerkin N. Aulbekov
     TO: Retired   FROM: 1st Sect. Turgai obkom

   3. **Aktiubinsk obkom** (1/22/85)
     OUT: Vasilii A. Liventsov IN: Yurii N. Trofimov
     TO: Retired   FROM: Sect. CC CPKaz (Agric)

   4. **Turgai obkom** (1/29/85)
     OUT: Yerkin N. Aulbekov   IN: Orazbek S. Kuanyshev
     TO: 1st Sect. Kzyl-Ordy   FROM: 1st Sect. Kokchetav
        obkom   obkom

Appendix VI (continued)

    IV.   BELORUSSIAN SSR (N = 0)

    V.   KIRGHIZ SSR (N = 0)

    VI. TURKMEN SSR (N = 0)

    VII. TADZHIK SSR (N = 0)

    VIII. UZBEK SSR (N = 1)

       1. **Tashkent obkom** (1/22/85)
        OUT: Mirzamakhmud Musakhanov IN: Timur A. Alimov
          TO: Retired   FROM: Chair Tashkent oblispolkom

Appendix VI (continued)

CHRONOLOGY OF OBKOM PERSONNEL CHANGES
UNDER CHERNENKO

Month/Year	Oblast	Republic
March 1984 (0)	-----	-----
April 1984 (1)	Primore Krai	RSFSR
May 1984 (0)	-----	-----
June 1984 (0)	-----	-----
July 1984 (1)	Rostov	RSFSR
August 1984 (0)	-----	-----
September 1984 (0)	-----	-----
October 1984 (0)	-----	-----
November 1984 (0)	-----	-----
December 1984 (0)	-----	-----
January 1985 (7)	Khmelnitskii	Ukrainian SSR
	Chernovtsy	Ukrainian SSR
	Kokchetav	Kazakh SSR
	Kzyl-Orda	Kazakh SSR
	Aktuibinsk	Kazakh SSR
	Turqai	Kazakh SSR
	Tashkent	Uzbek SSR
February 1985 (1)	Altai Krai	RSFSR

Appendix VI (continued)

CHANGES UNDER GORBACHEV

I. RSFSR (N = 29)

1. **Krasnodar krai** (6/4/85)
   OUT: Georgii Razumovskii   IN: Ivan Polozkov
   TO: Sect. CC CPSU   FROM: Head Section

2. **Stavropol Krai** (11/4/85)
   OUT: Vsevolod Murakhovskii IN: Ivan Boldyrev
   TO: 1st Dep Chair USSR   FROM: Inspector CC CPSU
   C of M

3. **Amur obkom** (6/29/85)
   OUT: Stepan Avramenko   IN: Leonid Sharin
   TO: Retired   FROM: Inspector CC CPSU

4. **Chelyabinsk obkom** (6/19/86)
   OUT: Gennadii Verednikov   IN: N. Shvyrev
   TO: Dep Chair USSR C of M   FROM: Unknown

5. **Ivanovo obkom** (7/15/85)
   OUT: Vladimir Kliuev   IN: Mikhail Kniaziuk
   TO: USSR Min of Light   FROM: Inspector CC CPSU
   Industry

6. **Kalinin obkom** (8/24/85)
   OUT: Pavel Leonov   IN: Vasilii Tatarchuk
   TO: Retired   FROM: USSR Dep Min of Agric

7. **Kemerovo obkom** (4/12/85)
   OUT: Leonid Gorshkov   IN: Nikolai (Y)ermakov
   TO: Dep Chair RSFSR CofM   FROM: 1st Dep Head Dept CC
                               CPSU (Heavy Ind/Power)

8. **Kirov obkom** (3/22/85)
   OUT: Ivan Bespalov   IN: Vadim Bakatin
   TO: Retired   FROM: Inspector CC CPSU

9. **Kostroma obkom** (1/4/86)
   OUT: Yurii Balandin   IN: Vladimir Toropov
   TO: Dep Chair USSR State   FROM: 1st Dep Chair Kostrama
   Cmtte (Agro-Ind)   oblispolkom

10. **Kurgan obkom** (6/25/85)
    OUT: Filipp Kniazev   IN: Aleksandr Plekhanov
    TO: Retired   FROM: Inspector CC CPSU

11. **Leningrad obkom** (7/1/85)
     OUT: Lev Zaikov   IN: Yurii Solov'ev
     TO: Sect. CC CPSU   FROM: USSR Min of Industrial
         (Defense Industry)   Construction

12. **Moscow obkom** (11/16/85)
     OUT: Vasilii Konotop   IN: Valentin Mesyats
     TO: Retired   FROM: USSR Min of Agriculture

13. **Orel obkom** (6/22/85)
     OUT: Fedor Meshkov   IN: (Y)egor Stroev
     TO: Retired   FROM: Inspector CC CPSU

14. **Riazan obkom** (12/14/85)
     OUT: Nikolai Priezzhev   IN: Pavel Smolsky
     TO: Retired   FROM: Dep Head Dept CC CPSU
                                              (Org/Party Work)

15. **Rostov obkom** (1/26/86)
     OUT: Aleksandr Vlasov   IN: Boris Volodin
     TO: USSR Min of Internal   FROM: Unknown
         Affairs (MVD)

16. **Saratov obkom** (4/11/85)
     OUT: Vladimir Gusev   IN: Aleksandr Khomiakov
     TO: 1st Dep Chair RSFSR   FROM: 1st Sect. Tambov obkom
         C of M

17. **Sverdlovsk** (4/1985)
     OUT: Boris (Y)eltsin   IN: Yurii Petrov
     TO: Head Dept CC CPSU   FROM: Unknown
         (Construction)

18. **Tambov obkom** (4/19/85)
     OUT: Aleksandr Khomiakov   IN: (Y)evgenii Podolskii
     TO: 1st Sect. Saratov ob.   FROM: Chair Tambov oblispolkom

19. **Tomsk obkom** (1/30/86)
     OUT: Aleksandr Melnikov   IN: V. I. Zarkaltsev
     TO: Head Dept CC CPSU   FROM: Inspector CC CPSU
         (Construction)

20. **Tula obkom** (8/6/85)
     OUT: Ivan Yunak   IN: Yurii Litvintsev
     TO: Retired   FROM: Inspector CC CPSU

21. **Vologda obkom** (7/20/85)
     OUT: Anatolii Drygin   IN: Valentin Kuptsov
     TO: Retired   FROM: Inspector CC CPSU

22. **Yaroslavl obkom** (6/1986)
     OUT: Fedor Loshchenkov   IN: Igor A. Tolstoukhov
     TO: Unknown   FROM: Unknown

Appendix VI (continued)

23. **Kamchatka obkom** (7/15/86)
     OUT: Kachin   IN: P. I. Reznikov
      TO: "other work"   FROM: 2nd Sect. Kamchatka obkom

24. **Chita obkom** (9/2/86)
     OUT: Mikhail I. Matafonov   IN: Nikolai I. Malkov
      TO: Retired   FROM: 1st Sect. Magadan obkom

25. **Magadan obkom** (9/15/86)
     OUT: Nikolai I. Malkov   IN: ?.?. Bogdanov
      TO: 1st Sect. Chita obkom   FROM: Unknown

26. **Novgorod obkom** (10/24/86)
     OUT: Nikolai A. Antonov   IN: Vladimir I. Nikulin
      TO: Retired   FROM: Inspector CC CPSU
                                           : Sect. Leningrad obkom

27. **Ulianovsk obkom** (12/16/86)
     OUT: Gennadii V. Kolbin   IN: Yurii G. Samsonov
      TO: 1st Sect. CC CPkaz   FROM: 2nd Sect. Ulianovsk obkom

28. **Voronezh obkom** (1/10/87)
     OUT: Vadim N. Ignatov   IN: ?. ?. Kabasin
      TO: Dep Chair USSR Agro-   FROM: Dep Head Dept CC CPSU
          Industrial Cmplx   (Org Party Work)

29. **Omsk obkom** (3/7/87)
     OUT: S. I. Maniakin   IN: Ye. D. Pokhitailo
      TO: Chair USSR People's   FROM: Chair Omsk oblispolkom
          Control Cmttee

II. UKRAINIAN SSR (N = 6)

1. **Zaporozhe obkom** (11/18/85)
     OUT: Mikhail Vsevolozhskii   IN: Anatolii Sazonov
      TO: Retired   FROM: Head Dept CC CPUk
                                           (Chemical Industry)

2. **Kiev obkom** (11/4/85)
     OUT: Vladimir Tsybul'ko   IN: Grigorii I. Revenko
      TO: Retired   FROM: Dep Head Dept CC CPSU
                                           (Org & Party Work)

3. **Ivano-Frankovsk obkom** (12/13/85)
     OUT: Ivan Liakhov   IN: I. G. Postoronko
      TO: Head Dept CC CPUk   FROM: Unknown
          (Org/Party Work)

4. **Dnepropetrovsk obkom** (3/18/87)
     OUT: V. G. Boiko   IN: ??
      TO: Ousted "serious   FROM: ??
          shortcomings"

Appendix VI (continued)

5. **Lvov obkom** (3/20/87)
   OUT: Dobrik   IN: ?. ?. Pogrebniak
   TO: Ousted "serious   FROM: Sect. CC CPUk
       failings"

6. **Ternopol obkom** (3/20/87)
   OUT: A. I. Kornienko   IN: V. Ye. Ostrozhinskii
   TO: Head Dept CC CPUk   FROM: 2nd Sect. Zhitomir obkom
       (Org-Party Work)

III. **KAZAKH SSR** (N = 9)

1. **Alma Ata obkom** (9/24/85)
   OUT: Kenes Aukhdiev   IN: M. S. Mendybaev
   TO: "Economic work"   FROM: Chair Kustanai oblispolkom

2. **Gurev obkom** (12/24/85)
   OUT: Onaibai Kushekov   IN: Askar A. Kulibaev
   TO: Retired   FROM: Chair Alma Ata gorispolkom

3. **Ural obkom** (6/13/86)
   OUT: Mustakhim Iksanov   IN: Nazhameden Iskaliyev
   TO: Retired   FROM: 1st Dep Chair Ural
                                        oblispolkom & Chair Urals
                                        oblast Agro-Ind Committee

4. **Taldy-Kurgan obkom** (6/1986)
   OUT: Abubakir A. Tynybaev   IN: V. G. Anufriev
   TO: Unknown   FROM: Unknown

5. **Chimkent obkom** (7/10/85)
   OUT: Asanbai Askarov   IN: Rysbek Myrzashev
   TO: Ousted   FROM: Chair Pavlodar oblispolkom

6. **Mangyshlak obkom** (11/15/85)
   OUT: Salamat Mukashev   IN: Yurii Kazachenko
   TO: Chair Presid of   FROM: Chair Mangyshlak oblispolkom
       KazSSR Sup Soviet

7. **Tselinograd obkom** (9/1/86)
   OUT: Nikolai Ye. Morozov   IN: Andrei Georgievich Braun
   TO: Retired   FROM: Chair Kokchetav oblispolkom

8. **Karaganda obkom** (11/15/86)
   OUT: Aleksandr Korkin   IN: V. I. Lokatunin
   TO: 1st Dep USSR Min of   FROM: Inspector, CC CPSU
       Coal Industry   prev.: 2nd Sect. Lipetsk
                                        obkom (RSFSR)

9. **Semipalatinsk obkom** (1/10/87)
   OUT: Sagidulla Kubashev   IN: K. B. Boztayev
   TO: 2nd Sect. CCCPKaz   FROM: Chair East Kazakhstan
                                        oblispolkom

Appendix VI (continued)

IV. **BELORUSSIAN SSR** (N = 4)

    1. **Minsk obkom** (3/29/85)
        OUT: Vladimir Mikulich   IN: Anatolii Malofeev
        TO: "other duties"   FROM: 1st Sect. Gomel obkom

    2. **Gomel obkom** (4/1/85)
        OUT: Anatolii Malofeev   IN: Aleksei Kamai
        TO: 1st Sect. Minsk obkom FROM: Chair Gomel oblispolkom

    3. **Vitebsk obkom** (1/6/86)
        OUT: Sergei Kabiak   IN: Vladimir Grigorev
        TO: Deceased [12/20/85]   FROM: Inspector CC CPSU

    4. **Brest obkom** (2/1987)
        OUT: Yefrem Sokolov   IN: ?. ?. Zelenovskii
        TO: 1st Sect. CC CPBelo   FROM: Chair Brest oblispolkom

V. **KIRGIZ SSR** (N = 4)

    1. **Naryn obkom** (12/1985)
        OUT: Maten Sydykov   IN: Iskender Muratalin
        TO: Retired   FROM: Head Dept CC CPKir
                                 (Agriculture)

    2. **Issyk-Kul' obkom** (6/27/85)
        OUT: Absamat Masaliev   IN: Apaz Dzhumagulov
        TO: Inspector CC CPSU   FROM: Sect. CC CPKir (Industry)

    3. **Issyk-Kul' obkom** (6/28/86)
        OUT: Apaz Dzhumagulov   IN: Anatolii Khrestenkov
        TO: Chair KirSSR C of M   FROM: 2nd Sect. Issyk-Kul'
                                 obkom

    4. **Talass obkom** (12/23/85)
        OUT: Karike Abdraev   IN: Essembek Duisheev
        TO: "another job"   FROM: 1st Sect. Issyk-Kul'
                                 raikom

VI. **TURKMEN SSR** (N = 4)

    1. **Ashkhabad obkom** (11/22/85)
        OUT: Poda Annaorazov   IN: Yurii Mogilevets
        TO: Retired   FROM: Chair Ashkhabad
                                oblispolkom

    2. **Mary obkom** (3/27/85)
        OUT: Ata Akgaev   IN: Chary Gedzhenov
        TO: Retired   FROM: 1st Sect. Kaakhka raikom

    3. **Tashauz obkom** (10/20/86)
        OUT: Bairamburdy Ataev   IN: Unknown
        TO: Expelled from posts   FROM: Unknown
           and from party for
           corruption

Appendix VI (continued)

4. **Ashkhabad obkom** (3/22/87)
   OUT: Mogilevets   IN: ?. ?. Chertishechev
   TO: 1st Dep Chair TurSSR   FROM: 2nd Sect. Ashkhabad
   CofM and Chair TurSSR   obkom
   State Agro-Ind Cmttee

VII. **TADZHIK SSR** (N = 2)

1. **Kuliab obkom** (1/4/86)
   OUT: Izatullo Khaeev   IN: Salokhiddin Khasanov
   TO: Chair TadSSR C of M   FROM: Chair Kuliab oblispolkom

2. **Leninabad obkom** (1/13/87)
   OUT: Rifiat Khodzhaev   IN: ?. ?. Mirkhalikov
   TO: Retired   FROM: Sect. CC CPTadzhikstan

VIII. **UZBEK SSR** (N = 7)

1. **Andizhan obkom** (8/3/85)
   OUT: Salidzhan Mamarasulov   IN: Makhmut Arikdzhanov
   TO: 1st Sect. Surkhandaria   FROM: CC CPSU apparatus
   obkom

2. **Surkhan-Daria obkom** (8/3/85)
   OUT: Abdukhalik K. Karimov   IN: Salidzhan Mamarasulov
   TO: Retired   FROM: 1st Sect. Andizhan obkom

3. **Syr-Daria obkom** (1/14/86)
   OUT: ?. ?. Antonov   IN: A. F. Klepikov
   TO: Sect. CC CPUz   FROM: 1st Dep Chair Tashkent
   oblispolkom

4. **Dzhizak obkom** (3/29/85)
   OUT: Khabibulla Shagazatov   IN: I. S. Umarov
   TO: Sect. CC CPUzb (Const)   FROM: Sect. Dzhizak obkom

5. **Khorezm obkom** (1/13/86)
   OUT: Madair Khudaibergenov   IN: M. M. Mirkasimov
   TO: Retired   FROM: 1st Sect. Almalyk gorkom

6. **Navoi obkom** (1/13/86)
   OUT: Vasilii (Y)esin   IN: Anatolii (Y)efimov
   TO: Dismissed   FROM: 1st Sect. Vyborg raikom
   (Leningrad oblast, RSFSR)

7. **Kashka-Daria obkom** (12/27/86)
   OUT: Nurmumin Turapov   IN: Abduvakhid K. Karimov
   TO: "other work"   FROM: Chair UzSSR Gosplan &
   Dep Chair UzSSR C of M

Appendix VI (continued)

CHRONOLOGY OF OBKOM PERSONNEL CHANGES
UNDER GORBACHEV

Month/Year	Oblast	Republic
March 1985 (4)	Kirov	RSFSR
	Minsk	Belorussian SSR
	Mary	Turkmen SSR
	Dzhizak	Uzbek SSR
April 1985 (5)	Kemerovo	RSFSR
	Saratov	RSFSR
	Tambov	RSFSR
	Sverdlovsk	RSFSR
	Gomel	Belorussian SSR
May 1985 (0)	-----	-----
June 1985 (5)	Krasnodar Krai	RSFSR
	Amur	RSFSR
	Kurgan	RSFSR
	Orel	RSFSR
	Issyk-Kul'	Kirgiz SSR
July 1985 (4)	Ivanovo	RSFSR
	Leningrad	RSFSR
	Vologda	RSFSR
	Chimkent	Kazakh SSR
August 1985 (4)	Kalinin	RSFSR
	Tula	RSFSR
	Andizhan	Uzbek SSR
	Surkhan-Daria	Uzbek SSR
September 1985 (1)	Alma Ata	Kazakh SSR
October 1985 (0)	-----	-----

Appendix VI (continued)

November 1985 (6)	Stavropol Krai	RSFSR
	Moscow	RSFSR
	Kiev	Ukrainian SSR
	Zaporozhe	Ukrainian SSR
	Mangyshlak	Kazakh SSR
	Ashkhabad	Turkmen SSR
December 1985 (5)	Riazan	RSFSR
	Ivano-Frankovsk	Ukrainian SSR
	Gurev	Kazakh SSR
	Naryn	Kirgiz SSR
	Talass	Kirgiz SSR
January 1986 (8)	Kostrama	RSFSR
	Rostov	RSFSR
	Tomsk	RSFSR
	Vitebsk	Belorussian SSR
	Kuliab	Tadzhik SSR
	Syr-Daria	Uzbek SSR
	Khorezm	Uzbek SSR
	Navoi	Uzbek SSR
February 1986 (0)	-----	-----
March 1986 (0)	-----	-----
April 1986 (0)	-----	-----
May 1986 (0)	-----	-----
June 1986 (5)	Chelyabinsk	RSFSR
	Yaroslavl	RSFSR
	Ural	Kazakh SSR
	Taldy-Kurgan	Kazakh SSR
	Issyk-Kul'	Kirgiz SSR

Appendix VI (continued)

July 1986 (1)	Kamchatka	RSFSR
August 1986 (0)	-----	-----
September 1986 (3)	Tselinograd	Kazakh SSR
	Chita	RSFSR
	Magadan	RSFSR
October 1986 (2)	Tashauz	Turkmen SSR
	Novgorod	RSFSR
November 1986 (1)	Karaganda	Uzbek SSR
December 1986 (2)	Ulianovsk	RSFSR
	Kashka-Daria	Uzbek SSR
January 1987 (3)	Semipalatinsk	Uzbek SSR
	Leninabad	Tadzhik SSR
	Voronezh	RSFSR
February 1987 (1)	Brest	Belorussian SSR
March 1987 (5)	Omsk	RSFSR
	Dnepropetrovsk	Ukrainian SSR
	Lvov	Ukrainian SSR
	Ternopol	Ukrainian SSR
	Ashkhabad	Turkman SSR

BIBLIOGRAPHY

Adams, Jan S. "Political Participation in the USSR: The Public Inspector," pp. 121–144 in Daniel N. Nelson, ed. *Local Politics in Communist Systems.* Lexington, KY: University Press of Kentucky, 1980.

Aitov, N. A. "The Dynamics of Social Mobility in the USSR," pp. 254–270 in Murray Yanowitch, ed. *The Social Structure of the USSR: Recent Soviet Studies.* Armonk, NY: M. E. Sharpe, Inc., 1986.

Armstrong, John A. *The Soviet Bureaucratic Elite: A Case Study of the Ukrainian Apparatus.* New York: Praeger Publishers, 1959.

Avtorkhanov, Abdurakhman. *The Communist Party Apparatus.* Chicago: Henry Regnery, 1966.

Azrael, Jeremy R. *Managerial Power and Soviet Politics.* Cambridge, Mass.: Harvard University Press, 1966.

Bandera, V. N., and Z. L. Melnyk, eds. *The Soviet Economy in Regional Perspective.* New York: Praeger Publishers, 1973.

Barghoorn, Frederic C. "Trends in Top Political Leadership in the USSR," in R. Barry Farrell, ed. *Political Leadership in Eastern Europe and the Soviet Union.* Chicago: Aldine, 1970.

Bater, James H. *The Soviet City: Ideal and Reality.* Beverly Hills, CA: Sage Publications, 1980.

Beck, Carl, et al., eds. *Comparative Communist Political Leadership.* New York: David McKay, 1973.

Beissinger, Mark R. "Economic Performance and Career Prospects in the CPSU Party Apparatus." Paper presented at the eighteenth national convention of the American Association for the Advancement of Slavic Studies, New Orleans, LA, November 20–23, 1986.

Bennigsen, Alexandre. "Islamic or Local Consciousness among Soviet Nationalities?" pp. 168–182 in Edward Allworth et al., eds. *Soviet Nationality Problems.* New York: Columbia University Press, 1971.

Bialer, Seweryn. *Stalin's Successors: Leadership, Stability, and Change in the Soviet Union.* Cambridge: Cambridge University Press, 1980.

Biddulph, Howard L. "Local Interest Articulation at CPSU Congresses," *World Politics* 36, no. 1 (October 1983): 28–52.

Blackwell, Robert E., Jr. "Career Development in the Soviet Obkom Elite: A Conservative Trend," *Soviet Studies* 24 (July 1972a): 26–39.

———. "Elite Recruitment and Functional Change: An Analysis of the Soviet Obkom Elite 1950–1968," *Journal of Politics* 34 (1972b): 124–152.

———. "The Soviet Political Elite—Alternative Recruitment Policies at the Obkom Level," *Comparative Politics* 6, no. 1 (October 1973a): 99–121.

———. "The Relationship between Social Background Characteristics, Career Specialization, Political Attitudes, and Political Behavior among Soviet Elites: A Research Design." Paper presented at the annual meeting of the American Political Science Association, New Orleans, LA, September 4–8, 1973b.

———. "Cadres Policy in the Brezhnev Era," *Problems of Communism* (March–April 1979): 29–42.

Blackwell, Robert E., Jr., and William E. Hulbary. "Political Mobility among Soviet Obkom Elites: The Effects of Regime, Social Backgrounds, and Career Development," *American Journal of Political Science* 17, no. 4 (1973): 721–743.

Breslauer, George W. *Krushchev and Brezhnev as Leaders: Building Authority in Soviet Politics.* London: George Allen and Unwin, 1982.

———. "The Nature of Soviet Politics and the Gorbachev Leadership," pp. 11–30 in Alexander Dallin and Condoleeza Rice, eds. *The Gorbachev Era.* Stanford, CA: Stanford Alumni Association, 1986a.

———. "Provincial Party Leaders' Demand Articulation and the Nature of Center-Periphery Relations in the USSR," *Slavic Review* 45, no. 4 (Winter 1986b): 650–673.

Brown, Archie. "Andropov: Discipline *and* Reform?," *Problems of Communism,* (Jan.-Feb. 1983): 18–31.

Brzezinski, Zbigniew K., and Samuel P. Huntington. *Political Power: USA/USSR.* New York: Viking Press, 1964.

Burg, Steven L. "Central Asian Elite Mobility and Political Change in the Soviet Union," *Central Asian Survey* 5, no. 3/4, (1986): 77–89.

Carlisle, Donald S. "The Uzbek Power Elite: Politburo and Secretariat (1938–1983)," *Central Asian Survey* 5, no. 3/4, (1986): 91–132.

Ciboski, Kenneth N. "The Significance of Party Organizations in the Careers of Top Soviet Leaders." Paper presented at the annual meeting of the Midwest Political Science Association, Chicago, April 1986.

Cleary, J. W. "Elite Career Patterns in a Soviet Republic," *British Journal of Political Science* 17, no. 4 (1974): 323–344.

Cole, J. P., and M. E. Harrison. *Regional Inequality in Service and Purchasing Power, 1940–1976.* London: University of London, 1978.

Colton, Timothy J. *The Dilemma of Reform in the Soviet Union,* rev. and enlarged ed. New York: Council on Foreign Relations, 1986.

Conquest, Robert. *The Great Fear: Stalin's Purge of the Thirties.* New York: Macmillan, 1968.

Dallin, Alexander, and Candoleeza Rice, eds. *The Gorbachev Era.* Stanford, CA: Stanford Alumni Association, 1986.

Daniels, Robert V. "Soviet Politics Since Khrushchev," in John W. Strong, ed. *The Soviet Union under Brezhnev and Kosygin.* New York: Van Nostrand, Reinhold, 1971.

Dellenbrandt, Jan Ake. "Regional Differences in Political Recruitment in the Soviet Republics," *European Journal of Political Research* 6 (June 1978): 181–201.

Donaldson, Robert H. "The 1971 Central Committee: An Assessment of the New Elite," *World Politics* (April 1972): 382–409.

Fainsod, Merle. *Smolensk under Soviet Rule.* New York: Random House, 1958.

Farrell, R. Barry, ed. *Political Leadership in Eastern Europe and the Soviet Union.* Chicago: Aldine Publishing Co., 1970.

Fitzpatrick, Sheila. "Stalin and the Making of a New Elite, 1928–1939." *Slavic Review* 38, no. 3 (September 1979): 377–402.

Fleron, Frederic. *Communist Studies and the Social Sciences: Essays on Methodology and Empirical Theory.* Chicago: Rand McNally, 1969.

———. "Representation of Career Types in the Soviet Political Leadership," pp. 108–139 in R. Barry Farrell, ed. *Political Leadership in Eastern Europe and the Soviet Union.* Chicago: Aldine Publishing Co., 1970.

———. "System Attributes and Career Attributes: The Soviet Leadership System, 1952 to 1965," in Carl Beck et al., eds. *Comparative Communist Political Leadership.* New York: David McKay, 1973.

Ford, Robert A. D. "The Soviet Union: The Next Decade," *Foreign Affairs* 62, no. 2 (Summer 1984): 1132–1144.

Frank, Peter. "The CPSU Obkom First Secretary: A Profile," *British Journal of Political Science* 1, no. 2 (1971): 173–190.

———. "Constructing a Classified Ranking of CPSU Provincial Committees," *British Journal of Political Science* 4, no. 3 (1974): 217–230.

Friedgut, Theodore H. "Community Structure, Political Participation, and Soviet Local Government: The Case of Kutaisi," pp. 261–296 in Henry W. Morton and Rudolf L. Tokes, eds. *Soviet Politics and Society in the 1970's.* New York: The Free Press, 1974.

Frolic, B. Michael. "Soviet Urban Political Leaders," *Comparative Political Studies* 2 (January 1970): 443–464.

Gehlen, Michael P. "The Soviet Apparatchiki," pp. 140–156 in R. Barry Farrell, ed. *Political Leadership in Eastern Europe and the Soviet Union.* Chicago: Aldine Publishing Co., 1970.

Gehlen, Michael P., and Michael McBride. "The Soviet Central Committee: An Elite Analysis," *American Political Science Review* 62 (1968): 1232–1241.

Gleason, Gregory. "Principles of Soviet Federalism anld Regional Policy." Paper presented at the eighteenth national convention of the American Association for the Advancement of Slavic Studies, New Orleans, November 20–23, 1986.

———. "Prefect or Paladin?: Centrist and Nationalist Leaders in Soviet Central Asia." Paper presented at thc 19th annual convention of the American Association for the Advancement of Slavic Studies, Boston, November 1987.

Granick, David. *The Red Executive: A Study of the Organization Man in Russian Industry.* Garden City, N.Y.: Anchor/Doubleday, 1960.

Hammer, Darrell P. *USSR: The Politics of Oligarchy.* Hinsdale, IL: Dryden Press, 1974.

Harasymiw, Bohdan. "Some Theoretical Considerations on Advancement within the Political Elite in Soviet-Type Systems," in T. H. Rigby and Bohdan Harasymiw, eds. *Leadership Selection and Patron–Client Relations in the USSR and Yugoslavia.* London: George Allen & Unwin, 1983.

———. *Political Elite Recruitment in the Soviet Union.* New York: St. Martin's Press, 1984a.

———. "Political Mobility in the Soviet Ukraine," *Canadian Slavonic Papers* 26 (June–September 1984b): 160–181.

Harris, Chauncy D. *Cities of the Soviet Union: Studies in Their Functions, Size, Density, and Growth,* no. 5 in the monograph series published for the Association of American Geographers. Chicago: Rand McNally, 1970.

Hauslohner, Peter. "Prefects as Senators: Soviet Regional Politicians Look to Foreign Policy," *World Politics* 33, no. 1 (October 1980): 197–233.

Hill, Ronald J. *Soviet Political Elites: The Case of Tiraspol.* New York: St. Martin's Press, 1977.

Hill, Ronald J. and Peter Frank. *The Soviet Communist Party,* 2d ed. London: George Allen and Unwin, 1983.

———. *The Soviet Communist Party,* 3d ed. Boston: Allen and Unwin, 1986.

Hodnett, Grey. "The Obkom First Secretaries," *Slavic Review* 24, no. 4 (December 1965): 636–652.

———. "Succession Contingencies in the Soviet Union," *Problems of Communism* 24, no. 2 (March–April 1975): 1–21.

———. *Leadership in the Soviet National Republics: A Quantitative Study of Recruitment Policy.* Oakville, Ont.: Mosaic Press, 1978.

———. "The Role of the Local Party Organs in Soviet Industrial Decision Making." Ph.D. dissertation, Harvard University, 1961.

———. *The Soviet Prefects: The Local Party Organs in Industrial Decision-Making.* Cambridge, MA: Harvard University Press, 1969.

———. "The Party Apparatchiki," pp. 47–92 in H. Gordon Skilling and Franklyn Griffiths, eds. *Interest Groups in Soviet Politics.* Princeton, NJ: Princeton University Press, 1972.

———. "The Brezhnev Era: The Man and the System," *Problems of Communism* 25, no. 2 (March–April 1976): 1–17.

———. *The Soviet Union and Social Science Theory.* Cambridge, MA: Harvard University Press, 1977.

———. "The Generation Gap and the Soviet Succession," *Problems of Communism* 28, no. 4 (July–August 1979): 1–16.

———. *Soviet Leadership in Transition.* Washington, DC: Brookings Institution, 1980.

———. "Soviet Succession: Issues and Personalities," *Problems of Communism* 31, no. 5 (September–October 1982): 20–40.

———. "Changes in Soviet Elite Composition," pp. 39–64 in Seweryn Bialer and Thane Gustafson, eds. *Russia at the Crossroads: The 26th Congress of the CPSU.* London: George Allen & Unwin, 1982.

Jozsa, Gyula. "Political 'Seilschaften' in the USSR," in T. H. Rigby and Bohdan Harasymiw, eds. *Leadership Selection and Patron–Client Relations in the USSR and Yugoslavia.* London: George Allen & Unwin, 1983.

Karpat, Kemal H. "Introduction: Elites and the Transmission of Nationality and Identity," *Central Asian Survey* 5, no. 3/4 (1986): 5–24.

Kim, Jae-On, and Charles W. Mueller. *Introduction to Factor Analysis,* number 13 in the series, *Quantitative Applications in the Social Sciences.* Beverly Hills, Cal.: Sage Publications, 1978.

Kress, John H. "Representation of Positions on the CPSU Politburo," *Slavic Review* 39, no. 2 (June 1980): 218–238.

Lamser, Vaclav. "A Sociological Approach to Soviet Nationality Problems," pp. 183–210 in Edward Allworth et al., eds. *Soviet Nationality Problems.* New York: Columbia University Press, 1971.

Lande, Carl H. "The Dyadic Basis of Clientelism," in Steffen W. Schmidt et al., eds. *Friends, Followers, and Factions.* Berkeley, CA: University of California Press, 1977.

Lapidus, Gail Warshofsky. "The Brezhnev Regime and Directed Social Change: Depoliticization as Political Strategy," pp. 26–38 in Alexander Dallin, ed., *The Twenty-fifth Congress of the CPSU: Assessment and Context.* Stanford, Cal.: Hoover Institution Press, 1977.

Lapidus, Gail Warshofsky. "Ethnonationalism and Political Stability: The Soviet Case," *World Politics* 36, no. 4 (July 1984): 555–580.

Lewis, Carol, and Stephen Sternheimer. *Soviet Urban Management.* New York: Praeger Publishers, 1979.

Lewis-Beck, Michael S. *Applied Regression: An Introduction,* number 22 in the series, *Quantitative Applications in the Social Sciences.* Beverly Hills, CA: Sage Publications, 1980.

Linden, Carl A. *Khrushchev and the Soviet Leadership: 1957–1964.* Baltimore: Johns Hopkins University Press, 1966.

Lodge, Milton. " 'Groupism' in the Post-Stalin Period," *Midwest Journal of Political Science* 12, no. 3 (August 1968): 330–351.

Matthews, Mervyn. "Some Problems of Elite Mobility," pp. 133–163 in Mervyn Matthews, *Privilege in the Soviet Union: A Study of Elite Life-Styles Under Communism.* London: George Allen and Unwin, 1978.

McAuley, Alastair. *Economic Welfare in the Soviet Union.* Madison, WI: University of Wisconsin Press, 1979.

McAuley, Mary. "The Hunting of the Hierarchy: RSFSR Obkom First Secretaries and the Central Committee," *Soviet Studies* (October 1974): 473–501.

Medvedev, Zhores A. *Gorbachev.* New York: W. W. Norton, 1986.

Meyer, Alfred G. "The Comparative Study of Communist Political Systems," in Frederic J. Fleron, Jr., ed. *Communist Studies and the Social Sciences.* Chicago: Rand McNally, 1969.

Meyer, Gerd. "The Impact of the Political Structure on the Recruitment of the Political Elite in the USSR," pp. 195–221 in L. J. Cohen and J. P. Shapiro, eds. *Communist Systems in Comparative Perspective.* Garden City, NY: Anchor Books, 1974.

Miller, John. "Nomenklatura: Check on Localism?", pp. 62–97 in T. H. Rigby and Bohdan Harasymiw, eds. *Leadership Selection and Patron-Client Relations in the USSR and Yugoslavia.* London: George Allen and Unwin, 1983.

Miller, John H. "Cadres Policy in Nationality Areas: Recruitment of CPSU First and Second Secretaries in non-Russian Republics of the USSR," *Soviet Studies* 29, no. 1 (January 1977): 3–36.

Mitchell, R. Judson. "Immobilism, Depoliticization, and the Emerging Soviet Elite," *Orbis* (Fall 1982): 591–610.

Moore, Barrington. *Terror and Progress USSR: Some Sources of Change and Stability in the Soviet Dictatorship.* Cambridge, MA: Harvard University Press, 1954.

Moses, Joel C. *Regional Party Leadership and Decision Making in the USSR.* New York: Praeger Publishers, 1974.

――――. "Regional Cohorts and Political Mobility in the USSR: The Case of Dnepropetrovsk," *Soviet Union* 8, part 1 (1976): 63–89.

――――. "Local Leadership Integration in the Soviet Union," pp. 12–53 in Daniel N. Nelson, ed. *Local Politics in Communist Countries.* Lexington, Ken.: The University Press of Kentucky, 1980.

――――. "Functional Career Specialization in Soviet Regional Elite Recruitment," in T. H. Rigby and Bohdan Harasymiw, eds. *Leadership Selection and Patron-Client Relations in the USSR and Yugoslavia.* London: George Allen & Unwin, 1983.

――――. "Regionalism in Soviet Politics: Continuity as a Source of Change, 1953–1982," *Soviet Studies* 37, no. 2 (April 1985): 184–211.

Nagle, John D. "The Soviet Political Elite, 1917–1971: Application of a Generational Model of Social Change." Paper presented at the annual meeting of the American Political Science Association, New Orleans, September 4–8, 1973.

Nechimias, Carol. "Regional Differentiation in Living Standards in the RSFSR: The Issue of Inequality," *Soviet Studies* 32 (July 1980).

Nelson, Daniel N. "Dilemmas of Local Politics in Communist States," *Journal of Politics* 41, no. 1 (1979): 23–54.

――――. "Conclusion: Participatory and Policymaking Dilemmas in Local Communist Politics," pp. 211–224 in Daniel N. Nelson, ed. *Local Politics in Communist Systems.* Lexington, Ken.: University Press of Kentucky, 1980.

Oliver, James H. "Turnover and 'Family Circles' in Soviet Administration," *Slavic Review* 32, no. 2 (September 1973): 527–545.

Potichnyi, Peter J. "Permanent Representations (Postpredstva) of Union Republics in Moscow, pp. 50–82 in Peter J. Potichnyi and Jane Shapiro Zacek, eds. *Politics and Participation Under Communist Rule.* New York: Praeger Publishers, 1983.

Rakowska-Harmstone, Teresa. "The Political Elite," pp. 146–189 in Teresa Rakowska-Harmstone, *Russia and Nationalism in Central Asia: The Case of Tadzhikistan.* Baltimore: Johns Hopkins University Press, 1970.

Rigby, T. H. "The Soviet Leadership: Towards a Self-Stabilizing Oligarchy?" *Soviet Studies* 22, no. 2 (October 1970): 167–191.

_____. "The Soviet Politburo: A Comparative Profile," *Soviet Studies* 24 (July 1972): 3–23.

_____. "Soviet Communist Party Membership under Brezhnev," *Soviet Studies* 28 (July 1976): 317–337.

_____. "The Soviet Regional Leadership: The Brezhnev Generation," *Slavic Review* 37, no. 1 (March 1978a): 1–24.

_____. "Personal and Collective Leadership: Brezhnev and Beyond," in Dmitri K. Simes et al. *Soviet Succession: Leadership in Transition.* Beverly Hills, CA: Sage Publications, 1978b.

_____. "How the Obkom Secretary Was Tempered," *Problems of Communism* (March–April 1980): 57–63.

_____. "Early Provincial Cliques and the Rise of Stalin," *Soviet Studies* 33, no. 1 (January 1981): 3–28.

Rigby, T. H., and Bohdan Harasymiw, eds. *Leadership Selection and Patron-Client Relations in the USSR and Yugoslavia.* London: George Allen and Unwin, 1983.

Ross, Dennis. "Coalition Maintenance in the Soviet Union," *World Politics* 32, no. 2 (January 1980): 258–280.

Rummel, R. J. *Applied Factor Analysis.* Evanston, Ill.: Northwestern University Press, 1970.

Rush, Myron. *Political Succession in the USSR.* Boston: Little, Brown & Co., 1965.

_____. "Succeeding Brezhnev," *Problems of Communism* (January–February 1983): 2–7.

Ryavec, Karl W. "The Soviet Bureaucratic Elite from 1964–1979: A Research Note," *Soviet Union* 12, no. 3 (1985): 322–345.

Schapiro, Leonard. *The Communist Party of the Soviet Union.* New York: Random House, 1960.

_____. *The Communist Party of the Soviet Union,* rev. ed. New York: Vintage Books, 1971.

Schlisinger, Joseph H. *Ambition and Politics: Political Careers in the United States.* Chicago: Rand McNally, 1966.

Schroeder, Gertrude E. "Regional Differences in Incomes and Levels of Living in the USSR," pp. 167–195 in V. N. Bandera and Z. L. Melnyk, eds. *The Soviet Economy in Regional Perspective.* New York: Praeger Publishers, 1973.

Schroeder, Gertrude E., and I. S. Koropeckyi. *The Economics of Soviet Regions.* New York: Praeger Publishers, 1981.

Schmidt, Steffen, et al., eds. *Friends, Followers, and Factions: A Reader in Political Clientelism.* Berkeley, CA: University of California Press, 1977.

Skilling, H. Gordon and Franklyn Griffiths. *Interest Groups in Soviet Politics.* Princeton, N.J.: Princeton University Press, 1971.

Silver, Brian. "Levels of Sociocultural Development among Soviet Nationalities: A Partial Test of the Equalization Hypothesis," *American Political Science Review* 68, no. 4 (December 1974): 1618–1637.

Stewart, Philip D. *Political Power in the Soviet Union: A Study of Decision-Making in Stalingrad.* New York: Bobbs-Merrill, 1968.

Stewart, Philip D., et al. "Political Mobility and the Soviet Political Process: A

Partial Test of Two Models," *American Political Science Review* 66 (1972): 1269–1290.

Stewart, Philip D., et al. "Soviet Regions and Economic Priorities: A Study of Politburo Perceptions," *Soviet Union* 11, no. 1 (1984): 1–30.

Stewart, Philip D., and Kenneth Town. "The Career-Attitude Linkage among Soviet Regional Elites: An Exploration of Its Nature and Magnitude." Paper delivered at the 1974 annual meeting of the American Political Science Association, Chicago, August 29–September 2, 1974.

Swearer, Howard R. *The Politics of Succession in the USSR.* Boston: Little, Brown & Co., 1964.

Tatu, Michel. "The Central Committee Elected at the Twenty-Seventh Party Congress: Halfway Towards Rejuvenation," *Radio Liberty Research,* RL 106/86 (March 10, 1986): 1–3.

Urban, Michael E. "The Structure of Elite Circulation in the Belorussian Republic: Centralization, Regionalism and Patronage." Paper presented at the eighteenth national convention of the American Association for the Advancement of Slavic Studies, New Orleans, November 20–23, 1986.

Welsh, William A. "Introduction," in Carl Beck et al., eds. *Comparative Communist Political Leadership.* New York: David McKay Co., Inc., 1973.

White, Paul M. *Soviet Urban and Regional Planning: A Bibliography with Abstracts.* London: Mansell, 1979.

Whitehouse, F. Douglas. "Demographic Aspects of Regional Economic Development in the USSR," pp. 154–166 in V. N. Bandera and Z. L. Melnyk, eds. *The Soviet Economy in Regional Perspective.* New York: Praeger Publishers, 1973.

Willerton, John P., Jr. "Clientelism in the Soviet Union: An Initial Examination," *Studies in Comparative Communism* 12, nos. 2–3 (1979): 159–183.

———. "Patronage Networks and Coalition Building in the Brezhnev Era," *Soviet Studies* 39, no. 2 (April 1987): 175–204.

Willerton, John P., Jr., and William M. Reisinger. "Elite Mobility and Regional Economic Performance in the Soviet Union: Hypotheses and Suggestive Analyses." Paper presented at the eleventh annual meeting of the Mid-Atlantic Slavic Conference, The American Association for the Advancement of Slavic Studies, Baruch College, New York, March 7, 1987.

Yaney, George L. "The Local Organs," in George L. Yaney, *The Systematization of Russian Government: Social Evolution in the Domestic Administration of Imperial Russia, 1711–1905.* Urbana: University of Illinois Press, 1973.

Yanowitch, M., and W. Fisher, eds. *Social Stratification and Mobility in the USSR.* White Plains, N.Y.: International Arts and Sciences Press, 1973.

Yaroshevski, Dov B. "Russian Regionalism in Turkestan," *Slavonic and East European Review* 65, no. 1 (January 1987): 77–100.

AUTHOR INDEX

SUBJECT INDEX